FRAGMENTS OF OLD COMEDY

III

LCL 515

FRAGMENTS OF OLD COMEDY

VOLUME III

PHILONICUS TO XENOPHON
ADESPOTA

EDITED AND TRANSLATED BY

IAN C. STOREY

HARVARD UNIVERSITY PRESS
CAMBRIDGE, MASSACHUSETTS
LONDON, ENGLAND
2011

Copyright © 2011 by the President and Fellows
of Harvard College
All rights reserved

First published 2011

Library of Congress Control Number 2010937704
CIP data available from the Library of Congress

ISBN 978-0-674-99677-9

*Composed in ZephGreek and ZephText by
Technologies 'N Typography, Merrimac, Massachusetts.
Printed on acid-free paper and bound by
The Maple-Vail Book Manufacturing Group*

CONTENTS

CONTENTS

vi

ABBREVIATIONS

A&R	*Atene e Roma*
Aevum (Ant.)	*Aevum Antiquum*
AFLB	*Annali della Facoltà di Lettere e Filosofia di Bari*
AHB	*Ancient History Bulletin*
AION (fil.)	*Annali dell'Istituto Universitario Orientale di Napoli. Sezione filologico-letteraria.*
AJPh	*American Journal of Philology*
Bakola	E. Bakola, *Cratinus and the Art of Comedy* (Oxford 2010)
BICS	*Bulletin of the Institute of Classical Studies*
C&M	*Classica et Mediaevalia*
Campbell *GL*	D. A. Campbell (ed.), *Greek Lyric*, 5 vols. (1982–1993)
Capps	E. Capps, "Epigraphical Problems in the History of Comedy," *CPh* 28 (1907) 179–99
CGA	A. López Eire (ed.), *Sociedad, Política y Literatura: Comedia griega antigua* (Salamanca 1997)
CGFP	C. Austin (ed.), *Comicorum Graecorum Fragmenta in Papyris Reperta* (Berlin/ New York 1973)

Companion	G. W. Dobrov (ed.), *Brill's Companion to the Study of Greek Comedy* (Leiden 2010)
CPh	*Classical Philology*
CQ	*Classical Quarterly*
CW	*Classical World*
Demianczuk	J. Demianczuk (ed.), *Supplementum Comicum* (Krakow 1912)
Dobrov (*BA*)	G. Dobrov (ed.), *Beyond Aristophanes* (Atlanta 1993)
Dobrov (*City*)	G. Dobrov, *The City as Comedy* (Chapel Hill, NC 1995)
Edmonds	J. M. Edmonds (ed./tr.), *The Fragments of Attic Comedy*, vol. I (Leiden 1957)
Euripides VII	C. Collard and M. Cropp, *Euripides Fragments:* Aegeus–Meleager (Cambridge, MA 2008)
Euripides VIII	C. Collard and M. Cropp, *Euripides Fragments:* Oedipus–Chrysippus, *other fragments* (Cambridge, MA 2008)
G&R	*Greece and Rome*
Geissler	P. Geissler, *Chronologie der altattischen Komödie*, 2nd ed. (Dublin/Zurich 1969)
GRBS	*Greek, Roman and Byzantine Studies*
GrGr	*Grammatici Graeci*, ed. G. Uhlig and others, 4 vols., in 6 (Leipzig 1867–1910)
ICS	*Illinois Classical Studies*
IG	*Inscriptiones Graecae*
JHS	*Journal of Hellenic Studies*
Kaibel	Extracts from Kaibel's unpublished writings on Old Comedy appear *ad loc.* in *PCG*

ABBREVIATIONS

Kassel-Austin [K.-A.]	= *PCG*
Kock	T. Kock (ed.), *Comicorum Atticorum Fragmenta*, vol. I (Lepizig 1880)
Koster	W. J. W. Koster (ed.), *Scholia in Aristophanem, Pars I: fasc. IA. Prolegomena de Comoedia* (Groningen 1975)
ΚΩΜΩΙΔΟ-ΤΡΑΓΩΙΔΙΑ	E. Medda, M. S. Mirto, and M. P. Pattoni (eds.), ΚΩΜΩΙΔΟΤΡΑΓΩΙΔΙΑ *Intersezioni del tragico e del comico nel teatro del V secolo a.C.* (Pisa 2006)
LCM	*Liverpool Classical Monthly*
MCr	*Museum Criticum*
Meineke	A. Meineke (ed.), *Fragmenta Comicorum Graecorum.* (Berlin 1839–1857)
MH	*Museum Helveticum*
Norwood	G. Norwood, *Greek Comedy* (London 1931)
Olson	S. D. Olson, *Broken Laughter* (Oxford 2007)
PAA	J. Traill (ed.), *Persons of Ancient Athens*, 20 vols. (Toronto 1994–)
PCG	R. Kassel and C. Austin (eds.), *Poetae Comici Graeci* (Berlin 1983–)
PCPhS	*Proceedings of the Cambridge Philological Society*
Pellegrino (*Utopie*)	M. Pellegrino, *Utopie e immagini gastronomiche nei frammenti dell' archaia* (Bologna 2000)
PMG	D. L. Page (ed.), *Poetae Melici Graeci* (Oxford 1962)
P. Oxy.	Oxyrhynchus Papyrus

PSI	*Pubblicazioni della Società italiana per la ricerca dei papyri greci e latini in Egitto*
QUCC	*Quaderni Urbinati di Cultura Classica*
Revermann	M. Revermann, *Comic Business* (Oxford 2006)
RFIC	*Rivista di Filologia e di Istruzione Classica*
Rivals	D. Harvey and J. Wilkins (eds.), *The Rivals of Aristophanes* (London 2000)
Rothwell	K. S. Rothwell, *Nature, Culture and the Origins of Old Comedy* (Cambridge 2007)
RPh	*Révue de Philologie*
SemRom	*Seminaria Romana*
SIFC	*Studi Italiani di Filologia Classica*
SPhV	*Studia Philologica Valentina*
Storey	I. C. Storey, *Eupolis: Poet of Old Comedy* (Oxford 2003)
TCP	A. H. Sommerstein, S. Halliwell, J. Henderson, and B. Zimmermann (eds.), *Tragedy, Comedy and the Polis* (Bari 1993)
Tessere	A. M. Belardinelli et al. (eds.). *Tessere. Frammenti della commedia greca: studi e commenti* (Bari 1998)
Thompson (*Birds*)	D.W, Thompson, *A Glossary of Greek Birds* (London 1936)
Thompson (*Fishes*)	D. W. Thompson, *A Glossary of Greek Fishes* (London 1947)

TrGF	B. Snell (corrected edition by R. Kannicht), *Tragicorum Graecorum Fragmenta*, vol. I (Göttingen 1986)
Tsantsanoglou	K. Tsantsanoglou, *New Fragments of Greek Literature in the Lexicon of Photius* (Athens 1984)
ZPE	*Zeitschrift für Papyrologie und Epigraphik*

FRAGMENTS OF OLD COMEDY

III

ΦΙΛΟΝΙΚΟΣ

Testimonium

i *IG* ii² 2325.137

Φιλόνικος I

PHILONICUS

This poet is known only from the entry on the victors' list for the Lenaea, immediately following that of Philyllius. At this point the list is recording victors in the 390s. The name is not that common in Athens: sixteen entries in PAA, *with only one other instance from the early fourth century,* PAA 940360, *a man involved in a liturgical* diadikasia, *c. 380.*

Testimonium

i [from the list of the victors at the Lenaea, c. 390]

Philonicus 1

ΦΙΛΩΝΙΔΗΣ

Aristophanes produced some of his comedies "through others," not only at the start of his career, when we could expect that youth and a lack of self-confidence might lead a novice to employ the talents of others, but also later in his career with the plays of his maturity, such as Birds and Frogs. Perhaps Aristophanes preferred to create comedy and eschewed the humdrum of actually putting it on, dealing with the temperaments of actors, chorus members, chorēgoi, and public officials. One of these producers was Philonides, a comic poet in his own right (T 1, 2), and if his name is correctly restored on T 4, a successful one at the Dionysia.

As Philonides' son Nicochares, a comic poet as well, is assigned to the deme of Cydathenaeum, the same deme to which Aristophanes belonged, it is very tempting to

Testimonia

i Suda φ 450

Φιλωνίδης· Ἀθηναῖος, κωμικὸς ἀρχαῖος· πρότερον δὲ ἦν γραφεύς.[1] τῶν δραμάτων αὐτοῦ ἦν Κοθόρνοι, Ἀπήνη, Φιλέταιρος.

4

PHILONIDES

*identify our Philonides with the member of a thiasos of
Heracles, based in the deme Cydathenaeum (T 3). Also sig-
nificant is the fact that Aristophanes' first play, Banquet-
ers, which one source (T 7b) says was produced through
Philonides, featured a chorus of men holding a feast in
honour of Heracles (Orion p. 49.8). Of the other names on
T 3, four are mentioned in Aristophanes' extant work (Si-
mon, Lysanias, Antitheus, Amphitheus), while Hegemon is
the name of a comic poet and writer of parodies. It seems
that there was a complex web of intertextual and meta-
theatrical comic references which we can only dimly grasp.*

We know of three titles, but only Buskins *has any frag-
ments. The allusion to Theramenes [F 6], who was nick-
named "Buskin" (cothurnus), implies that this comedy be-
longs around 405.*

Testimonia

i Philonides: of Athens, poet of Old Comedy. Previously
he was a scribe [or "fuller"]. His plays include *Buskins,
Mule-Car, Good Friend.*

---

1 Two MSS read γναφεύς or κναφεύς (fuller).

5

ii *Suda* ν 407

Νικοχάρης· Φιλωνίδου τοῦ κωμικοῦ, Ἀθηναῖος, κωμικός, σύγχρονος Ἀριστοφάνους.

iii *IG* ii² 2343

Σίμωνος Κυδαθ ἱερέως Ἡρακλέος καὶ κοινō θιασωτῶν·
Φιλώνδης Εὐθύνομος Θεοφῶν Πυθαῖος Λυσανίας Ἀντίθεος Ἀμφίθεος Ἡγήμων Ἀρχέστρατος Με[λα]νωπίδης Μελανωπίδης Θεοφάνης Τελέστης, Ἀπολλόδωρος, Ναυσίστρατος

iv *IG* ii² 2325.64

Φιλ[ωνίδης

v

(a) Hypothesis II *Wasps*

ἐδιδάχθη ἐπὶ ἄρχοντος Ἀμεινίου διὰ Φιλωνίδου ἐν τῇ πθ′ Ὀλυμπιάδι. β′ ἦν εἰς Λήναια. καὶ ἐνίκα πρῶτος Φιλωνίδης Προάγωνι. Λεύκων Πρέσβεσι.

(b) Hypothesis I *Birds*

ἐπὶ Χαρίου . . . εἰς Λήναια τὸν Ἀμφιάραον ἐδίδαξε διὰ Φιλωνίδου.

ii Nicochares: the son of Philonides the comic poet, of Athens, a comic poet, a contemporary of Aristophanes.

iii Of Simon of Cydathenaeum, priest of Heracles, and the members of the *thiasos:* Philonides, Euthynomus, Theophon, Pythaeus, Lysanias, Antitheus, Amphitheus, Hegemon, Archestratus, Melanopides, Melanopides, Theophanes, Telestes, Apollodorus, Nausistratus.

iv [list of victors at the Dionysia]

   Phil[onides.[1]

   [1] Possibly "Philyllius."

v

(a) It [*Wasps*] was produced in the 89th Olympiad, in the archonship of Ameinias [423/2] through Philonides. It was second at the Lenaea. Philonides won first prize with *Preview,* Leucon ‹was third› with *Envoys*.[1]

   [1] Unless the writer of the hypothesis has jumbled the results of the Lenaea and Dionysia of 422, there is clearly an error here. Since at *Wasps* 1015–50 Aristophanes is summarising his own career, it is likely that Aristophanes was the advertised poet for *Wasps* and that *Preview* was put on "through Philonides," thus allowing Aristophanes to compete with two plays at the same festival.

(b) In the archonship of Charias [415/4] . . . at the Lenaea he produced *Amphiaraus* through Philonides.

(c) Hypothesis I *Frogs*

τὸ δὲ δρᾶμα . . . ἐδιδάχθη ἐπὶ Καλλίου τοῦ μετὰ
Ἀντιγένη διὰ Φιλωνίδου εἰς Λήναια.

vi *Clouds* 528–33

ἐξ ὅτου γὰρ ἐνθάδ᾽ ὑπ᾽ ἀνδρῶν, οὓς ἡδὺ καὶ λέγειν,
ὁ σώφρων τε χὠ καταπύγων ἄριστ᾽ ἠκουσάτην,
κἀγώ, παρθένος γὰρ ἔτ᾽ ἦν κοὐκ ἐξῆν πώ μοι
    τεκεῖν,
ἐξέθηκα, παῖς δ᾽ ἑτέρα τις λαβοῦσ᾽ ἀνείλετο,
ὑμεῖς δ᾽ ἐξεθρέψατε γενναίως κἀπαιδεύσατε,
ἐκ τούτου μοι πιστὰ παρ᾽ ὑμῶν γνώμης ἔσθ᾽ ὅρκια.

vii

(a) Σ Aristophanes *Clouds* 531a

δηλονότι ὁ Φιλωνίδης καὶ ὁ Καλλίστρατος οἱ ὕστερον
γενόμενοι ὑποκριταὶ τοῦ Ἀριστοφάνους.

(b) Σ *Clouds* 531b

ἕτερος ὑποκριτὴς ἀνελάβετο τοῦτο, ὁ Φιλωνίδης.

(c) Σ *Wasps* 1018a

τὰ μὲν οὐ φανερῶς· . . . δι᾽ ἑτέρων ποιητῶν λάθρα,
ἐπειδὴ διὰ Φιλωνίδου καὶ Καλλιστράτου καθίει τινὰ
τῶν δραμάτων

(c) The play [*Frogs*] . . . was produced at the Lenaea in the archonship of Callias who followed Antigenes [406/5] through Philonides.

vi Ever since the time when my *Good Son and the Asshole*[1] was so well received by men whom it is pleasant even to mention, when I, who was still an unwed maiden and not ready to give birth, gave it up, and another woman took it in and claimed it, and you people nobly brought it up and educated it, from that time I have had a reliable testament to your judgement.

[1] Referring to his first play, *Banqueters*, which finished second in 427.

vii

(a) That is, Philonides and Callistratus, who were later actors for Aristophanes.

(b) Another actor took this up, Philonides.

(c) "Not openly at first": . . . secretly through other poets, since he would put on some of his plays through Philonides and Callistratus.

viii

(a) Anonymous *On Comedy* (Koster III.38–40)

ἐδίδαξε δὲ πρῶτος ἐπὶ ἄρχοντος Διοτίμου διὰ Καλ-
λιστράτου. τὰς μὲν γὰρ πολιτικὰς τούτῳ φασὶν αὐτὸν
διδόναι, τὰ δὲ κατ' Εὐριπίδου καὶ Σωκράτους Φιλω-
νίδῃ.

(b) Anonymous *On Actors* (Koster Xc)

ὑποκριταὶ Ἀριστοφάνους Καλλίστρατος καὶ Φιλω-
νίδης, δι' ὧν ἐδίδασκε τὰ δράματα ἑαυτοῦ, διὰ μὲν
Φιλωνίδου τὰ δημοτικά, διὰ δὲ Καλλιστράτου τὰ
ἰδιωτικά.

(c) *Life of Aristophanes* (Koster XXVIII.7–10)

εὐλαβὴς δὲ σφόδρα γενόμενος τὴν ἀρχὴν ἄλλως τε
καὶ εὐφυὴς τὰ μὲν πρῶτα διὰ Καλλιστράτου καί
Φιλωνίδου καθίει δράματα· διὸ καὶ ἔσκωπτον αὐτὸν
Ἀριστώνυμός τε Ἀμειψίας "τετράδι" λέγοντες "γεγο-
νέναι" κατὰ τὴν παροιμίαν ἄλλοις πονοῦντα.

(d) Tzetzes on *Clouds* 518

νόμος ἦν Ἀθηναίοις μὴ τεσσαρακονταετῆ τινα γεγο-
νότα μήτε δικηγορεῖν μήτε δημηγορεῖν, ἀλλὰ μηδὲ
δράματα ὑπαναγινώσκειν ἐς θέατρον. τούτῳ τῷ νόμῳ
καὶ ὁ κωμικὸς οὗτος εἰργόμενος πρότερον διὰ τὸ μὴ
τεσσαρακονταετὴς ἔτι ὑπάρχειν τὰ ἑαυτοῦ τῶν κωμῳ-
διῶν δράματα διὰ Φιλωνίδου καὶ Καλλιστράτου

viii

(a) He [Aristophanes] produced first in the archonship of Diotimus [428/7] through Callistratus. They say that he gave his political comedies to this man, and those against Euripides and Socrates to Philonides.[1]

(b) Callistratus and Philonides were actors for Aristophanes, through whom he put on his own plays, through Philonides his public plays, and his personal ones through Callistratus.

(c) At the start of his career being especially cautious as well as especially talented, he [Aristophanes] produced his first plays through Callistratus and Philonides. That is why Aristonymus [F 3] and Ameipsias [F 27] would make fun of him, saying that he was "born on the fourth," a proverb of those who laboured for others.

(d) The Athenians had a law that no one under forty years of age could conduct litigation or speak publicly before the people, and also could not produce plays in the theatre. Bound by this law and because he was not yet forty years old, this comic poet [Aristophanes] had his own plays performed in the theatre through Philonides and Callistratus.

[1] This entry contradicts the scholiast's identification (T 7b) of the producer of *Banqueters* as Philonides and the assignment in T 8b of the political plays to Philonides and the personal ones to Callistratus. Certainly *Babylonians, Acharnians, Birds,* and *Lysistrata,* which were produced through Callistratus, would seem to be "political."

THE POETS OF OLD COMEDY

Fragments

ΑΠΗΝΗ

ΚΟΘΟΡΝΟΙ

1 Athenaeus 247e

ἐγὼ δ᾽ ἀπόσιτος ὢν τοιαῦτ᾽ οὐκ ἀνέχομαι.

2 Athenaeus 228f

ὑποδέχεσθαι καὶ βατίσι καὶ τηγάνοις.

ὀσφρομένην τῶν τηγάνων.

12

PHILONIDES

Fragments

MULE-WAGON

This comedy is known only from its mention by the Suda *(T 1). There may have been some on-stage comedy with a cart drawn into the playing area (cf.* Agamemnon *906), or some comic business with an ass, such as that in* Wasps *or* Frogs.

BUSKINS

The cothurnus *was a high, loose-fitting soft boot that could be worn on either foot. Later it would become associated with the tragic actor, but in the fifth century it was worn by women. Males in drama wearing a* cothurnus *distinguished themselves from a "normal" male, e.g., Dionysus at* Frogs *47. Because it fit either foot, the nickname "cothurnus" was applied to the politician Theramenes, who invariably came out on the right side of any issue (Xenophon* Hellenica *2.3.30, Pollux 7.91). F 6 shows that he was mentioned in the play. He does appear in comedy as early as Eupolis'* Cities *(F 251—late 420s), but assuming that the nickname is a result of Theramenes' deft manoeuvrings in 406 (see* Frogs *534–40), we may want to date this comedy close to* Frogs *(D-405?).*

1 Without food I am not putting up with this.

2 To entertain with skates and frying pans.

A woman sniffing the frying pans.

3 Pollux 10.115

ὥσπερ οἱ δίμυξοι τῶν λύχνων

4 Photius (b, z) α 2024

περὶ δ' ὧν σὺ λέγεις, λόγος ἐστὶν ἐμοὶ πρὸς
   Ἀθηναίους κατὰ χειρός,
ὃν ἐγὼ λογιοῦμ' ἐξ ἀτελείας, τῷ δήμῳ δ' οὐδὲν
   ἀνοίσω.

5 Pollux 9.29

παναγὴς γενεά, πορνοτελῶναι, Μεγαρεῖς δεινοί,
   πατραλοῖαι.

6 The Antiatticist p. 100.1

Θηραμένης· τὴν κλητικὴν. Φιλωνίδης Κοθόρνοις.

ΠΡΟΑΓΩΝ

ΦΙΛΕΤΑΙΡΟΣ

ΑΔΗΛΩΝ ΔΡΑΜΑΤΩΝ

7 Helladius, cited at Photius *Library* 279.530a15–18

ὅρκους δὲ μοιχῶν εἰς τέφραν ἐγὼ γράφω.

3 Just like lamps with the double wicks.

4 Concerning what you say, I have a personal account with the Athenians, which I shall consider as settled, and I shall not charge it to the people.

5 A thoroughly cursed generation: tax-farmers, nasty Megarians, murderers.

6 Theramenes: in the vocative case, Philonides in *Buskins*.

PREVIEW

The hypothesis to Wasps *assigns a comedy of this name to Philonides as the first-place winner at L-422, but all other references to and citations from a "Preview" attribute the play to Aristophanes. In view of Philonides' attested career as a producer of Aristophanes' comedies, we should regard this comedy as the work of Aristophanes.*

GOOD FRIEND

This comedy is attested only by the Suda *(T 1). Plays of this title are known for six writers of later comedy.*

UNASSIGNED FRAGMENTS

7 The oaths of adulterers I write on ashes.[1]

[1] A parody of Sophocles F 811, "As for the oaths of women, I write them in water." *Clouds* 1083 reveals that singeing with ashes was part of the punishment of adulterers.

8 Athenaeus 23e

κατάκειμαι δ', ὡς ὁρᾶτε, δεκαπάλαι.

9 Athenaeus 67d

τὰ καταχύσματ' αὐτοῖσιν ὄξος οὐκ ἔχει.

10 Pollux 2.24

ὦ πολυτρίχου πώγωνος

11 Photius (z) α 2782

Ἀργείους ὁρῶ

ΑΜΦΙΣΒΗΤΗΣΙΜΟΝ

17 Pollux 3.18

νυνὶ δὲ Κρόνου καὶ Τιθωνοῦ παππεπίπαππος
νενόμισται.

8 As you [pl.] see, I have been lying down for quite some time.

9 Their sauces have no vinegar in them.

10 O my thick beard.

11 I see Argives.

Brief fragments: (F 12) "the edge" (of a blade), (F 13) "one who laughs at," (F 14) "sharp" (of wine), (F 15) "fond of villainy," (F 16) "hand washings."

DISPUTED FRAGMENT

17 Now he is considered the great-great-grandfather of Cronus and Tithonus.[1]

[1] One MS of Pollux names the comic poet as Nicophon [F 23], not Philonides.

ΦΙΛΥΛΛΙΟΣ

Philyllius was a minor comic poet of the very late fifth and early fourth centuries. F 8 makes fun of Laispodias, a figure of the 410s, but who is mentioned as late as Strattis' Cinesias (F 19), produced not long after Frogs (L-405). At the other end, his victory at the Lenaea (T 3) belongs to the late 390s. Thus a career from 405 to 390 seems reasonable. We have ten titles, seven of which have fragments surviving. The last two listed by the Suda (T 1), Atalanta *and* Helen, *are out of alphabetical sequence, and as neither possesses any attested fragments, are probably wrongly attributed. Three comedies seem to have been burlesques of myth (Aigeus, Auge, Nausicaa), or possibly parodies of*

Testimonia

i *Suda* φ 457

Φιλύλλιος, Ἀθηναῖος, κωμικὸς τῆς παλαιᾶς κωμῳδίας. τῶν δραμάτων αὐτοῦ ἐστιν Αἰγεύς, Αὔγη, Ἄντεια (ἑταίρας ὄνομα), Δωδεκάτη, Ἡρακλῆς, Πλύντρια ἢ Ναυσικάα, Πόλις, Φρεωρύχος, Ἀταλάντη, Ἑλένη.

18

PHILYLLIUS

tragedy, since we know of tragedies of all three titles by Sophocles and Euripides. We are told that Anteia *was the name of a hetaera, and three other plays appear to have had contemporary settings (*Cities, Twelfth Day, Well-Digger*).*

There was some confusion over the authorship of two comedies, Anteia *and* Cities. *The first was attributed to Eunicus or Philyllius, and we do have one fragment of an* Anteia *by Eunicus.* Cities *was assigned variously to Philyllius, Eunicus, and (surprisingly) Aristophanes. Eunicus and Philyllius may have written comedies with the same title, which were then confused, or one may have acted as the producer for the other.*

Testimonia

i Philyllius: of Athens, poet of Old Comedy. His plays are: *Aigeus, Auge, Anteia* (name of a hetaera), *Twelfth Day, Heracles, Washer-Woman* or *Nausicaa, City, Well-Digger, Atalanta, Helen.*

19

ii *Suda* δ 1155

Διοκλῆς . . . ἀρχαῖος κωμικός, σύγχρονος Σαννυρίωνι
καὶ Φιλυλλίῳ.

iii *IG* ii² 2325.136

Φιλύλλιος I

iv *IG* ii² 2325.64

Φιλ[ύλλιος

v Σ Aristophanes *Wealth* 1194

ὅτι Λυκόφρων, ὡς ὁ Ἐρατοσθένης φησὶν, ᾠήθη πρῶ-
τον τοῦτον δᾷδας ᾐτηκέναι. πεποίηκε δὲ καὶ ἐν Ἐκκλη-
σιαζούσαις αὐτό. ἀλλὰ γὰρ Στράττις πρὸ ἀμφοτέρων
τούτων τοὺς Ποταμίους διδάσκων εἰς Φιλύλλιον ἀνα-
φέρει τὸ πρᾶγμα·

vi Strattis F 38

ὑμεῖς τε πάντες ἔξιτ᾽ ἐπὶ τὸ Πύθιον,
ὅσοι πάρεστε μὴ λαβόντες λαμπάδας
μηδ᾽ ἄλλο μηδὲν ἐχόμενον Φιλυλλίου.

ΑΙΓΕΥΣ

ii Diocles: . . . a poet of Old Comedy, a contemporary of Sannyrion and Philyllius.

iii [from the list of victors at the Lenaea, early fourth century]

Philyllius 1

iv [list of victors at the Dionysia]

Phil[yllius.[1]

[1] Or "Phil[onides."

v As Eratosthenes said [F 7], Lycophron . . . believed that he [Aristophanes] was the first to have requested torches. He has done this also in *Assembly-Women*. But Strattis [F 38], putting on *Potamians* before either of these two dramas, attributes the practice to Philyllius.

vi All of you here present, go away, off to the shrine of Pythian Apollo, taking no lamps or anything else that belongs to Philyllius.

AEGEUS

The father of Theseus was the subject of tragedies by both Sophocles and Euripides, while Theseus appears in satyr drama (Euripides' Theseus*) and comedy (Cratinus'* Runaways, *a* Theseus *by both Aristonymus and Theopompus). It is not immediately apparent what story of Aegeus' life would extend itself to comic treatment. The tragedies concerned his relationship with Medea and her attempt to poison Theseus.*

THE POETS OF OLD COMEDY

Fragment

1 Stephanus of Byzantium p. 197.1

ὁ πάππος ἦν μοι γαλεὸς ἀστερίας

ANTEIA

Testimonia

i

(a) Athenaeus 567c

καὶ ἄλλα δὲ πολλά, ὦναιδές, δράματα ἀπὸ ἑταιρῶν
ἔσχε τὰς ἐπιγραφάς, Θάλαττα Διοκλέους, Φερεκρά-
τους Κοριαννώ, Εὐνίκου ἢ Φιλυλλίου Ἄντεια, Μενάν-
δρου δὲ Θαὶς καὶ Φάνιον, Ἀλέξιδος Ὀπώρα, Εὐβού-
λου Κλεψύδρα.

(b) Athenaeus 586e

ἀπὸ δὲ Ἀντείας καὶ ὅλον δρᾶμα ἐπιγραφόμενον, ὡς
προεῖπον, Εὐνίκου ἢ Φιλυλλίου Ἄντειά ἐστιν.

PHILYLLIUS

Fragment

1 My grandfather was a speckled dogfish.

Brief fragment: (F 2) "without grain."

ANTEIA

The play is known only from its inclusion in the Suda's *list (T 1) and from Athenaeus' attribution of the comedy to "Eunicus or Philyllius." One fragment (F 1) is assigned to an* Anteia *by Eunicus.*

Testimonia

i

(a) Many other plays, you disgusting man, also took their titles from hetaerae: *Thalatta* (Sea) by Diocles, Pherecrates' *Corianno*, *Anteia* by Eunicus or Philyllius, Menander's *Thais* and *Phanion*, *Opora* (Bounty) by Alexis, *Clepsydra* (Water-Clock) of Eubulus.

(b) But, as I mentioned above, there is an entire play named from Anteia; it is *Anteia* by Eunicus or Philyllius.

ΑΤΑΛΑΝΤΗ

ΑΥΓΗ

Fragments

3 Athenaeus 408e

καὶ δὴ δεδειπνήκασιν αἱ γυναῖκες· ἀλλ' ἀφαιρεῖν
ὥρα 'στὶν ἤδη τὰς τραπέζας, εἶτα παρακορῆσαι,
ἔπειτα κατὰ χειρῶν ἑκάστῃ καὶ μύρον τι δοῦναι.

4 Athenaeus 110f

αὐτὸς φέρων πάρειμι πυρῶν ἐκγόνους τριμήνων
γαλακτόχρωτας κολλάβους θερμούς.

5 Athenaeus 485b

πάντα γὰρ ἦν
μέστ' ἀνδρῶν <καὶ> μειρακίων
πινόντων, ὁμοῦ † δ' ἄλλων
γρᾳδίων μεγάλαισιν οἴ-
νου χαίροντα λεπασταῖς.

ATALANTA

It has been argued above that this might be mistakenly attributed to Philyllius. Atalanta was a frequent subject of both tragedy and comedy—as many as six Athenian and two Sicilian comedies bore this title (or the plural); for Old Comedy see the titles by Callias and Strattis.

AUGE

Auge, daughter of Aleos from Arcadia, was sexually involved with Heracles, in one version after an evening of hospitality, and became the mother of the hero Telephus. The concealed birth of Telephus and her self-defence formed the subject of Euripides' tragedy Auge, *and the three extant fragments here do suggest a theme of entertainment.*

Fragments

3 The ladies have in fact finished dinner. It is time now to clear away the tables, next to sweep up, then to provide water for the hands and scent for each woman.

4 I [masc.] am here in person bringing the offspring of spring wheat, hot rolls as white as milk.

5 The whole place was crammed with men and young men drinking, and near . . . of other old women enjoying great limpet cups of wine.

ΔΩΔΕΚΑΤΗ

Fragment

6 Pollux 10.70

> σοὶ μὲν οὖν τήνδ᾽, ἀμφορεῦ,
> δίδωμι τιμήν, πρῶτα μὲν τοῦτ᾽ αὐτ᾽ ἔχειν
> ὄνομα μετρητὴν μετριότητος οὕνεκα.

ΕΛΕΝΗ

PHILYLLIUS

TWELFTH DAY

If Hesychius (δ 2708) is correct in identifying "the twelfth day" as the celebration of the Choes (wine pots), held as part of the Anthesteria on the twelfth day of the month of Anthesterion, then we have a comedy whose setting was a day of festive and competitive drinking throughout the city. The last scenes of Acharnians *are set against the background of this celebration. The feast may be the occasion from which a plot of romantic intrigue proceeded.*

Fragment

6 To you, amphora, I give this honour, first that you bear the name "measurer" because you measure out in moderation.

HELEN

Helen was a figure in tragedy, first in Trojan Women *(415) and then in Euripides' revolutionary presentation of her in* Helen *(412) and finally in* Orestes *(408). She does not appear to have been the title character in comedy until the poets of Middle Comedy (Anaxandrides, Alexis), but she will certainly have appeared in Cratinus'* Dionysalexander *and probably in* Nemesis. *Both Sophocles'* Demand for Helen's Return *and his* Wedding of Helen *are thought to have been satyr plays. Platon wrote a* Menelaus *and a* Men of Laconia. *An Apulian bell krater (375–50, see V 20) shows a woman on shipboard taking leave of another man on shore. Some have identified this as a comic presentation of Helen and Menelaus.*

ΗΡΑΚΛΗΣ

Fragment

7 Athenaeus 171d

βούλεσθε δῆτ' ἐγὼ φράσω τίς εἰμ' ἐγώ;
ἡ τῶν προτενθῶν Δορπία καλουμένη.

ΠΛΥΝΤΡΙΑΙ Η ΝΑΥΣΙΚΑΑ

Two obvious sources for this comedy are the memorable episode in Odyssey 6, *when Nausicaa and her young companions do the laundry for the palace and awaken the sleeping Odysseus in the bushes, and Sophocles' early play,* Nausicaa *or* Washer-Women. *If this was, as some suggest, a*

HERACLES

*F 7 shows that the prologue was spoken by Dorpia, a
personification of the first day of the Apaturia, a three-day
meeting of the "clans" (phratries—cf. the play of that ti-
tle by Leucon) held during the autumn. That first day
(Dorpia) featured communal feasts of the members of the
phratry. How Heracles was worked into what seems to be
a contemporary setting is not clear, but if Dionysus can
come to Athens to join the navy (Eupolis' Officers) or fetch
back a dead tragic poet, it would not be out of the question
for Heracles (or an impersonator?) to appear at a festive
banquet. At Birds 1668–70 Heracles complains that, as a
bastard son of Zeus, he has never been introduced to his
father's phratry.*

Fragment

7 Do you people want me to tell you who I am? I am the
one called Dorpia of the Fore-Tasters.[1]

---

[1] Fore-tasters (*protenthai*) seem to have been a guild of of-
ficials who tasted food before others at the Apaturia.

WASHER-WOMEN OR NAUSICAA

*satyr play, then the humorous aspects of this encounter
were an early theme for comic drama. In Sicily Epichar-
mus wrote an Odysseus Shipwrecked and Phormus an Al-
cinous, which may have some bearing here. The Middle
Comic poet Eubulus wrote a Nausicaa, of which one frag-
ment remains. The mention of Laispodias (F 8) suggests a
date in the 410s.*

Fragment

8 Σ Aristophanes *Birds* 1569

Λαισποδίας . . . μέμνηται δὲ αὐτοῦ . . . Φιλύλλιος δὲ
ἐν ταῖς Πλυντρίαις ὡς φιλοδίκου.

ΠΟΛΕΙΣ

Fragments

9 Athenaeus 381a

> ὅ τι ἂν τύχῃ
> \<ὁ\> μάγειρος ἀδικήσας, τὸν αὐλητὴν λαβεῖν
> πληγάς.

Fragment

8 Philyllius mentions him [Laispodias] in his *Washer-Women* as fond of litigation.[1]

[1] Laispodias (*PAA* 600730) was a general in the late 410s (Thucydides 6.105.2). He was a frequent target in comedy, principally for some visible peculiarity with his legs (*Birds* 1569, Eupolis *Demes* F 107, Phrynichus F 17, Strattis F 19, Theopompus F 40).

CITIES

Athenaeus twice attributes this comedy to "Philyllius or whoever wrote the Cities*" (92e, 381a), once just to Philyllius (104f), once to "Philyllius or Eunicus or Aristophanes" (86e), and once to "Philyllius or Aristophanes" (140a). This last is odd since the only other* Cities *we know of is that of Eupolis c. 420. That comedy had an individuated chorus of cities from the Athenian* archē, *but we have no hint of the identity of the cities here, assuming that they did constitute the chorus. The Doric dialect in F 10 indicates that there was an ethnic character in the play, perhaps one with difficulty in reading.*

Fragments

9 Whenever the cook happens to do something wrong, the *aulos* player <must> get beaten.[1]

[1] See Eubulus F 60 for something very similar. This may be proverbial.

10 Pollux 10.58

ἐκ τᾶς πινακίδος διαμπερέως, ὅ τι κα λέγοι
τὰ γράμμαθ᾽, ἑρμήνευε.

11 Pollux 10.126

σπαθᾶν τὸν ἱστὸν οὐκ ἔσται σπάθη.

12 Athenaeus 86e

πουλυπόδειον, σηπιδάριον, κάραβον, ἀστακόν,
    ὄστρειον,
χήμας, λεπάδας, σωλῆνας, μῦς, πίννας, κτένας ἐκ
    Μυτιλήνης·
† αἴρετ᾽ ἀνθρακίδας† τρίγλη, σαργός, κεστρεύς,
    πέρκη, κορακῖνοι.

13 Pollux 7.110

ἀνθρακοπώλης, κοσκινοποιός, κηπεύς, κουρεύς

ΦΡΕΩΡΥΧΟΣ

10 Read out ‹for me› what is written on the notice board from beginning to end.

11 There won't be a batten to strike the beam.

12 A little octopus, a tiny squid, a crawfish, lobster, an oyster, clams, limpets, razor shells, mussels, pinnas, scallops from Mytilene, and get me (?) little broilers, a red mullet, a sargue, a grey mullet, a perch, a tilapia.

13 A coal seller, sieve maker, gardener, barber.

Brief fragments: (F 14) "ring maker," (F 15) "Copis," (F 16) "greedy scrooge."

WELL-DIGGER

The best-known well in Greek drama is that into which Cnemon falls in Menander's Bad-Tempered Man, *but the title and two fragments do not take us very far.*

THE POETS OF OLD COMEDY

Fragments

17 Eustathius *On the* Odyssey p. 1553.10

προὔδωκεν αὐτὸν ὁ τόρος· ἦν γὰρ ἀσθενής.

18 Athenaeus 640e

ἀμυγδάλια, καρύδι', ἐπιφορήματα

ΑΔΗΛΩΝ ΔΡΑΜΑΤΩΝ

19 Clement of Alexandria *Miscellany* 5.46.3–6

ἕλκειν τὸ βέδυ σωτήριον προσεύχομαι,
ὅπερ μέγιστόν ἐστιν ὑγιείας μέρος,
τὸ τὸν ἀέρ' ἕλκειν καθαρόν, οὐ τεθολωμένον.

20 Athenaeus 63a

οὐκ εἰμὶ τέττιξ οὐδὲ κοχλίας, ὦ γύναι.

21 Pollux 7.29

τὸ κάταγμα κροκυδίζουσαν αὐτὴν κατέλαβον.

22 Σ Aristophanes *Wealth* 179b

ἦ τις κάμηλος ἔτεκε τὸν Φιλωνίδην;

PHILYLLIUS

Fragments

17 The drill let him down—it was weak after all.

18 Almonds, nuts, desserts.

UNASSIGNED FRAGMENTS

19 I pray that I may draw a lifesaving breath. This is the most important element of health, to breathe clean and unpolluted air.

20 Woman, I am not a cicada or a snail.

21 I found her plucking away at a flock of wool.

[Auge?]

22 Did some she-camel give birth to Philonides?[1]

[1] Philonides (*PAA* 957480), son of Onetor, hence his nickname Onos (ass), was a large, awkward, not very bright, but rich Athenian, said to be the lover of the hetaera Nais. See *Wealth* 179, 303; Nicochares F 4; and the comedy *Philonides* by the Middle Comic poet Aristophon.

23 Athenaeus 31a

παρέξω Λέσβιον,
Χῖον σαπρόν, Θάσιον, <   > Βίβλινον,
Μενδαῖον, ὥστε μηδένα κραιπαλᾶν.

24 Athenaeus 52b

ᾠά, κάρυ', ἀμυγδάλαι

25 Athenaeus 700f

]σω καὶ θρυαλλίδ', ἢν δέῃ.

26 Athenaeus 63a

μαινίδες <   > σκόμβροι, κοχλίαι, κορακῖνοι

23 I will be providing wine from Lesbos, some mellow Chian, Thasian . . . wine from Byblus, wine from Mende, so no one gets a hangover.

24 Eggs, nuts, almonds.

25 ⟨I will bring a two-wicked lamp⟩ and wicks, if you need them.

26 Sprats, mackerel, snails, tilapia.

Brief fragments: (F 27) "I shall grind," (F 28) "illegally," (F 29) "torches" (used of lamps), (F 32) "objects of desire," (F 31) "semiplaited," (F 32) "lukewarm," (F 33) "to wind thread off the reel."

ΦΡΥΝΙΧΟΣ

*Two dates are given for his debut: "in the 87th Olympiad"
[436–2–T 1] and "the archonship of Apollodorus" [429–T
2]. As the latter is very probably giving us the occasion of a
poet's first play, and not just the fact that both Eupolis and
Phrynichus produced a play in the same year, the latter
date (429) is to be preferred. The hypothesis to* Frogs *(T 8)
shows that he was still active in 405. Ten titles are known—
in T 1* Satyrs *and* Tragic Actors *have for some reason inter-
rupted the alphabetical sequence, and then* Satyrs *was in-
advertently repeated.*

*Two of his comedies have the same title as plays by
Ameipsias. While two comic poets may well have each
written a play called "Revellers," that each wrote a "Con-
nus" about the well-known musical figure of the 420s seems
less likely. Five fragments of a* Revellers *are attributed to
Phrynichus, none to a play by Ameipsias, although T 7
definitely names Ameipsias as the winning poet at D-414
with a comedy of that name. For* Connus, *three fragments
are attributed to Phrynichus and six to Ameipsias. A hy-
pothesis to* Clouds *(Ameipsias T 5) fixes the production of
Ameipsias'* Connus *at D-423. I suspect some sort of rela-
tionship between Phrynichus and Ameipsias, either as col-
laborators in comedy, or that Ameipsias produced one or
two of Phrynichus' comedies, as Philonides did for Aris-*

PHRYNICHUS

tophanes. If Phrynichus is the real author of Revellers, *it will have allowed him to stage two plays at one festival (D-414), as Aristophanes seems to have done with Philonides' help at L-422.*

We can pin down some of Phrynichus' dates: a comedy in 429, probably Cronus, *since Diopeithes (F 9) is known to have been active in the late 430s and a comedy of this title would fit well with the burlesques of myth in the 430s, especially Cratinus'* Wealth-Gods, Connus *at D-423,* Revellers *and* Hermit *at D-414,* Muses *at L-405. For* Ephialtes *(or* Nightmare?*) and* Lady Grass-Cutters, *the references to Meidias (F 4, 43) should put these comedies in the 410s.* Satyrs *is most easily placed in the late 420s or very early 410s, while* Tragic Actors *and* Initiates *remain less easy to date.*

*His was not as prolific a career (ten plays in twenty-five years) as Aristophanes' or Eupolis', and his high point seems to have been the 410s. He did win a victory at the Lenaea (T 6), perhaps even in his first attempt in 429; if not then, certainly in 428. But his first victory at the Dionysia (T 5) seems not to have come until 420 or after. An early play (*Cronus?*) contained a parody of the story of Andromeda, with a drunken old woman threatened by the sea monster (T 9, F 77).*

As far as we can tell from the few fragments and play

titles, he seems to have written comedy of the same sort as Aristophanes, although Cronus *suggests a burlesque of myth. Two titles* (Muses, Tragic Actors) *imply a theme of poetry and poets, but most of the titles suggest comedy with a contemporary Athenian setting, in two instances with a god present (Dionysus in F 10, Hermes in F 61). He makes frequent jokes at real people (nineteen in eighty-six fragments—compare that with fewer than twelve in three hun-*

Testimonia

i *Suda* φ 763

Φρύνιχος, Ἀθηναῖος, κωμικὸς τῶν ἐπιδευτέρων τῆς ἀρχαίας κωμῳδίας. ἐδίδαξε γοῦν τὸ πρῶτον ἐπὶ πϛ´ Ὀλυμπιάδος. δράματα δὲ αὐτοῦ ἐστι ταῦτα· Ἐφιάλτης, Κόννος, Κρόνος, Κωμασταί, Σάτυροι, Τραγῳδοὶ ἢ Ἀπελεύθεροι, Μονότροπος, Μοῦσαι, Μύστης, Ποάστριαι, Σάτυροι.

ii Anonymous *On Comedy* (Koster III.9–13, 32–34)

τούτων δέ εἰσιν ἀξιολογώτατοι Ἐπίχαρμος, Μάγνης, Κρατῖνος, Κράτης, Φερεκράτης, Φρύνιχος, Εὔπολις, Ἀριστοφάνης.
Φρύνιχος †† <Πολυ>φράδμονος ἔθανεν ἐν Σικελίᾳ.
Εὔπολις Ἀθηναῖος. ἐδίδαξεν ἐπὶ ἄρχοντος Ἀπολλοδώρου, ἐφ' οὗ καὶ Φρύνιχος.

*dred fragments of Pherecrates). One ancient source (T 11)
records that he was criticised for crude jokes, the poor
quality of his plays, stealing material from other poets, and
irregularities in his use of metre. But these are all likely de-
rived from comments in comedy, like that in the opening of
Frogs (T 10).*

Recent bibliography: Harvey, in Rivals *91–134; M. Chan-
try,* RPh *75 (2001) 239–47.*

Testimonia

i Phrynichus: of Athens, a poet belonging to the second
generation of Old Comedy. For he produced for the first
time in the 86th Olympiad [436–2]. These are his plays:
*Ephialtes, Connus, Cronus, Revellers, Satyrs, Tragic Ac-
tors or Freed-men, Hermit, Muses, Initiate, Lady Grass-
Cutters, Satyrs.*

ii The most noteworthy of these are Epicharmus,
Magnes, Cratinus, Crates, Pherecrates, Phrynichus, Eu-
polis, and Aristophanes.

Phrynichus the son of ‹Poly›phradmon died in Sicily.[1]

[1] This is likely not the comic poet, but Phrynichus the early
tragic poet, whose father was named Polyphradmon (Σ *Birds* 749
= *TrGF* 3 T 10g). It would be no surprise if a dramatist of his repu-
tation became part of the cultural entourage at the court of Syra-
cuse, or there may be a confusion with Aeschylus who did die in
Sicily.

Eupolis of Athens produced in the archonship of Apol-
lodorus [430/29], the same year as Phrynichus.

iii *The Names and Plays of the Poets of Old Comedy*
(Koster VIII.7)

Φρυνίχου δράματα ι′.

iv *Suda* π 1708

Πλάτων, Ἀθηναῖος, κωμικός, γεγονὼς τοῖς χρόνοις
κατὰ Ἀριστοφάνην καὶ Φρύνιχον, Εὔπολιν, Φερεκρά-
την.

v *IG* ii² 2325.61

Φρύ[νιχος

vi *IG* ii² 2325.124

Φρύνιχος II

vii Hypothesis II *Birds*

ἐδιδάχθη ἐπὶ Χαρίου διὰ Καλλιστράτου ἐν ἄστει, ὃς
ἦν δεύτερος τοῖς Ὄρνισι, πρῶτος Ἀμειψίας Κωμα-
σταῖς, τρίτος Φρύνιχος Μονοτρόπῳ.

viii Hypothesis I *Frogs*

ἐδιδάχθη ἐπὶ Καλλίου τοῦ μετὰ Ἀντιγένη διὰ Φιλω-
νίδου εἰς Λήναια. πρῶτος ἦν· δεύτερος Φρύνιχος Μού-
σαις· Πλάτων τρίτος Κλεοφῶντι.

iii Of Phrynichus ten plays.

iv Platon: of Athens, comic poet, lived at the time of Aristophanes and Phrynichus, Eupolis, Pherecrates.

v [from the list of victors at the Dionysia, c. 420]
  Phry[nichus

vi [from the list of victors at the Lenaea, early 420s]
  Phrynichus 2

vii The play [*Birds*] was produced in the archonship of Charias [415/4] through Callistratus at the Dionysia. He [Aristophanes] was second with *Birds,* Ameipsias was first with *Revellers*, and Phrynichus third with *Hermit.*

viii The play [*Frogs*] was produced in the archonship of Callias [406/5], who came after Antigenes, through Philonides at the Lenaea. He [Aristophanes] was first, Phrynichus second with *Muses,* and Platon third with *Cleophon.*

ix *Clouds* 553–56

Εὔπολις μὲν τὸν Μαρικᾶν πρώτιστον παρείλκυσεν
ἐκστρέψας τοὺς ἡμετέρους Ἱππέας κακὸς κακῶς,
προσθεὶς αὐτῷ γραῦν μεθύσην τοῦ κόρδακος οὕνεχ᾽,
    ἣν
Φρύνιχος πάλαι πεπόηχ᾽, ἣν τὸ κῆτος ἤσθιεν.

x *Frogs* 12–15

τί δῆτ᾽ ἔδει με ταῦτα τὰ σκεύη φέρειν,
εἴπερ ποήσω μηδὲν ὧνπερ Φρυνίχοις
εἴωθε ποιεῖν καὶ Λύκις κἀμειψίας
σκεύη φέρουσ᾽ ἑκάστοτ᾽ ἐν κωμῳδίᾳ;

xi Σ *Frogs* 13

Φρύνιχος· Δίδυμός φησιν ὅτι νῦν Φρυνίχου τοῦ κωμι-
κοῦ μέμνηται, ὡς παρ᾽ ἕκαστα ἐν ταῖς κωμῳδίαις
φορτικευομένου. ἔστι δὲ πατρὸς Εὐνομίδου. κωμῳδεῖ-
ται δὲ καὶ ὡς ξένος, καὶ ἐπὶ φαυλότητι ποιημάτων, καὶ
ὡς ἀλλότρια λέγων καὶ ὡς κακόμετρα. εἰσὶ δὲ καὶ
ἄλλοι τρεῖς Φρύνιχοι. Φρύνιχος δὲ ὁ κωμικὸς οὐδὲν
τούτων ἐποίησεν ἐν τοῖς σῳζομένοις αὐτοῦ· εἰκὸς δὲ ἐν
τοῖς ἀπολωλόσιν εἶναι αὐτοῦ τοιοῦτόν τι.

xii Σ *Clouds* 555/56

ἦν Φρύνιχος· φαίνεται †ὑπεύθυνος† Φρύνιχος· μήποτε
οὖν ἐκείνην <εἰσήγαγε> χλευάζων ὡς γραῦν ἐκκειμέ-

ix First that wretched Eupolis dragged his wretched *Maricas* on stage, turning our *Knights* inside out, tacking onto it a drunken crone for the sake of a vulgar dance, the same old woman that Phrynichus portrayed once, the one whom the sea monster was devouring.

x (XANTHIAS) Why then did I have to carry all this stuff, if I am not going to do any of the jokes that Phrynichus is used to doing, and Lycis and Ameipsias as well? They have baggage-carrying in every comedy.

xi "Phrynichus": Didymus says that he is talking about Phrynichus the comic poet at this point, for making crude jokes in each of his comedies. His father was Eunomides. He is made fun of as a foreigner, for the poor quality of his plays, for using other people's material, and for faulty metrics. There are three other men named Phrynichus. In his surviving works, Phrynichus the comic poet does none of these things. It is likely that there was something like this in his lost plays.

xii "Whom Phrynichus": Phrynichus seems . . . Perhaps he brought her on stage making fun of an old woman set

νην τῷ κήτει, καὶ ἴσως ἐν ὑπερβολῇ ἂν λέγοι αὐτός,
ὅτι "τὸ κῆτος ἤσθιεν."

ἦν Φρύνιχος· εἰσήγαγε γραῦν Φρύνιχος ὑπὸ κή-
τους ἐσθιομένην κατὰ μίμησιν Ἀνδρομέδας διὰ γέλω-
τα τῶν θεατῶν. ἦν δὲ αὐτὸς κωμῳδίας ποιητής.

xiii Σ *Birds* 749

τέσσαρες δὲ ἐγένοντο Φρύνιχοι. ὁ μὲν εἷς οὗ νῦν
μνημονεύει, Πολυφράδμονος παῖς, ποιητὴς ἡδὺς ἐν
τοῖς μέλεσιν. ὁ ἕτερος, Χοροκλέους παῖς, ὑποκριτής.
τρίτος, Φρύνιχος ὁ κωμικός, οὗ μέμνηται Ἕρμιππος
ἐν Φορμοφόροις ὡς ἀλλότρια ὑποβαλλομένου ποιή-
ματα. τέταρτος δέ ἐστιν Ἀθηναῖος τὸ γένος ὁ στρατη-
γήσας τὰ περὶ Σάμον καὶ Ἀστυόχῳ προσθέμενος,
ἐπιχειρήσας δὲ τῇ τοῦ δήμου καταλύσει. περὶ ὧν ἐν
τοῖς Βατράχοις ἱκανῶς εἰρήκαμεν.

xiv "Marius Victorinus" (Aphthonius) *Art of Grammar*
2.6

heptametrum catalecticum choriambicum purum, quod
Phrynichum comicum, auctorem eius artis, tradidisse et
sui nominis appellatione signasse dicunt.

xv "Marius Victorinus" (Aphthonius) *Art of Grammar* 2.9

tetrametrum . . . catalecticum copiosum est apud Phryni-
chum, auctorem comoediae veteris.

out for a sea monster, or perhaps he himself was speaking in exaggeration, "the sea monster was devouring."

"Whom Phrynichus": Phrynichus brought on stage an old woman being devoured by a sea monster in the manner of Andromeda for the amusement of the spectators. He was a comic poet.

xiii There were four men named Phrynichus. The first is the one he mentions here, the son of Polyphradmon, a poet of sweet choral songs. The next is the son of Chorocles, an actor. There is a third Phrynichus, the comic poet whom Hermippus mentions in *Basket-Bearers* [F 64] as passing other people's work off as his own. The fourth is the Athenian, who served as general in the campaign at Samos, associated with Astyochus, and attempted to bring down the democracy. About these men we have said enough in *Frogs*.

xiv Pure choriambic heptameter catalectic, which they say that Phrynichus the comic poet, the creator of this metre, passed along and indicated that by calling it by his name.

xv [on the ionic meter] The tetrameter catalectic is frequent in Phrynichus, a writer of Old Comedy.

xvi "Marius Victorinus" (Aphthonius) *Art of Grammar* 2.10

trimetrum autem . . . quos phynichion vocatur.

xvii Marius Plotius Sacerdos *Art of Grammar* 3.7

choriambicum dimetrum acatalectum, quod phrynichium nuncupatur, incipit a dispondeo et desinit in choriambum vel in hippium, id est epitritum.

ΕΦΙΑΛΤΗΣ

Both the actual title and especially its meaning are obscure. The play is cited six times, four times as "Ephialtes" and twice as "Epialtes." Eustathius (On the Iliad p. 561.16) cites the orators for the distinction in Attic Greek between "Epialtes" (a supernatural being such as a nightmare or incubus, or a nighttime fever) and "Ephialtes" (a proper name). PAA bears this out, recording seven instances of Ephialtes as a proper name (the most famous being the democratic leader assassinated in 461), and none for Epialtes. F 1 has a character announce his identity (in the prologue?—cf. F 19 for Monotropos), the text of which is corrupt but seems to turn on a pun between Ephialtes and epialas (turn one's hand to). Suggestions include a personified Nightmare introducing the comedy, the shade of the murdered democrat, and the ideal of the "beautiful youth" of F 3.

Another possibility is that we have an intertextual reference here. First "Ephialtes" is the name of the fellow

xvi ⟨There is⟩ also a ⟨paeonic⟩ trimeter . . . which they call a "phrynichean."

xvii The choriambic dimeter acatalectic, which is called a "phrynichean," begins with a double spondee and ends in a choriamb or in a hippius, that is an epitrite.

xviii On a vase by the Cleophon painter (V 1), dated to the mid-420s, we see two singers on each side, and in the middle an *aulos* player (Amphilochus) and a figure (the poet) labelled "Phrynichus." Harvey argues strongly that this is the comic poet.

EPHIALTES (NIGHTMARE?)

slave of Eupolis (T 11), who attempted to steal some of Eupolis' plays but was deterred by Eupolis' watchful dog. This might reflect some borrowing by one poet from another (see T 11, 13)—did Phrynichus and Eupolis collaborate with (or plagiarise) one another at an early point in their careers? Or is Phrynichus' comedy the source of this story? Then at Wasps 1038 *Aristophanes claims that in a previous comedy (probably at L-423) he "took on the chills and fevers, who would choke their fathers by night and smother their grandfathers, get into the beds of those of you who were uninvolved, cobble together affidavits and summonses and depositions, so that many people woke up in fear and headed straight for the polemarch." This is usually taken to be an attack by Aristophanes (in his* Merchant-Ships?) *on informers, but a comedy by Phrynichus called* Nightmare, *perhaps competing with Aristophanes at L-423, would be an alternative explanation for "taking on the chills and fevers."*

THE POETS OF OLD COMEDY

Fragments

1 Σ Aristophanes *Wasps* 1348a

† ὄνομα δέ τῶ τοῦτ' ἦν ἔσωθεν γην τε μὴ
ἔστω φιάλτης ἀνδραγαθίας οὕνεκα,
ἔτι ἐπιάλας χρηστὰ λέ ἀπωλόμην †.

2 Athenaeus 184f

οὐ τουτονὶ μέντοι σὺ κιθαρίζειν ποτὲ
αὐλεῖν τ' ἐδίδαξας;

3 Athenaeus 165b

ἔστιν δ' αὐτούς γε φυλάττεσθαι τῶν νῦν
χαλεπώτατον ἔργον.
ἔχουσι γάρ τι κέντρον ἐν τοῖς δακτύλοις,
μισάνθρωπον ἄνθος ἥβης·
εἶθ' ἡδυλογοῦσιν ἄπασιν ἀεὶ κατὰ τὴν ἀγορὰν
περιόντες.
5 ἐπὶ τοῖς ‹δὲ› βάθροις ὅταν ὧσιν, ἐκεῖ τούτοις οἷς
ἡδυλογοῦσιν
μεγάλας ἀμυχὰς καταμύξαντες καὶ συγκύψαντες
ἅπαντες
γελῶσιν.

PHRYNICHUS

Fragments

1 This was . . . name . . . let it be "Ephialtes" because of his courage . . . I perished.

2 But didn't you teach this man here to play the lyre and the *aulos*?

3 To protect ourselves from them is the most difficult task of all today. For they possess a sort of sting in their fingers, this hostile flower of youth. Then they walk around the marketplace, always speaking pleasantly to everyone, but when they're in the seats, there they inflict deep scratches and huddling all together laugh at those to whom they talk so pleasantly.

4

(a) Σ Aristophanes *Birds* 1297

κόβαλός τε ἐλέγετο εἶναι καὶ πτωχαλαζὼν, ὡς Φρύνιχος ἐν Ἐπιάλτῃ.

(b) Σ Lucian *Tragic Zeus* 48

ὡς πονηρὸν δὲ καὶ τῶν δημοσίων νοσφιστὴν Φρύνιχος καὶ Πλάτων διαβάλλουσιν.

ΚΟΝΝΟΣ

Fragment

6 Photius ε 889

τί δαί; τὸν ἐνεργμόν;

ΚΡΟΝΟΣ

The title suggests a burlesque of myth, and we may cite the appearance of the Titans as the chorus in Cratinus' Wealth-Gods *and presumably having some role in Myrtilus'* Titan-Pans, *also Aristonymus'* The Sun is Cold, *and Ocean in* Prometheus. *A comedy called "Cronus" might fo-*

4

(a) He [Meidias] is said to be a scoundrel and a pretentious beggar, so Phrynichus in *Epialtes*.

(b) Phrynichus and Platon [F 116] accuse him of being a wicked man and a scoundrel and a stealer of public funds.

Brief fragment: (F 5) "coiner."

CONNUS

The play title is the same as that of Ameipsias' comedy of D-423, of which four fragments remain. These two plays may be the same comedy, with Phrynichus perhaps acting as producer. Or (more likely) "Connus" may be a misreading of "Cronus" (see below).

Fragment

6 What now? The lyre peg?

Brief fragments: (F 7) "until," (F 8) "unlearned."

CRONUS

cus on his association with the Golden Age (Cratinus F 176), and here the presence of Dionysus (F 10) might be natural in a utopian comedy. Alternatively, could a comic poet have staged the forced regurgitation of the brothers and sisters of Zeus? Birth comedies of gods and heroes are a common theme of both satyr plays and comedy, and if comedies can present the birth of Helen from an egg (Nemesis) and the birth of Athena from the forehead of Zeus,

Fragments

9 Σ Aristophanes *Birds* 988

ἀνὴρ χορεύει καὶ τὰ τοῦ θεοῦ καλά.
βούλει Διοπείθη μεταδράμω καὶ τύμπανα;

10 Hesychius σ 324

ἄγαμαι, Διονῦ, σου στόματος, ὡς σεσέλλισαι
† κεκομμένα πολλάκις.

11 Erotianus υ 18

†κείνη μεμνήσθω με ξύλον ὑποτεταγός†

ΚΩΜΑΣΤΑΙ

A play of this title by Ameipsias won first prize at the Dionysia of 414, but as no fragments are cited from it, it is often thought that Phrynichus' Revellers and that of Ameipsias are the same comedy. It must be admitted, how-

*why not the rebirth of the Olympians? PCG VIII 1062
presents a papyrus from a comedy in which Rhea com-
plains about her husband's behaviour in swallowing their
newborn children.*

Fragments

9 The fellow is dancing and all is well with the gods. Do
you want me to run after Diopeithes and some tambou-
rines?[1]

[1] Comedy makes fun of Diopeithes (*PAA* 363095) for being
obsessed with oracles (*Knights* 1085, *Birds* 988, Teleclides F 7,
Ameipsias F 10). He was also active in politics—see Pericles *Plu-
tarch* 32.1 for his decree against "those who do not believe in the
gods."

10 I do admire your way of speaking, Dionysus, how you
pretend and boast (?) so often.

11 . . . a piece of wood placed beneath.

Brief fragments: (F 12) "leek," (F 13) "cock-seller's shop."

REVELLERS

*ever, that a title of "Revellers" would not have been an un-
common one in comedy. Early critics regarded the play's
subject as the drunken parody of the Mysteries at the house
of Poulytion in 415, but that could have been too dangerous
a topic even for comedy.*

THE POETS OF OLD COMEDY

Fragments

14 Pollux 4.55

ἐγὼ δὲ νῶν δὴ τερετιῶ τι πτιστικόν.

15 Athenaeus 474b

εἶτα κεραμεύων ἂν οἴκοι σωφρόνως Χαιρέστρατος
ἑκατὸν ⟨ἂν⟩ τῆς ἡμέρας †ἔκλαιεν† οἴνου κανθάρους.

16 Photius (b, Sᶻ) α 1993

ἡμῖν δ᾽ ἀνίει σὺ τἀγαθὰ
τοῖς τήνδ᾽ ἔχουσι τὴν πόλιν ἵλεως

17 Σ Aristophanes *Birds* 1569

τοῦτον δὲ τὸν Λαισποδίαν καὶ στρατηγῆσαί φησι
Θουκυδίδης ἐν τῇ η΄. μέμνηται δὲ αὐτοῦ Φρύνιχος ἐν
Κωμασταῖς ὡς πολεμικοῦ γεγονότος.

18 Hesychius ε 3309

Κολακοφοροκλείδης

ΜΟΝΟΤΡΟΠΟΣ

Fragments

14 And I shall hum a winnowing song for the pair of us.

15 Then Chaerestratus the potter working soberly at home would . . . a hundred cups of wine a day.

16 You [sing.], graciously send up good things for us who hold this city.

17 Thucydides in Book 8 [86.9] says that this Laispodias was also a general. Phrynichus mentions him in *Revellers* as being a man of war.

18 Suck-up—thieving—clides.[1]

---

[1] A comic coinage based on *kolax* (suck-up) + *phoro* (rob) + *clides*. According to Hesychius it refers to a certain Hieroclides, but Chronopoulos (*Eikasmos* 17 [2006] 139–43) argues that a Phereclides (*PAA* 920100) is meant. See also Hermippus F 39.

HERMIT

There seems to have been a vogue of comedies in the 410s about the flight from life in the city. Pherecrates produced his Wild-Men *with a chorus of uncivilised men in 420,* Birds *is about two Athenians escaping to the birds for a life without the worries (mainly legal) of the city, and a figure of folklore, Timon of Athens, is mentioned here (F 19), at* Birds *1549 (of Prometheus who hates the gods as "a Timon, pure and simple"), and again by the women in* Lysistrata *(805–20), as "abodeless among trackless thorns." Some sources treat him as a historical figure (*PAA* 890660).*

Testimonia

i See T 7 above.

ii Σ Aristophanes *Birds* 997

καθεῖται δὲ καὶ ὁ Μονότροπος ἐπὶ τοῦ αὐτοῦ †χωρίου†, εἴρηται.

χρόνου ὡς Dobree, Χαβρίου Tyrwhitt.

Fragments

19 Photius (b, z) α 375

ὄνομα δέ μούστι Μονότροπος
        ζῶ δὲ Τίμωνος βίον,
ἄγαμον, †ἄζυγον†, ὀξύθυμον, ἀπρόσοδον,
ἀγέλαστον, ἀδιάλεκτον, ἰδιογνώμονα.

3 ἄζυγον codd., ἄδουλον Hermann.

20 Pollux 3.48

        τηλικουτοσὶ γέρων
ἄπαις ἀγύναικος.

21 Σ Aristophanes *Birds* 11

{A.} μεγάλους πιθήκους οἶδ᾽ ἑτέρους τινὰς λέγειν,
Λυκέαν, Τελέαν, Πείσανδρον, Ἐξηκεστίδην.

PHRYNICHUS

The main character of this comedy calls himself "Mono-tropos" (of solitary ways) and is certainly the literary ante-cedent of Cnemon in Menander's Bad-Tempered Man. *If the later comedy is any guide, Phrynichus' play would have involved an encounter with this unapproachable fig-ure. F 29 would suggest an incident of violence, F 19–20 perhaps a theme of marriage.*

Recent bibliography: P. Ceccarelli, in Rivals *461–63.*

Testimonia

i See T 7 above.

ii *Hermit* was produced in the same year(?) [as *Birds*], ⟨as⟩ it is said.

Fragments

19 My name is "Hermit," and I am living a life of Timon, without a wife, without a slave (?), sharp-tempered, don't come near me, I don't laugh, I don't talk, I know my own mind.

20 An old man of my generation, childless, wifeless.

21 (A) I know certain other great baboons to mention: Lyceas, Teleas, Peisander, Execestides.

{B.} ἀνωμάλους εἶπας πιθήκους
ὁ μέν γε δειλός, ὁ δὲ κόλαξ, ὁ δὲ νόθος

22 Σ Aristophanes *Birds* 997

{A.} τίς δ᾽ ἔστιν ὁ μετὰ ταῦτα φροντίζων; {B.}
Μέτων,
ὁ Λευκονοιεύς. {A.} οἶδ᾽, ὁ τὰς κρήνας ἄγων.

23 *Suda* ν 217

ἀλλ᾽ ὑπερβέβληκε πολὺ τὸν Νικίαν
στρατηγίας πλήθει †καὶ εὑρήμασιν.

24 Athenaeus 248c

ὁ δ᾽ ὀλιγόσιτος Ἡρακλῆς ἐκεῖ τί δρᾷ;

25 Pollux 7.178

ἔπειτ᾽ ἐπειδὰν τὸν λύχνον κατακοιμίσῃ

26 Athenaeus 74a

κἀντραγεῖν σικύδιον

(B) You have mentioned a strange variety of baboons
. . . one is a coward, another a sponger, one a bastard.[1]

[1] It is not certain how many "baboons" were mentioned or which description belongs to which figure. Regarding Λυκέαν as dittography from λέγειν reduces the "baboons" to three and thus matches l. 4.

22 (A) Who is the next man who has good ideas?

(B) Meton, of Leuconoe.[1]

(A) I know him, the man who is responsible for the springs.

[1] A deme of the tribe Leontis.

23 But he has far surpassed Nicias in the wealth (?) of his generalship and in his schemes.

24 What is the light-feeding Heracles doing over there?

25 Then whenever he puts the light to bed.

26 And to munch on a small cucumber.

27 Σ Aristophanes *Birds* 1297

δοκεῖ δὲ καὶ ψήφισμα τεθεικέναι μὴ κωμῳδεῖσθαι
ὀνομαστί τινα, ὡς Φρύνιχος ἐν Μονοτρόπῳ φησί·
    ψῶρ᾽ ἔχε Συρακόσιον, ἐπιφανὲς γὰρ αὐτῷ καὶ
    μέγα τύχοι. ἀφείλετο γὰρ κωμῳδεῖν οὓς
    ἐπεθύμουν.
διὸ πικρότερον αὐτῷ προσφέρονται.

31 Photius p. 397.7

παρθένοι Ὑακινθίδες

ΜΟΥΣΑΙ

This comedy was produced along with Frogs *at L-405,
winning the second prize. The title plus F 32 suggests a
comedy with a literary theme and raises the question of
whether poets were aware of or influenced by what others*

27 He [Syracosius] seems also to have passed a decree that no one be made fun of by name, as Phrynichus says in *Hermit*:

> Mange, get Syracosius. May he get a lot of it and very visible too. For he has taken away those whom I [they?] wanted to make fun of.[1]

That's why they attack him even more bitterly.

[1] One of the most disputed passages in the study of Old Comedy. The decree is clearly a deduction from the comic text, but how much of the actual citation belongs to Phrynichus? Does the last sentence belong rather to the commentator? If so, how did the commentator draw his conclusion about the "decree"? If there was such a decree, the plays of 414 show no sign of it. Was it restricted in its scope, i.e., no mention of those involved in the scandals of 415? Or is the whole thing a scholiast's fiction? Syracosius (*PAA* 853435) was politically active in the late 420s and 410s (*Birds* 1297; Eupolis F 220).

31 [of the daughters of Erechtheus, sacrificed for the city]
　　Maidens of Hyacinthus' Hill.

Brief fragments: (F 28) "to bake bread," (F 29) "he hits on the jaw," (F 30) "gives the breast."

MUSES

were proposing. F 33 reveals a trial, but since the "you" is singular, it cannot be the Muses who judge the issue. A poet is very likely the one on trial, possibly another comic poet (Aristophanes?) or Euripides, for mistreating the Muses. If the latter, the Muses could be the chorus, pursuing Euripides in the manner of the Furies after Orestes. The Muses were canonically nine in number, but there should be no problem in seeing their number raised to twenty-four for a comic chorus. Harvey makes the attractive suggestion

Fragments

32 Hypothesis to Sophocles *Oedipus at Colonus*

μάκαρ Σοφοκλέης, ὃς πολὺν χρόνον βιοὺς
ἀπέθανεν εὐδαίμων ἀνὴρ καὶ δεξιός·
πολλὰς ποιήσας καὶ καλὰς τραγῳδίας
καλῶς ἐτελεύτησ᾽, οὐδὲν ὑπομείνας κακόν.

33 Harpocration p. 165.6

ἰδού, δέχου τὴν ψῆφον· ὁ καδίσκος δέ σοι
ὁ μὲν ἀπολύων οὗτος, ὁ δ᾽ ἀπολλὺς ὁδί.

34 Pollux 7.203

ὦ κάπραινα καὶ περίπολις καὶ δρομάς

35 Pollux 10.86

κἂν ὀξυβάφῳ †χρεῖσθαι† τρεῖς χοίνικας ἢ δύ᾽
    ἀλεύρων.

ΜΥΣΤΑΙ

that as Euripides has "his" Muse at Frogs *1306, other poets could have had "their" Muses to increase the number. He wonders also if Apollo is the judge in F 33, pointing out a possible wordplay on "acquit"* (apolyson)*, "condemn"* (apollys)*, and the name "Apollo."*

Fragments

32 Sophocles was a man blessed. He lived a long life, and died a happy and accomplished man. He came to a fine end, after writing many fine tragedies, never suffering anything bad.

33 Here, you [sing.] take the pebble for voting. You see, this is the jar that acquits, and this the one that condemns.

34 You she-goat, you streetwalker, you cruiser.

35 And to . . . two or three pecks of white meal in a saucer.

Brief fragment: (F 36) "young tunny."

INITIATES

The title "Initiates" might suggest a number of approaches. Frogs *also had a chorus of initiates, called* mystai *at lines 336, 370, but we have no way of knowing whether Phrynichus' comedy was earlier or later than* Frogs *or whether it had any connection with it at all. Bergk would date the play in the wake of the successful celebration of the Mysteries in 407, the first time in several years, while an ironical interpretation of the title might place the comedy in the mid-410s at the time of the scandal of 415.*

Fragments

37 Photius p. 583.16

μάστιγα δ᾽ ἐν χεροῖν ἔχων †τευταθαι.

38 Eustathius *On the Iliad* p. 1112.36

ἐβουλόμην ἂν ἧμιν ὥσπερ καὶ πρὸ τοῦ

ΠΟΑΣΤΡΙΑΙ

Fragments

39 Photius (b, z) α 1511

σὺ δ᾽ εἰσιοῦσα δουλικῶς ἐνσκεύασαι
καὶ τἄνδον ἀνακάλλυνον.

40 Athenaeus 110e

αὐτοπυρίταισί τ᾽ ἄρτοις καὶ λιπῶσι στεμφύλοις.

41 Priscian *Institutes of Grammar* 17.126

ὥσπερ ἐμὸν αὐτῆς ἴδιον

42 Athenaeus 424c

κύλικ᾽ ἀρύστιχον

Fragments

37 With whip in hand get busy (?).

38 I would be wishing for us just as in the past.

LADY GRASS-CUTTERS

A poastria *was a woman cutting grass or herbs or labour-ing in the fields. The plural title presumably denotes a cho-rus of such working women—compare Hermippus'* Bread-Women. *Archippus F 46 mentions "grass cutters" along with gardeners and donkey drivers as examples of manual labourers. Henderson* (Rivals *141*) *wonders if this is the play with "the drunken old woman . . . whom the sea mon-ster was eating," but that would have to be an early play by Phrynichus, and Meidias (F 43) is a* kōmōidoumenos *of the 410s.*

Fragments

39 You [fem.], go inside, dress yourself up as a slave, and start sweeping up indoors.

40 With loaves of whole wheat bread and glistening olive paste.

41 Just as my very own ⟨son?⟩.

42 A ladle cup.

43 Σ Aristophanes *Birds* 1297

λέγει δὲ ἐν Ποαστρίαις ὁ αὐτός, ὡς καὶ περὶ ἀλέκτορας αὐτοῦ ἐσπουδακότος.

ΣΑΤΥΡΟΙ

Fragments

46 Phrynichus *Selection* 232

ὁτιὴ πρὶν ἐλθεῖν αὐτὸν εἰς βουλὴν ἔδει
καὶ ταῦτ᾽ ἀπαγγείλαντα πάλιν πρὸς τὸν θεὸν
ἥκειν· ἐγὼ δ᾽ ἀπέδραν ἐκεῖνον †δευριανὸν δεῖ†

47 Σ Aristophanes *Birds* 1463

Κορκυραῖαι δ᾽ οὐδὲν <   >
ἐπιβάλλουσιν μάστιγες.

48 Σ Aristophanes *Clouds* 1154b

βοάσομαί τἄρα τὰν ὑπέρτονον
βοάν.

---

[1] Parodied from Sophocles' *Peleus* [F 491], also at *Clouds* 1154.

PHRYNICHUS

43 The same one [Phrynichus] says in his *Lady Grass-Cutters* that he [Meidias] was very keen on fighting-cocks.

Brief fragments: (F 44) "eviction," (F 45) "pigpen."

SATYRS

Satyrs are not unknown in Old Comedy and can be attested in as many as five comedies of the 430s and 420s, the best-known being Cratinus' Dionysalexander. *If "the god" of F 46 is Dionysus, this is one more comedy which brought him on stage as a character. The mention of the Council (boulē) and of "whips from Corcyra" would suggest that the comedy is not a burlesque of myth, but had a contemporary setting. If Dionysus is a character, then the comedy will have resembled* Babylonians, Frogs, *or Eupolis'* Officers, *where Dionysus finds himself in present-day Athens. Sophocles'* Peleus *is parodied at F 48 and again at* Clouds *1154 (D-423), while Philoxenus (F 49) is a kōmōidoumenos of the late 420s (*Clouds *686,* Wasps *81–84, Eupolis F 249). Thus a date in the late 420s for* Satyrs *seems reasonable.*

Fragments

46 Because he should have gone first to the Council, announced the news, and then have come back to the god. But I got away from him . . .

47 Whips from Corcyra do not inflict.

48 So then I shall give out a shout exceeding loud.[1]

49 Σ Aristophanes *Wasps* 82b

ὁ Φιλόξενος ἐκωμῳδεῖτο ὡς πόρνος . . . Φρύνιχος Σατύροις.

ΤΡΑΓΩΙΔΟΙ Η ΑΠΕΛΕΤΘΕΡΟΙ

Testimonia

i Athenaeus 115b

εἰπόντος . . . τινος καὶ δρᾶμα ἐπιγράφεσθαι Φρυνίχου Ἀπελευθέρους.

ii Photius (z) α 2328

ἀπελεύθερος· Ἑλληνικὸν τὸ ὄνομα. καὶ δράματα ἄττα οὕτως ἐπιγεγράπται.

Fragments

52 Athenaeus 287b

ὦ χρυσοκέφαλοι βεμβράδες θαλάσσιαι

49 Philoxenus is made fun of as a male prostitute . . . Phrynichus in *Satyrs*.

Brief fragments: (F 50) "the owner" [of a slave], (F 51) "conch."

TRAGIC ACTORS or FREEDMEN

In comedy tragōidos *means: tragic poet, tragic actor, or member of the tragic chorus. The title suggests another comedy with a literary theme. If "craft" in F 56 is the poet's craft, then someone was being portrayed as "bad" or "wretched at it." It does not have to be Euripides; it could easily be a rival comic poet. F 58 mentions the "arrangement of verses," again supporting a criticism of a poet as part of the play. Were the tragic actors and the freedmen of the titles the same group and thus the chorus, or were the tragic actors perhaps competing characters against a chorus of freedmen?*

Testimonia

i When someone said that there was also a play by Phrynichus titled "Freedmen."

ii "Freedman": a Greek term, and there are some plays with this title.

Fragments

52 O anchovies from the sea, with golden heads.

53 Athenaeus 654b

περιστέριον δ᾽ αὐτῷ τι λαβὲ τριωβόλου.

54 Pollux 7.195

σὺ δὲ τιμιοπώλης ὥς γ᾽ Ἀχιλλεὺς οὐδὲ εἷς.

55 Athenaeus 389f

τὸν Κλεόμβροτόν τε τοῦ
Πέρδικος υἱόν.

56 Priscian *Institutes of Grammar* 18.274

αἰτίαν ἔχει
πονηρὸς εἶναι τὴν τέχνην.

57 Photius (b, z) α 1609

ἄσιτος, ἄποτος, ἀναπόνιπτος

58 Harpocration p. 91.18

τῇ διαθέσει τῶν ἐπῶν

59 Photius (z) α 3188

καὶ τέμαχος αὐξίδος

60 Athenaeus 229a

ἡδὺ δ᾽ ἀποτηγανίζειν ἄνευ συμβολῶν.

53 Buy a little dove for him for three obols.

54 You ask a great price, as much as Achilles.[1]

[1] The point seems to be that Achilles asked for and received a great ransom for the body of Hector, but in Homer *Iliad* 24 the ransom is assembled by Priam before he goes to Achilles, and Achilles' reaction at 24.559 is anger, although at 24.578–79 he does accept the gifts. The comparison must depend on a later version where Achilles demanded a hefty ransom.

55 Cleombrotus the son of Perdix.[1]

[1] *Perdix* also means "partridge." As a partridge was a proverbial deceiver (Thompson *Birds* 235–36), this should be the force of calling Cleombrotus "son of a partridge." The name is known in a prominent family of Acharnae in the 4th c. (*PAA* 577035).

56 He is accused of being bad at his craft.

57 Without food, without drink, with hands unwashed.

58 In the arrangement of his lines.

59 And a slice of young bonito.

60 It is pleasant to eat straight from the pan without making any contribution.

ΑΔΗΛΩΝ ΔΡΑΜΑΤΩΝ

61 Plutarch *Alcibiades* 20.6

{Α.} ὦ φίλταθ' Ἑρμῆ, καὶ φυλάσσου, μὴ πεσὼν
αὑτὸν περικρούσῃ καὶ παράσχῃς διαβολὴν
ἑτέρῳ Διοκλείδῃ βουλομένῳ κακόν τι δρᾶν.
{ΕΡΜ.} φυλάξομαι· Τεύκρῳ γὰρ οὐχὶ βούλομαι
μήνυτρα δοῦναι τῷ παλαμναίῳ ξένῳ.

62 Plutarch *Nicias* 4.8

ἦν γὰρ πολίτης ἀγαθός, ὡς εὖ οἶδ' ἐγώ,
κοὐχ ὑποταγεὶς ἐβάδιζεν, ὥσπερ Νικίας.

63 Photius (S^z) α 3097

τιμοῦντι κἀτιμοῦντι τοὺς βελτίονας

64 Athenaeus 53a

ἀμυγδαλῆ τῆς βηχὸς ἀγαθὸν φάρμακον.

65 Athenaeus 59c

ἢ μαζίου τι μικρὸν ἢ κολοκυντίου

66 Pollux 4.181

ἔμει καταμηλῶν· φλέγματος γὰρ εἶ πλέως.

UNASSIGNED FRAGMENTS

61 (A) My dear Hermes, do watch out that you don't fall over and break something off, and so provide a scandal for some other Dioclides who wants to cause trouble.

(HERMES) I shall indeed watch out, for I do not wish to provide any reward money for that murderous foreigner Teucrus.[1]   [*Hermit, Revellers*?]

[1] Dioclides (*PAA* 931775) and Teucrus (*PAA* 881010) were two informers involved in the affair of the Herms in 415.

62 For he was a good citizen, as I well know, and he didn't walk around with a hangdog look like Nicias.

[*Hermit*?]

63 For [to?] someone honouring and dishonouring their betters.

64 Almond is a good remedy for a cough.

65 A little bit of barley cake and a small cucumber.

66 Insert the probe and vomit, because you're full of phlegm.

67 Σ Aristophanes *Peace* 344a

πολὺς δὲ συβαριασμὸς αὐλητῶν ‹◡› ἦν.

68 Diogenes Laertius 4.20

οὐ γλύξις οὐδ' ὑπόχυτος, ἀλλὰ Πράμνιος.

69 Athenaeus 47f

        ἑπτάκλινος οἶκος ἦν καλός,
εἶτ' ἐννεάκλινος ἕτερος οἶκος.

70 Σ Aristophanes *Wasps* 300b

τριώβολόν γ' ὅσουπερ ἡλιάζομαι.

71 Pollux 2.17

ἦσαν δὲ καὶ γυναῖκες ἀφήλικες.

72 Pollux 2.82

ἐπήκοος γενοῦ

73 Athenaeus 52b

        τοὺς δὲ γομφίους
ἅπαντας ἐξέκοψεν, ὥστ'
οὐκ ἂν δυναίμην Ναξίαν
   ἀμυγδάλην κατᾶξαι.

67 There was a great racket from the *aulos* players.
[*Revellers*?]

68 Not sweet wine, nor adulterated wine, but Pramnian.
[*Muses, Tragic Actors*?]

69 There was a splendid room with space for seven couches, and another room with nine.   [*Revellers*?]

70 Three obols, what I get for jury duty.

71 There were also young women.

72 You [sing.] be mindful.

73 He has knocked out all my molars, and now I won't be able to crack a Naxian almond.[1]

1 At Eupolis F 271 (*Officers*), a character (very probably Dionysus) asks, "Allow me to munch some Naxian almonds." If the speaker here is Dionysus, then we might assign this fragment to *Cronus* (cf. F 10) and see it as another instance of the comic illtreatment of Dionysus. At *Frogs* 546–48 Dionysus imagines that Xanthias might knock his teeth out, and at *Frogs* 571–72 the enraged innkeeper threatens to strike the molars of the figure they think is Heracles.

74 Athenaeus 44d

λάρους θρηνεῖν, ἐν οἷσι Λάμπρος ἐναπέθνησκεν,
ἄνθρωπος ⟨ὢν⟩ ὑδατοπότης, μινυρὸς ὑπερσοφιστής,
Μουσῶν σκελετός, ἀηδόνων ἠπίαλος, ὕμνος Ἅιδου.

75 Photius (b, z) α 1599

ἐν χαλεπαῖς ὀργαῖς ἀναπηροβίων †γερόντων

76 Hephaestion *Handbook* 12.3

ἃ δ' ἀνάγκη 'σθ' ἱερεῦσιν καθαρεύειν φράσομεν.

77 Pollux 6.19

πότις γυνή

78 Σ^RV Aristophanes *Clouds* 967b

Παλλάδα περσέπολιν δεινάν· ἀρχὴ ᾄσματος Στησι-
χόρου, ὡς Ἐρατοσθένης φησίν. Φρύνιχος αὐτοῦ τού-
του τοῦ ᾄσματος μέμνηται ὡς Λαμπροκλέους ὄντος.

74 ⟨They say⟩ the seagulls sang the lament, in whose presence Lamprus passed away, a teetotaller, whinger, and too clever by half, mummifier of the Muses, a nightingales' nightmare, a song of Death.[1]   [*Muses, Tragic Actors*?]

[1] Lamprus (*PAA* 601647) was a celebrated musician and was said to have been the music teacher of the young Sophocles. This would date him to the 470s, but Phrynichus, the tragic poet of the same era, could still be mentioned by the comic poets in the 420s and later.

75 In the cranky moods of old men with withered lives.

76 We shall explain what the priests must purify.
        [*Initiates*?]

77 A drunken woman. [See T 9, 12]

78 "Pallas the terrible, sacker of cities": the beginning of a song by Stesichorus, as Eratosthenes [F 101] says. Phrynichus mentions that this song is by Lamprocles [*PMG* 735b; Campbell *GL* IV 320–21].

Brief fragments: (F 79) "human means," (F 80) "fixed gaze," (F 81) "you are filthy," (F 82) "sunken eyes," (F 83) "groom-to-be," (F 84) "female tenants," (F 85) "toothless," (F 86) "to be in heat."

ΠΛΑΤΩΝ

Platon, like Aristophanes, spans the transition between Old Comedy (or at least the stereotypical picture we have of a topical, free-spirited, personally abusive genre) and later comedy. Eusebius (T 5) places him with Cratinus in the 450s, but this is far too early and may be the result of a confusion of archon names. We can trace his career from the mid-420s (see T 7) until the 380s, a career roughly the same as that of Aristophanes. The two secure dates are L-405 (Cleophon) and 391 (Phaon), but we can assign rough dates to other comedies: to the late 420s, Pesiander, *on a date of L-421,* Victories; *to the 410s,* Sophists, Festivals, Hyperbolus *(419 or 418),* The Man in Great Pain; *to 410–405,* Costumes, Greece *or* Islands; *to the 390s,* Envoys, Laius; *and to the early 380s,* Women from the Festival. *He is credited (T 1, 3) with twenty-eight comedies. The* Suda *gives thirty titles, to which we may add the previously unknown comedy* Rhabdouchoi, *translated here as "Security."* Daedalus *and* Io *are doubtful entries, and* Security *may be an alternative title (for* Poet *or* Victories?).*

T 8 presents some interesting information about Platon's career as a comic poet. If Aristophanes is a useful parallel (three years between first production and first production in his own name), and if only three comedies were being performed between 425 and 421, then Security

PLATON

belongs in the early 410s. That Platon, like Aristophanes, used other men as producers is confirmed by his own statement at F 106 that he was "imitating the Arcadians" when "because of poverty" he had others put on his plays. It might explain also the debate over the authorship of Alliance, attributed to both Platon and Cantharus, if Cantharus was one of those "others."

For some ancient writers (T 16–17) Platon was seen as either the founder or the main exponent of what would be called Second or Middle Comedy, the latter perhaps most usefully seen as a chronological term to cover the period from Aristophanes to Menander (385–325). Platon did write various sorts of comedy: politically themed, burlesques of myths, plays about love and romance, comedies about poetry and the theatre. Are these chronological? Did Platon begin by writing the comedy that we see as "typically" Old and then move on to the burlesques of myth and romantic themes, or did he write a variety of comedies throughout his career? If the former, should he be regarded as the "founder" of Middle Comedy?

Political plays include his three demagogue comedies (Peisander, Hyperbolus, Cleophon), where we note that, unlike Aristophanes and Eupolis, Platon did not disguise his targets under suggestive nicknames (Cleon~Paphlagon in Knights, *Hyperbolus~Maricas* in *Maricas*), *but both in the title and in the dialogue (F 184) used the actual names. Platon continues the stereotype of the demagogue in comedy: dubious citizenship (F 182, 185), dishonest and self-seeking in politics (F 58), homosexual prostitute in his youth (F 60, 202), unpleasant and foreign manner of speaking (F 61, 183). The comedies* Greece or Islands, Envoys, *and* Alliance *may also have had political themes. If* Envoys *does indeed have a topical relevance, its date in the late 390s shows that Platon was still writing political comedy in the latter part of his career. At F 115 he claims to "have been the first to wage war on Cleon."*

Burlesques of myth include Adonis, Europa, Zeus Badly Treated *(Heracles was a speaking character in F 46),* A Long Night *(the original of Plautus'* Amphitryo?), Laius, Menelaus, Wool-Carders or Cercopes, Daedalus *and* Io *(if these two are in fact by Platon), and* Phaon. *It is not clear whether these plays remained in the world of myth throughout (like Cratinus'* Dionysalexander) *or the characters from myth were brought into the contemporary world (like Dionysus in* Frogs *or Eupolis'* Officers). *F 46 shows Heracles at what would seem to be an Athenian dinner party, while* Phaon *gives us Aphrodite describing the offerings needed for the women "to see Phaon" (F 188) and a character reading the latest cookbook by Philoxenus of Leucas (F 187).*

One final group of plays was concerned with poetry and the theatre. Here the titles are suggestive: Laconians or Poets *(F 69–70, 72),* Poet, Costumes *(see F 136, 138, 140, 142),* Security, Sophists *(F 143, 149, 151), and* Victories *(F 86 refers intertextually to Aristophanes'* Peace). *In two fragments from* Peisander *(F 106–7), Platon calls attention to the practice of producing comedies through other men.* Riff-Raff *(F 175) mentions the tragic actor Mynniscus as being fond of fish. F 179 of the same comedy enjoins people to "drink much water," and we recall the theme of drink that dominates Cratinus'* Wine-Flask. *F 29 from* Festivals *thanks someone for "saving us from the sigma of Euripides."*

Platon does seem to have been in the vanguard of the change that came over comedy in the early fourth century, but he did not abandon completely political themes (Envoys) or personal jokes in the 390s and 380s (F 14, 65, 127, 130, 133, 200–201, 238). The burlesques of myth and social comedies that we can date do belong to the last part of his career, but it must remain a cautious assumption that he began his career in the manner of Aristophanes and Eupolis, and moved with (or led) the times to what would be called "Second" or "Middle" Comedy.

Recent bibliography: R. Rosen, ZPE 76 (1988) 223–28, in Dobrov (BA) 119–37; W. Luppe, Nikephoros 1 (1988) 185–89, Nikephoros 2 (1989) 121–24; Z. Biles, ZPE (1999) 182–88; J. L. Sanchez Llopis, in CGA 329–37; S. Pirotta, Plato Comicus: die fragmentarischen Komödien (2009).

THE POETS OF OLD COMEDY

Testimonia

i

(a) *Suda* π 1708

Πλάτων, Ἀθηναῖος, κωμικός, γεγονὼς τοῖς χρόνοις κατὰ Ἀριστοφάνην καὶ Φρύνιχον, Εὔπολιν, Φερεκράτην. δράματα δὲ αὐτοῦ κη΄ ταῦτα· Ἄδωνις, Ἀφ᾽ ἱερῶν, Γρῦπες, Δαίδαλος, Ἑορταί, Ἑλλὰς ἢ Νῆσοι, Εὐρώπη, Ζεὺς κακούμενος, Ἰώ, Κλεοφῶν, Λάϊος, Λάκωνες ἢ Ποιηταί, Μέτοικοι, Μύρμηκες, Μαμμάκυθος, Μενέλεως, Νῖκαι, Νὺξ μακρά, Ξάνται ἢ Κέρκωπες, Περιαλγής, Ποιητής, Πείσανδρος, Πρέσβεις, Παιδίον, Σοφισταί, Συμμαχία, Σκευαί, Σύρφαξ, Ὑπέρβολος, Φάων. ἔστι δὲ λαμπρὸς τὸν χαρακτῆρα.

(b) [Andronicus] *On the Classification of Poets* (Koster XXIII.9–18)

ἡ δὲ μέση τις καὶ αἰνιγματώδης, ἧς ἐπίσημος Πλάτων ὁ τὸν χαρακτῆρα λαμπρότατος, οὐχ ὁ φιλόσοφος, ἀλλ᾽ ἕτερός τις καὶ αὐτὸς Ἀθηναῖος, οὗτινος τὰ δράματα τάδε λέγονται· Γρῦπες, Κλεοφῶν, Πρέσβεις, Παιδίον, Σοφισταί, Συμμαχία, Σκευαί, Ἄδωνις, Ἀφιέρων, Δαίδαλος, Ἑλλάς, Ἑορταί, Εὐρώπη, Ζεὺς κακούμενος, Ἰώ, Λάιος, Λάκωνες, Μύρμηκες, Μέτοικοι, Μαμμάκουθος, Ξάνται, Νῖκαι, Νὺξ Μακρά, Πείσανδρος, Περίαλγος, Ποιητής, Σύρφαξ, Ὑπέρβολος.

84

PLATON

Testimonia

i

(a) Platon: of Athens, comic poet, who lived around the time of Aristophanes and Phrynichus, Eupolis and Phere-crates.[1] His plays are twenty-eight in number: *Adonis, Women from the Festival, Griffins, Daedalus, Feasts, Greece or Islands, Europa, Zeus Badly Treated, Io, Cleophon, Laius, Laconians or Poets, Metics, Ants, Dolt, Menelaus, Victories, A Long Night, Wool-Carders or Cercopes, The Man in Great Pain, Poet, Peisander, Envoys, The Little Kid, Sophists, Alliance, Costumes, Riff-Raff, Hyperbolus, Phaon.* His style of writing was quite brilliant.

[1] W. Luppe (*Nikephoros* 1 [1988] 185–89) argues that these five poets all competed together at the Lenaea of 420, finishing in the order given.

(b) Middle ‹comedy› was something allusively insulting, of which the best known was Platon, very brilliant in his style. He was not the philosopher, but another man, also an Athenian. These are said to be his plays: *Griffins, Cleophon, Envoys, The Little Kid, Sophists, Alliance, Costumes, Adonis, Women from the Festival, Daedalus, Greece, Feasts, Europa, Zeus Badly Treated, Io, Laius, Laconians, Ants, Metics, Dolt, Wool-Carders, Victories, A Long Night, Peisander, The Man in Great Pain, Poet, Riff-Raff, Hyperbolus.*

THE POETS OF OLD COMEDY

ii *Canons of the Comic Poets*

κωμῳδοποιοὶ ἀρχαίας ζ΄· Ἐπίχαρμος, Κρατῖνος, Εὔπολις, Ἀριστοφάνης, Φερεκράτης, Κράτης, Πλάτων.

iii *The Names and Plays of the Poets of Old Comedy* (Koster V.5)

Πλάτωνος δράματα κη΄.

iv Marcellinus *Life of Thucydides* 29

συνεχρόνισε δ᾽, ὥς φησι Πραξιφάνης ἐν τῷ περὶ ἱστορίας, Πλάτωνι τῷ κωμικῷ, Ἀγάθωνι τραγικῷ, Νικηράτῳ ἐποποιῷ καὶ Χοιρίλῳ καὶ Μελανιππίδῃ.

v Eusebius (Jerome) p. 111.26 (Helm)

Cratinus et Plato comoediarum scriptores clari habentur.

Eusebius (Armenian) p. 193 (Karst)

Kratinos und Platon, die Komiker, gingen um diese Zeit auf.

vi Syncellus *Chronography* p. 297.3 Mosshammer

Κρατῖνος καὶ Πλάτων οἱ κωμικοὶ ἤκμαζον.

ii There were seven poets of Old Comedy: Epicharmus, Cratinus, Eupolis, Aristophanes, Pherecrates, Crates, Platon.

iii The plays of Platon, 28.

iv As Praxiphanes says in his *On History* [F 18], he [Thucydides] lived at the same time as Platon the comic poet, Agathon the tragedian, Niceratus who wrote epic, and as Choerilus and Melanippides.

v [for the year 454/3] Cratinus and Platon, writers of comedy, were well known.

[for the year 453/2] Cratinus and Platon, the comic writers, belong to this period.[1]

[1] This is far too early for Platon. Luppe (*Philologus* 114 [1970] 4) argues that the ancients confused the archonship of Ariston (454/3) with that of Aristion (421/0).

vi The comic poets Cratinus and Platon were at their height.

vii Cyril of Alexandria *Against Julian* 1.13

ὀγδοηκοστῇ ὀγδόῃ Ὀλυμπιάδι τὸν κωμῳδὸν Ἀριστο-
φάνην, Εὔπολίν τε καὶ Πλάτωνα γενέσθαι φασίν.

viii P. Oxy. 2737.44–51

Ἐρατοσθένης περὶ Πλάτωνος ὅτι ἕως μὲν [ἄλ]λοις
ἐδίδου τὰς κωμῳδίας εὐδοκίμει, δι᾽ αὐτοῦ δὲ πρῶτον
διδάξας τοὺς Ῥαβδούχους καὶ γενόμενος τέταρτος
ἀπεώσθη πάλιν εἰς τοὺς Ληναϊκούς.

ix *IG* ii² 2325.63

Πλά[των

x Hypothesis I *Frogs*

ἐδιδάχθη ἐπὶ Καλλίου τοῦ μετὰ Ἀντιγένη διὰ Φιλω-
νίδου εἰς Λήναια. πρῶτος ἦν· δεύτερος Φρύνιχος Μού-
σαις· Πλάτων τρίτος Κλεοφῶντι.

xi Horace *Satires* 2.3.11–12

quorsum pertinuit stipare Platona Menandro? Eupolin
Archilochum, comites educere tantos?

xii Dion of Prusa 16.9

Ἀθηναῖοι γὰρ εἰωθότες ἀκούειν κακῶς, καὶ νὴ Δία ἐπ᾽
αὐτὸ τοῦτο συνιόντες εἰς τὸ θέατρον ὡς λοιδορηθη-

vii In the 88th Olympiad [428/7–425/4] they say that Aristophanes the comic poet was active, also Eupolis and Platon.

viii Eratosthenes says about Platon that as long as he gave his comedies to others, he was successful, but when he produced *Security* in his own name for the first time and finished fourth, he was shunted back to the Lenaea.

ix [from the list of victors at the Dionysia, in the 410s]

Pla[ton

x It [*Frogs*] was produced in the archonship of Callias [406/5], who came after Antigenes, through Philonides at the Lenaea. He [Aristophanes] was first, Phrynichus second with *Muses*, and Platon third with *Cleophon*.

xi What was the purpose of packing Platon along with Menander, of bringing along such companions as Eupolis or Archilochus?[1]

1 It is uncertain whether "Platona" refers to Plato the philosopher or Platon the comic poet.

xii The Athenians were accustomed to hearing bad things about themselves and by Zeus they went to the theatre for

THE POETS OF OLD COMEDY

σόμενοι, καὶ προτεθεικότες ἀγῶνα καὶ νίκην τοῖς ἄμει-
νον αὐτὸ πράττουσιν, οὐκ αὐτοὶ τοῦτο εὑρόντες, ἀλλὰ
τοῦ θεοῦ συμβουλεύσαντος, Ἀριστοφάνους μὲν ἤκου-
ον καὶ Κρατίνου καὶ Πλάτωνος, καὶ τούτους οὐδὲν
κακὸν ἐποίησαν.

xiii Plutarch *Table-Talk* 711f

οὕτω δεήσει γραμματικὸν ἑκάστῳ τὸ καθ᾽ ἕκαστον
ἐξηγεῖσθαι, τίς ὁ Λαισποδίας παρ᾽ Εὐπόλιδι καὶ ὁ
Κινησίας παρὰ Πλάτωνι καὶ ὁ Λάμπων παρὰ Κρα-
τίνῳ

xiv Diogenes Laertius 3.109

καὶ ὁ τῆς ἀρχαίας κωμῳδίας ποιητής.

xv

(a) Tzetzes *Distinctions among Poets* (Koster XXIa) 82–
84

τῆς δευτέρας ἦν ὁ ψόγος κεκρυμμένος,
ἧς ἦν Κρατῖνος, Εὔπολις, Φερεκράτης,
Ἀριστοφάνης, Ἕρμιππός τε καὶ Πλάτων.

(b) Tzetzes *Proem* (Koster XIa I.98)

οὕτως ἡ πρώτη κωμῳδία τὸ σκῶμμα εἶχεν ἀπαρα-
κάλυπτον· ἐξήρκεσε δὲ τὸ ἀπαρακαλύπτως οὑτωσὶ
κωμῳδεῖν μέχρις Εὐπόλιδος . . . ἀλλὰ ψήφισμα θέν-

this very purpose to be insulted. They established a competition and awarded a prize to the one who did this best. This was not their own doing, but rather on the advice of a god, they would listen to Aristophanes and Platon and Cratinus and would take no action against them.

xiii We would need a learned scholar beside each guest to explain each reference, e.g., who Laispodias was in Eupolis [F 107], and Cinesias in Platon [F 200], and Lampon in Cratinus [F 62, 125].

xiv [on various men named "Platon"] There is also the poet of Old Comedy.

xv

(a) Indirect insult was characteristic of second ⟨comedy⟩, of which there were Cratinus, Eupolis, Pherecrates, Aristophanes, Hermippus, and Platon.

(b) First comedy had personal jokes that were open and direct, and this direct humour was accepted until the time of Eupolis . . . but when Alcibiades passed a law to

τος Ἀλκιβιάδου κωμῳδεῖν ἐσχηματισμένως καὶ μὴ
προδήλως αὐτός τε ὁ Εὔπολις Κρατῖνός τε καὶ Φερε-
κράτης καὶ Πλάτων, οὐχ ὁ φιλόσοφος, Ἀριστοφάνης
τε σὺν ἑτέροις τὰ συμβολικὰ μετεχειρίσαντο σκώμ-
ματα, καὶ ἡ δευτέρα κωμῳδία τῇ Ἀττικῇ ἀνεσκίρ-
τησεν.

(c) Tzetzes *Prolegomena to Lycophron* (Koster XXIIb 39)

κωμῳδοὶ πραττόμενοί εἰσιν οὗτοι οἷοι Ἀριστοφάνης,
Κρατῖνος, Πλάτων, Εὔπολις, Φερεκράτης καὶ ἕτεροι.

xvi Anonymous *On Comedy* (Koster IV 16–17)

γέγονε δὲ τῆς μὲν πρώτης κωμῳδίας ἄριστος τεχνίτης
οὗτος ὁ Ἀριστοφάνης καὶ Εὔπολις, τῆς δὲ δευτέρας
Πλάτων, τῆς δὲ τρίτης Μένανδρος.

xvii Σ Dionysius Thrax (Koster XVIIIa 37)

τρεῖς διαφορὰς ἔδοξεν ἔχειν ἡ κωμῳδία· καὶ ἡ μὲν
καλεῖται παλαιά, ἡ ἐξ ἀρχῆς φανερῶς ἐλέγχουσα, ἡ
δὲ μέση, ἡ αἰνιγματωδῶς, ἡ δὲ νέα, ἡ μηδ' ὅλως τοῦτο
ποιοῦσα πλὴν ἐπὶ δούλων ἢ ξένων. καὶ τῆς μὲν πα-
λαιᾶς πολλοὶ γεγόνασιν, ἐπίσημος δὲ Κρατῖνος ὁ καὶ
πραττόμενος, μετέσχον δέ τινος χρόνου τῆς παλαιᾶς
κωμῳδίας Εὔπολίς τε καὶ Ἀριστοφάνης· τῆς δὲ μέσης
καὶ αὐτῆς μὲν πολλοὶ γεγόνασιν, ἐπίσημος δὲ Πλά-
των, οὐχ ὁ φιλόσοφος, ἀλλ' ἕτερός τις· ὁμοίως δὲ
κἀκείνου τὰ δράματα οὐ φαίνεται

make fun of people indirectly and not plainly, Eupolis and Cratinus and Pherecrates and Platon (not the philosopher) and Aristophanes with the rest fashioned their jokes allusively and so second comedy was at its height.

(c) The comic poets that are studied are those such as Aristophanes, Cratinus, Platon, Eupolis, Pherecrates, and the others.

xvi Of "first comedy" the best writer was Aristophanes, and also Eupolis, of "second" Platon, and of "third" Menander.

xvii Comedy has three forms. What is called "Old Comedy" is comedy that which from the start attacks openly, "Middle" that ⟨which attacks⟩ allusively, and "New" that which does not do this at all except for slaves and foreigners. There were many poets of Old Comedy, especially Cratinus, who is still studied. For a while Eupolis and Aristophanes were part of Old Comedy. Of Middle Comedy there were also many poets, especially preeminent is Platon, not the philosopher, but another writer. But his plays also are not extant.

xviii Hephaestion *Handbook* 15.12

γίνεται δὲ καὶ τριπενθημιμερὲς ἐκ τούτων τὸ καλού-
μενον Πλατωνικόν, ἐν ᾧ τὰ μὲν ἑκατέρωθεν δύο δακτυ-
λικά εἰσι πενθημιμερῆ, τὸ δὲ μέσον ἰαμβικόν.

xix Πλάτων ὁ τῆς ἀρχαίας
κωμῳδίας ποιητής
Λυσικλῆς ἐποίει.

ΑΔΩΝΙΣ

Fragments

1 Hesychius υ 451

εἶτ᾽ οὐχ ὑπέρου μοι περιτροπὴ γενήσεται;

2 Photius (z) ined.

περὶ τῶν δὲ πλευρῶν οὐδεμίαν ὥραν ἔχεις.

xviii Out of these [the encomiologic and the iambelegus] comes the tripenthemimer called the "Platonicum," in which the two ⟨metra⟩ on either side are dactylic penthemimers and the ⟨metron⟩ in the middle is an iambic. This has been used by Platon in his *Wool-Carders* [cites F 96].

xix [on the base of a statue found at Ostia, first century BC]

Platon the Old/Comic poet./Sculpted by Lysicles.

ADONIS

Adonis seems to have been a favourite subject of fourth-century comedy—this title is known for other poets, including Nicophon in 388, and we may add Women at the Adonia *by Philippides;* Σ Lysistrata *389 cites* Women at the Adonia *as an alternative title for that comedy. The epic poet Panyassis (F 28) relates a story of the birth of Adonis from a myrrh tree and a contest between Aphrodite and Persephone over his guardianship. This could have been a good subject for a comedy. Or it may have had to do with his female followers and the celebration of his festival (see* Lysistrata *387–98 and Menander's* Samian Woman *38–46).*

Fragments

1 Won't that just be the grinding of the pestle for me?

2 You have no concern for your [my?] ribs.

3 Athenaeus 456a

ὦ Κινύρα, βασιλεῦ Κυπρίων ἀνδρῶν δασυπρώκτων,
παῖς σοι κάλλιστος μὲν ἔφυ θαυμαστότατός τε
πάντων ἀνθρώπων, δύο δ' αὐτὸν δαίμον' ὀλεῖτον,
ἡ μὲν ἐλαυνομένη λαθρίοις ἐρετμοῖς, ὁ δ' ἐλαύνων.

ΑΙ ΑΦ'ΙΕΡΩΝ

Fragments

9 Athenaeus 446de

οὐδ' ὅστις αὐτῆς ἐκπίεται τὰ χρήματα.

10 Pollux 10.190

δότω τὴν κιθάραν τις ἔνδοθεν
καὶ τοὐπιπόρπαμα.

3 Cinyras, king of the Cypriots, men with hairy butts, a son has been born to you, the fairest and most amazing of all men, but two deities will destroy him, the goddess who is driven on secret oars and the god who does the driving.[1]

[1] These three lines are in dactylic hexameter, the metre of epic, but used in comedy for oracles and prophecies. Athenaeus claims that the "two deities" are Aphrodite and Dionysus, each of whom was allegedly in love with Adonis, but the presence of Dionysus in the story of Adonis is not attested elsewhere. Photius (*Library* 151b 5–7) describes Adonis as *androgynos* and makes him a lover of Aphrodite and Apollo.

Brief fragments: (F 4) "Adonis," (F 5) "to excrete," (F 6) "heap," (F 7) "desertion," (F 8) "cheese grater."

WOMEN FROM THE FESTIVAL

Not much can be said about this comedy. The title reveals a chorus of women in the context of a festival—cf. Aristophanes' two plays called Thesmophoriazusae *and his* Women Pitching Tents. *The mention of Pamphilus embezzling funds should date this comedy to the early 380s. Pirrotta (76–77) includes this play with* Adonis *and* Phaon *as having a women's chorus and a religious parody.*

Fragments

9 Nor is there a man who will drink up all her money.

10 Let someone from inside give <me?> a lyre and the formal robe.

11 Hesychius α 7749

πόθεν ὁρμιὰ καὶ κάλαμος;

12 The Antiatticist p. 106.28

λέπει τραχεῖαν ἔχων

13 Pollux 7.57

μαλλωτὰς χλανίδας

14 Σ Aristophanes *Wealth* 174

καὶ νὴ Δί᾽ εἰ Πάμφιλόν γε φαίης
κλέπτειν τὰ κοίν᾽ ἅμα τε συκοφαντεῖν.

ΓΡΥΠΕΣ

Fragments

15 Zenobius *Common Proverbs* 2.31

ἀνηρπάκασ᾽ ἁπαξάπαντ᾽ αὐτῷ κανῷ.

16 Photius (b, z) α 499

αἰαῖ· γελῶν ἐπηκροώμην ‹ - › πάλαι.

11 Where is my rod and fishing line?

12 He is thrashing with a rough ⟨whip⟩.

13 Cloaks lined with wool.

14 Yes, by Zeus, as if you were to say that Pamphilus embezzles public money and also acts as an informant.[1]

1 Pamphilus (*PAA* 762665) was a wealthy general of the 390s and early 380s, convicted of mishandling public money in 389 or 388. See *Wealth* 174. The Aristophanic scholiast cites the fragment from Plato's *Amphiareus* (otherwise unknown), emended by Meineke to *hai eph' hierōn* (women from the festival).

GRIFFINS

Griffins were fabled birds of the east, "animals like lions, but with wings and the beak of an eagle" (Pausanias 1.24.6). At Prometheus *803 they are "the sharp-beaked voiceless hounds of Zeus." Herodotus (4.13.1) relates their appearance in Greek lore to the journeys of Aristeas of Proconnesus. If they are the chorus of this comedy (see Rothwell on animal choruses in comedy), they would have provided an arresting spectacle. Does F 15 suggest griffins behaving like Harpies?*

Fragments

15 They have carried off everything basket and all.

16 Oh, I have been aware of ⟨his? their?⟩ laughter for a long time.

17 Athenaeus 368e

ἰχθῦς, κωλᾶς, φύσκας

ΔΑΙΔΑΛΟΣ

ΕΛΛΑΣ Η ΝΗΣΟΙ

All the fragments are cited as "Platon in Greece"; only the Suda (T 1) records the comedy as having a double title. Photius, citing F 25, says "Platon in Islands." Aristophanes (or Archippus—authorship was disputed in antiquity) wrote an Islands *and perhaps, as with* Daedalus *and also at F 14,* Aristophanes *and Platon were confused with one another.*

The title(s) suggest a comedy with a contemporary setting and theme. F 20 presents a woman representing herself in tragic language as "sightless and feeble," who may be Greece herself. F 21 mentions "our laws," while F 23 has someone chain up a proxenos, that is the local representative of a foreign state. But the most interesting fragment is F 23, where the speaker is possibly Poseidon threatening someone to give back control of the sea. But is he speaking to another god (Zeus?), or to a Spartan, an Athenian, or a fictional character in the play, and in what circumstances?

17 Fish, ham bones, sausages.

Brief fragment: (F 18) "having raised the price."

DAEDALUS

Daedalus by Platon is attested by the Suda (T 1). The scholiast to Clouds 663a assigns to a Daedalus by Platon three lines, the first two of which are more commonly attributed to Daedalus by Aristophanes (F 174), a comedy cited over a dozen times. Thus while an Aristophanic Daedalus is not in doubt, that Platon wrote one is considerably more so. The third line in the Aristophanic scholiast appears as Platon F 293 (dubium).

GREECE or ISLANDS

Pirrotta (98–99) makes a good case that the speaker of F 23 is a demagogue, revelling in his power, and engaged in an agon.

The comedy is generally dated to the crucial years of naval fighting during the War, 410–405, although Dover would identify the background to F 23 as that following the victory of Conon at Cnidus in 394. The combative tone of F 21 and the metre (iambic tetrameter catalectic) might suggest an agon as the context.

Some have classed this comedy with Eupolis' Cities and Aristophanes' Babylonians as comedies taking an anti-imperialistic theme, but such an attitude on the part of the comic poet does not stand up to close scrutiny. It is possible that we have an individuated chorus, with some or all of the chorus of islands named and perhaps visually identified.

THE POETS OF OLD COMEDY

Fragments

19 Pollux 10.142

βούλει τήνδε σοι πλεκτὴν καθῶ
κἄπειτ᾽ ἀνελκύσω σε δεῦρο;

20 Photius (b, z) α 1147

αὐτὴ δ᾽ ἀμαυρὸς ἀσθενής τ᾽ ἐγιγνόμην

21 Photius p. 638.5

εἴξασιν ἡμῖν οἱ νόμοι τούτοισι τοῖσι λεπτοῖς
ἀραχνίοις, ἃν ἐν τοῖσι τοίχοις ἡ φάλαγξ ὑφαίνει.

22 Pollux 10.167

λαβὼν οὖν
τὸν σκύλακα τὸν τοῦ προξένου κἄπειτα δῆσον
αὐτόν.

23 Σ Homer *Iliad* 1.135

– ∪ – εἰ μὲν σὺ τὴν θάλατταν ἀποδώσεις ἑκών·
εἰ δὲ μή, ‹᾽γὼ› ταῦτα πάντα συντριαινῶν ἀπολέσω.

ΕΟΡΤΑΙ

Fragments

19 Do you [sing.] want me to let down this rope and then haul you up here?

20 (WOMAN) For myself I was becoming obscure and feeble.

21 Our laws are like the thin cobwebs which the spider spins along the walls.

22 So take the representative's chain and tie him up.[1]

1 Meineke argued that "representative" (*proxenos*) should in fact be a proper name. Pirrotta (97) identifies four men of this name in the late 5th and early 4th c.

23 ... if you [masc. sing.] will willingly yield up the sea; but if not, I shall strike with my trident and destroy all this.

Brief fragments: (F 24) "sea swell," (F 25) "to reckon the value of," (F 26) "sacrificial gear."

FESTIVALS

If a plural title denotes the chorus, we may have had a group of personified Athenian festivals, but equally well the play might have featured some characters making the rounds of the various festivals. In Old Comedy we get parodies of the Rural Dionysia and Anthesteria in Acharnians, *the Thesmophoria, and either the Lenaea or the Mysteries in* Frogs. Lysistrata *also bore the alternative title of* Women

103

THE POETS OF OLD COMEDY

Fragments

27 Clement of Alexandria *Miscellanies* 7.33.1

τῶν γὰρ τετραπόδων οὐδὲν ἀποκτείνειν ἔδει
ἡμᾶς τὸ λοιπόν, πλὴν ὑῶν. τὰ γὰρ κρέα
ἥδιστ᾽ ἔχουσιν, κοὐδὲν ἀφ᾽ ὑὸς γίγνεται
πλὴν ὑστριχὶς καὶ πηλὸς ἡμῖν καὶ βοή.

28 Athenaeus 308a

              ἐξιόντι γὰρ
ἁλιεὺς ἀπήντησεν φέρων μοι κεστρέας,
ἰχθῦς ἀσίτους καὶ πονηροὺς ἔν γ᾽ ἐμοί .

29 Σ Euripides *Medea* 476

           εὖ γέ σοι ⟨γένοιθ᾽⟩, ἡμᾶς ὅτι
ἔσωσας ἐκ τῶν σῖγμα τῶν Εὐριπίδου.

30 Σ Aristophanes *Birds* 798

τὸν μαινόμενον, τὸν Κρῆτα, τὸν μόγις Ἀττικόν.

31 Σ Aristophanes *Acharnians* 352

καὶ τὰς ὀφρῦς σχάσασθε καὶ τὰς ὄμφακας.

32 Athenaeus 367b

ὁπόθεν ἔσοιτο μᾶζα καὶ παροψίδες.

at the Adonia. *F 27 seems to imply some business about dietary regulations.*

Dieitrephes (F 30—PAA 323750) was a comic target of the 420s and 410 (Birds 798–800, Cratinus F 251), who is not heard from after Thracian mercenaries under his command committed a massacre at Mycalessus in 412/1. Thus this comedy probably belongs to the 410s.

Fragments

27 In future we ought to kill no four-footed beasts, except for pigs, because they provide the most delicious meat, and we have nothing left from a pig except the bristle, the mud, and the squeal.

28 As I was going out, a fisherman met me carrying some mullets, fish that don't eat, inferior in my opinion.

29 ⟨May things go⟩ well for you, since you saved us from the sigma of Euripides.[1]

[1] A reference to *Medea* 476 (*esōsa s' hōs isasin*—I saved you as ⟨all Greeks⟩ know).

30 [of Dieitrephes] That crazy man, the Cretan, hardly an Athenian.

31 Relax your [pl.] eyebrows and that sour-grape look.

32 From where a barley cake and some side dishes might come.

33 Photius (b, z) α 1334

ἔπειτα κλίνην ἀμφικέφαλον πυξίνην

34 Eustathius *On the Odyssey* p. 1403.33

κατηδέσθημεν ἂν
καὶ κατεκόπημεν εὐθύς.

35 Pollux 10.135

ἐφέρεσθε δὲ
τὰ ῥάμματα.

36 Σ Aristophanes *Peace* 73b

ὡς μέγα μέντοι †πάλαι† τὴν Αἴτνην ὄρος εἶναί
    φασι τεκμαίρου,
ἔνθα τρέφεσθαι τὰς κανθαρίδας τῶν ἀνθρώπων
    λόγος ἐστὶν
οὐδὲν ἐλάττους.

37 Eustathius *On the Odyssey* p. 1547.58

ὁ δὲ τὸν ἐγκέφαλόν τις
ἐξαύσας καταπίνει.

ΕΥΡΩΠΗ

33 Next a two-headed couch made of boxwood.

34 We would have immediately been chopped to bits and eaten up.

35 You [pl.] were making the seams.

36 Guess how large they say Mount Etna is, where the story goes that the beetles raised there are as big as men.[1]

[1] Etna was famous for its beetles. In comedy see Epicharmus F 65 and the opening scene of *Peace,* where the giant dung beetle on which Tyrgaeus flies to Olympus is from Etna (73).

37 And another man took up a bit of brain and gulped it down.

Brief fragments: (F 38) "to ride on a mule," (F 39) "coward-ice," (F 40) "goads," (F 41) "wicker basket," (F 42) "stylo-bate."

EUROPA

The best-known ancient versions of the story of Europa, sister of Cadmus, who was abducted by Zeus disguised as a white bull, are the poem by Moschus (2nd c. BC) and the amusing sketch in Lucian's Dialogues of the Sea-Gods *(15). The story is as old as Homer (Iliad 14.321–22), and in drama Europa was the principal character in Aeschylus'* Fates or Europa, *in which she is worried about the fate of her son Sarpedon at Troy. Hermippus also wrote a comedy with this title. The comic poets are much more likely to have fastened on her encounter with the bull, which was*

Fragments

43 Athenaeus 367c

{A.} γυνὴ καθεύδουσ᾽ ἐστὶν ἀργόν. {B.} μανθάνω.
{A.} ἐγρηγορυίας δ᾽ εἰσὶν αἱ παροψίδες,
αὐταὶ μόνον κρεῖττον πολὺ χρῆμ᾽ εἰς ἡδονὴν
ἢ τᾶλλα {B.} βίνου γάρ τινες παροψίδες
εἰσ᾽, ἀντιβολῶ σε;

44 Athenaeus 328f

ἁλιευόμενός ποτ᾽ αὐτὸν εἷλον ἀνδράχνη
μετὰ πρημνάδων, κἄπειτ᾽ ἀφῆχ᾽, ὅτι ἦν βόαξ.

   1 εἶδον ACE, εἷλον Meineke.

ΖΕΥΣ ΚΑΚΟΥΜΕΝΟΣ

Athenaeus, citing F 47, records that Heracles was a charac-
ter in the comedy, and it is a natural assumption that he is
the second speaker also in F 46. The scene is perhaps a
brothel, where Heracles is invited to pass the time before
dinner playing cottabus *with a female, likely a hetaera.*
How Zeus was worked into this comedy is not immediately

either the agent of Zeus or Zeus himself disguised. F 43 implies that Europa was asleep at some point in the comedy, while someone (Zeus or just some chance passer-by?) begins a list of sexual double entendres on paropsides *("side dishes" or "hors d'oeuvres").*

Fragments

43 (A) A sleeping woman is an inactive thing. (B) I agree.

(A) But when she is awake, her "hors d'oeuvres" are a much better route to pleasure than the main course.

(B) Then my question to you is, are there "hors d'oeuvres" of sex?[1]

[1] The text, especially of l. 4, is in some dispute, and all of ll. 2–5 may belong to A.

44 Once while fishing I caught one along with some little tunny fish using some purslane, and then I threw it back because it was a grunt fish.

Brief fragment: (F 45) "I [they?] did not know what to do."

ZEUS BADLY TREATED

clear, but the particple kakoumenos *may be related to the legal charge of* kakōsis, *or parental abuse. A scene in* Birds *shows that Zeus has not had his son Heracles admitted to a phratry; thus comedy could explore the less than satisfactory relationship between father and son. Some of the fragments (F 51–52, 54) have to do with words and cleverness,*

109

Fragments

46 Athenaeus 666d

πρὸς κότταβον παίζειν, ἕως ἂν σφῷν ἐγὼ
τὸ δεῖπνον ἔνδον σκευάσω. {ΗΡΑΚΛΗΣ.} πάνυ
    βούλομαι.
† ἀλλὰ νεμος ἔστ† {Α.} ἀλλ' εἰς θυείαν παιστέον.
{ΗΡ.} φέρε τὴν θυείαν, αἶρ' ὕδωρ, τὰ ποτήρια
5 παράθετε. παίζωμεν δὲ περὶ φιλημάτων.
{Α.} <   > ἀγεννῶς οὐκ ἐῶ
παίζειν. τίθημι κοττάβεια σφῷν ἐγὼ
τασδί τε τὰς κρηπῖδας ἃς αὕτη φορεῖ,
καὶ τὸν κότυλον τὸν σόν. {ΗΡ.} βαβαιάξ, οὑτοσὶ
10 μείζων ἀγὼν τῆς Ἰσθμιάδος ἐπέρχεται.

3 αλλα νεμος ἐστ cod., ἀγὼν ἐμός ἐστ' Kaibel, ἀλλ' ἄγγος
ἔστ'; Kock.

47 Athenaeus 667b

            ἀγκυλοῦντα δεῖ σφόδρα
τὴν χεῖρα πέμπειν εὐρύθμως τὸν κότταβον.

48 Athenaeus 478c

τὸν κότυλον φέρει

*and we may have a comic opposition of the theme of brawn
(Heracles) and brain (who?), as in Sophocles'* Philoctetes
and Euripides' Antiope. *Lucian's two later sketches* Tragic
Zeus *and* Zeus under Fire *may owe something to com-
edy's presentation of the king of the Olympians. Oellacher
and Coppiola date the play to 429 or 428 and regard it, not
as a mythological burlesque, but as an attack on the person
and family of Pericles ("Zeus" at Cratinus F 73, 118, 258).
F 47 reminds one of the teaching scene in* Wasps, *where the
father is instructed in elegant behaviour. Is the boorish
Heracles the pupil here?*

Fragments

46 (A) To play at cottabus, while I go inside and get din-
ner ready for the two of you.

(HERACLES) Excellent idea, but is there a basin?[1]

(A) You'll have to play using a mortar.

(HERACLES) Bring [sing.] the mortar, draw [sing.]
some water, put out [pl.] some cups. Let us play for kisses.

(A) ‹Kisses?› I will not let you play for such low stakes.
As the stakes in cottabus I propose the boots which she is
wearing and this drinking cup of yours.

(HERACLES) Bloody hell, that's a more serious con-
test than the Isthmian Games.

[1] Or "that's my game."

47 You must bend your wrist all the way back and then
fling the cottabus smoothly.

48 You win the drinking cup [or "he brings"].

111

49 Athenaeus 119b

ὥσθ᾽ ἅττ᾽ ἔχω ταῦτ᾽ ἐς ταρίχους ἀπολέσω.

50 Pollux 10.17

κεράτινον εἶχε σκευοφόριον καμπύλον.

51 Athenaeus 677a

καίτοι φορεῖτε γλῶτταν ἐν ὑποδήμασιν,
στεφανοῦσθ᾽ ὑπογλωττίσιν, ὅταν πίνητέ που·
κἂν καλλιερῆτε, γλῶτταν ἀγαθὴν πέμπετε.

52 Orion *Anthology* 1

γλώττης ἀγαθῆς οὐκ ἔστ᾽ ἄμεινον οὐδὲ ἕν.

ἡ γλῶττα δύναμιν τοὺς λόγους ἐκτήσατο,
ἐκ τῶν λόγων δ᾽ ἅττ᾽ αὐτὸς ἐπιθυμεῖς ἔχεις.

53 Σ Lucian *Companions for Hire* 21

ἐπὶ ⟨τὰ⟩ Μανδροβούλου χωρεῖ.

54 Photius (b, Sᶻ) α 1386

τὼ προσεμφερῆ τὴν σοφίαν

55 Photius (b, Sᶻ) α 3399

ἀφροδίσιος λόγος

49 And so I will waste all that I have on salted fish.

50 He had a curved baggage pole made of horn.

51 What's more, you wear a tongue in your shoes; when-ever you go drinking, you wear a crown with tongue wort; and if your sacrifice is auspicious, you "give good tongue."

52 There is nothing better than a good tongue.

The tongue possesses power by its words; from words you get what you desire.

53 It's going the way of Mandrobulus.[1]

[1] Of things that get progressively worse.

54 The two of them similar in cleverness.

55 A tale of sex.

ΙΩ

Fragment

56 Athenaeus 657a

πρόσφερε δεῦρο δὴ τὴν κεφαλὴν τῆς δέλφακος.

ΚΛΕΟΦΩΝ

Aristophanes is considered to have pioneered the dema-gogue comedy with his Knights *in 424, with Kleon dis-guised (slightly) as "Paphlagon." In this he was followed by Eupolis, who caricatured Hyperbolus under the name of Maricas (L-421). But Platon seems not to have concealed his target under a false name, but openly titled his com-edy and the lead character in it with the victim's actual name (Peisander, Hyperbolus, Cleophon). The hypothesis to* Frogs *(T 10) shows that this comedy finished third at the Lenaea of 405.*

Cleophon (PAA 578250), by profession a lyre maker, was the leading demagogue during the last years of the War and would be put to death by the Thirty in 405/4. He was certainly active by 416, as ostraka bearing his name at-test. He is made fun of at Thesmophoriazusae *805 (411), and he has been identified by some as the unnamed dema-gogue at Eupolis* Demes *F 99.23–34 (417).* Frogs *674–85, the ode from the parabasis, describes him as having "a*

PLATON

IO

Sannyrion also wrote an Old Comedy with this title, while Io appears as a character in Prometheus *with horns denoting the heifer into which she has been transformed. But we cannot determine what aspect of the myth was the subject of Platon's play.*

Fragment

56 So bring here the head of the sow.

CLEOPHON

Thracian swallow perched on his lips," and it has been suggested that his mother was Thracian and that he had a distinctive accent in his speech. As we know his father to have been Cleippides, a general of the 420s, the accusations of foreign birth and irregular citizenship must be comic fictions, one of which is reported as "fact" by Aeschines (2.76). An attractive explanation is that Cleophon (and his brother Philinus) were the children of Cleippides and a Thracian women, born shortly before Pericles' law of 451 that both of one's parents must be Athenian to qualify one for citizenship. Anyone of that age with a non-Athenian mother would have been suspect and thus available for caricature. Aristotle's statement that he came into the assembly after the battle of Arginusae (405) drunk and wearing a breastplate is likely derived from comedy.

The fragments of Platon's comedy are not greatly informative. F 58–59 very probably refer to Cleophon—for his abuse of public funds see Lysias 19. If F 60 is spoken

Testimonia

i See Platon T 10.

ii Σ Aristophanes *Frogs* 679

Κλεοφῶν στρατηγὸς τῶν Ἀθηναίων. καὶ εἰς τοῦτον τὸν δημαγωγὸν ὅλον δρᾶμα φέρεται Πλάτωνος καὶ ἐπιγράφεται ὁμωνύμως αὐτῷ Κλεοφῶν.

Fragments

57 Athenaeus 315b

σὲ γάρ, γραῦ, συγκατῴκισεν σαπρὰν
ὀρφῷσι σελαχίοις τε καὶ φάγροις βοράν.

58 Eustathius *On the Odyssey* p. 1441.23

ἵν' ἀπαλλαγῶμεν ἀνδρὸς ἁρπαγιστάτου.

59 Bachmann's *Lexicon* p. 114.15

ἀλλ' αὖτ' ἀπαρτὶ τἀλλότρι' οἰχήσῃ φέρων.

60 Phrynichus *Sophistic Preparation* p. 12.4

ἐψάθαλλε λεῖος ὤν

116

*of Cleophon, it continues comedy's recurrent portrayal of
the demagogues as having been homosexual prostitutes in
their youth. F 61 suggests strongly that Cleophon's mother,
like Hyperbolus' in Eupolis'* Maricas *and Hermippus'* Bak-
ery-Women, *was a character in the comedy. If so, she may
also be the old woman addressed in F 57. Is the "he" of that
fragment Cleophon, accused of ill-treating his mother in
her old age?*

Testimonia

i See Platon T 10.

ii Cleophon was an Athenian general. An entire play has
been written against this demagogue by Platon and titled
"Cleophon" after him.

Fragments

57 For he has placed you there, old woman, as rotting
food to sea perch and sharks and bream.[1]

[1] In Archippus' *Fishes* (F 28) the gourmand Melanthius is
handed over to the fishes as food. Was Kleophon's mother a fish
seller in the agora?

58 So that we may be rid of a most thieving fellow.

59 Just the opposite, you [masc. sing.] will go away taking
other people's property.

60 When he was beardless he would excite himself.

61 Σ Aristophanes *Frogs* 681

Θρηκία χελιδὼν· ἵνα διαβάλλῃ αὐτὸν ὡς βάρβαρον. κωμῳδεῖται δὲ ὡς υἱὸς Θράσσης. οὗτος δὲ ἦν ὁ καλούμενος Κλεοφῶν ὁ λυροποιός. καὶ Πλάτων ἐν Κλεοφῶντι δράματι βαρβαρίζουσαν πρὸς αὐτὸν πεποίηκε τὴν μητέρα. καὶ αὐτὴ δὲ Θρᾷσσα ἐλέγετο.

62 Athenaeus 76f

Σέλευκος δ' ἐν ταῖς Γλώσσαις καὶ γλυκυσίδην τινὰ καλεῖσθαί φησι σύκῳ τὴν μορφὴν μάλιστα ἐοικυῖαν· φυλάσσεσθαι δὲ τὰς γυναῖκας ἐσθίειν διὰ τὸ ποιεῖν ματαισμούς, ὡς καὶ Πλάτων ὁ κωμῳδιοποιός φησιν ἐν Κλεοφῶντι.

ΛΑΙΟΣ

Fragments

65 Athenaeus 68c [1–4], Σ *Wealth* 179 [1, 5–6]

οὐχ ὁρᾷς ὅτι
ὁ μὲν Λέαγρος, Γλαύκωνος ὢν μεγάλου γένους,

61 "Thracian swallow": so that he might attack him as a foreigner. He is made fun for being the son of a Thracian woman. This is the man called "Cleophon," the lyre maker. Platon in his play *Cleophon* depicts his mother talking to him in a foreign tongue. She was said to be a Thracian.

62 Seleucus in his *Glossary* [F 45 Müller] says that there is a flower called "peony" which looks very much like a fig, and which women avoid eating because it gives them gas, as Platon the comic poet says in *Cleophon*.

Brief fragments: (F 63) "money," (F 64) "whip."

LAIUS

The story of Laius, the ill-fated father of Oedipus, would certainly have been part of the lost Theban epics of the seventh/sixth centuries BC. Aeschylus wrote a play called "Laius," the first of his "Theban plays" of 467, while Meletus composed a trilogy "The Oedipus Story" and Euripides a Chrysippus, *about Laius' affair with the attractive son of Pelops. Thus comedy could have used any one of a number of plotlines: the affair with Chrysippus, his disobedience of the oracle not to have children (the verb "be strong" in F 66 is used of women in labour), or the fateful encounter with Oedipus. The mention of Leagrus and Philonides (F 65) should put the play in the late 390s or early 380s.*

Fragments

65 Do you [sing.] not see that Leagrus, from the great house of Glaucon, walks about, the silly foolish cuckoo,

119

<ἀβελτερο>κόκκυξ ἠλίθιος περιέρχεται,
σικυοῦ πέπονος εὐνουχίου κνήμας ἔχων;
5 Φιλωνίδην δ' οὐ τέτοκεν ἡ μήτηρ ὄνον
τὸν Μελιτέα, κοὐκ ἔπαθεν οὐδέν;

66 Photius (b, z) α 1168

ἀπαμβρακοῦ καὶ μὴ προδῷς σαυτήν

ΛΑΚΩΝΕΣ Η ΠΟΙΗΤΑΙ

The double title is found only in the Suda (T 1); all other citations are to Platon's Laconians *only. Pirrotta describes this play as a Literaturenkomödie, since the second title "Poets" fits well with the mention of the tragic poet Sthenelus (F 72) and with the search for an "angular phrase" (F 69). F 70 reveals an unidentified character returned from the dead. It is an attractive speculation, but still only a speculation, that this is again Aeschylus, a character in* Frogs *and in Pherecrates'* Tiddlers. *He could be the "this one" of F 69, the quarry used by an inferior artist (Sthenelus?). Aristophanes mentions both Aeschylus and Sthenelus in two fragments of his* Gerytades *(F 158, 161). At* Clouds *1399 Aeschylus is "a mover and prier of new verses."*

with shins like a seedless cucumber? And did not Philonides' mother give birth to that ass from Melite, and suffer no ill effects?[1]

[1] Leagrus (*PAA* 602660) is very likely the rival litigant mentioned at Andocides 1.117–21, of a wealthy and distinguished family (*APF* 90–91). Philonides (*PAA* 957480), son of Onetor, hence his nickname Onos (ass), was a large, awkward, not very bright, but rich Athenian, said to be the lover of the hetaera Nais. See *Wealth* 179, 303; Platon F 65; Nicochares F 4; Theopompus F 5; and the comedy *Philonides* by the Middle Comic poet Aristophon.

66 Be strong and do not give up on yourself [fem.].

Brief fragments: (F 67) "cloudy," (F 68) "yes!".

LACONIANS or POETS

The date is difficult to determine. F 71 is very much in the spirit of Middle Comedy and lacks any of the vigour and punch of an Old Comic dialogue. However, Sthenelus is a poet of the fifth century, active between 422 and c. 408. Pirrotta (164) is content with the decade 410–400. Cobet proposed an ingenious theory that when Aristophanes (Peace 700–701) says that Cratinus "died when the Laconians invaded," he is referring not to the Spartan invasion of 431 etc., but to the performance of Platon's Laconians, thus dating the comedy to 424–422.

How do we harmonise the two titles, and which (if either) denotes the chorus? Laconians seem more likely to have provided a chorus, especially so the poet could exploit a number of stereotypes: the military lifestyle, the personal

Fragments

69 Σ Oribasius *Medical Collection* XI A 63

ὅταν δέωμαι γωνιαίου ῥήματος,
τούτῳ παριστῶ καὶ μοχλεύω τὰς πέτρας.

70 Σ Aristophanes *Birds* 471

{A.} καὶ μὴν ὅμοσόν μοι μὴ τεθνάναι. {B.} τὸ σῶμ᾽
  ἐγώ,
ψυχὴν δ᾽ ἀνήκειν ὥσπερ Αἰσώπου ποτέ.

71 Athenaeus 665b

{A.} ἄνδρες δεδειπνήκασιν ἤδη; {B.} σχεδὸν
  ἅπαντες. {A.} εὖ γε·
τί οὐ τρέχων ⟨σὺ⟩ τὰς τραπέζας ἐκφέρεις; ἐγὼ δὲ
νίπτρον παραχέων ἔρχομαι. {B.} κἀγὼ δὲ
  παρακορήσων.
{A.} σπονδὰς δ᾽ ἔπειτα παραχέας τὸν κότταβον
  παροίσω.
5 τῇ παιδὶ τοὺς αὐλοὺς ἐχρῆν ἤδη πρὸ χειρὸς εἶναι,
καὶ προαναφυσᾶν. τὸ μύρον ἤδη παράχεον βαδίζων
Αἰγύπτιον, κᾆτ᾽ ἴρινον· στέφανον ἔπειθ᾽ ἑκάστῳ
δώσω φέρων τῶν ξυμποτῶν. νεοκρᾶτά τις ποιείτω.
{B.} καὶ δὴ κέκραται. {A.} τὸν λιβανωτὸν ἐπιτιθεὶς †
  εἶπε
10 σπονδὴ μὲν ἤδη γέγονε, καὶ πίνοντές εἰσι πόρρω.

habits of the Spartans (Birds 1280–83), or the sexual impli-cations of lacōnizein.

Fragments

69 Whenever I need an angular phrase, I stand beside this one (?) and pry out the stones.

70 (A) Well then swear to me that you are not dead.
(B) I am in body, but I have brought my soul back up like that of Aesop.

71 (A) Have the men already had their dinner?
(B) Nearly all.
(A) Good. Why don't you run inside and take the tables away? I will go and pour out water for washing.
(B) And I to sweep up.
(A) Then when I have poured out the drink for libation, I shall put out the *cottabus*. The slave girl should have had her *auloi* out by now and started tuning up already. Now I shall go and pour out some scent from Egypt and then that made from iris root. Next I shall bring and give a garland to each one of the guests. Someone, get some new wine ready.
(B) It's already mixed.
(A) Put out the incense and tell . . .

They have already done the libation and are well on

καὶ σκόλιον ᾖσται, κότταβος δ' ἐξοίχεται θύραζε.
αὐλοὺς δ' ἔχουσά τις κορίσκη Καρικὸν μέλος ‹τι›
μελίζεται τοῖς συμπόταις, κἄλλην τρίγωνον εἶδον
ἔχουσαν, εἶτ' ᾖδεν πρὸς αὐτὸ μέλος Ἰωνικόν τι.

72 Harpocration p. 272.14

καὶ ἐν ταῖς διδασκαλίαις εὑρίσκεται ὁ Σθένελος τρα-
γῳδίας ποιητής. ἐκωμῴδει δὲ αὐτὸν ὁ τοὺς Πλάτωνος
Λάκωνας γράψας ὡς τἀλλότρια ἐπισφετεριζόμενον.

73 Athenaeus 380e

πάσας παραφερέτω

MAMMAKYΘOI

with the drinking. A drinking song has been sung, and the *cottabus* has been taken away. A young girl is playing a Carian melody on the *auloi* for the guests, and I saw another one with a spindle harp, and she was singing an Ionian tune along with it.

72 Sthenelus a tragic poet is found in the production records. The author of Platon's *Laconians* made fun of him for plagiarising other people's material.[1]

[1] A tragic poet (*TrGF* I 32), whose poetry is described by Aristotle as "clear and uninspired" (*Poetics* 1458a), he is also made fun of at F 136, and at Aristophanes *Wasps* 1313 and F 158.

73 Let ⟨someone⟩ hand out all ⟨the cups⟩.

Brief fragments: (F 74) "column heads," (F 75) "locusts."

DOLTS

There is considerable doubt whether there is in fact a comedy so called by Platon. Hesychius (T 2) attributes it to Platon, while the Aristophanic scholiast (T 1) comments that "some say" it is a play by Platon. Athenaeus (571b) quotes Metagenes F 4 from "the Breezes *of Metagenes or the* Dolt *by Aristagoras," and at 335a cites an iambic line "from the* Dolt *or* Breezes *of Metagenes." It is not immediately clear whether we have two different plays by two different poets or a single play with alternative titles, and whether this comedy has anything to with the* Dolts *attributed to Platon.*

THE POETS OF OLD COMEDY

Testimonia

i Σ Aristophanes *Frogs* 990

Μαμμάκυθοι· Ἀρίσταρχός φησιν ὠνοματοπεποιῆ-
σθαι. πῶς οὖν, Δημήτριός φησιν, εἰ μὴ σύνηθες αὐ-
τοῖς τὸ ὄνομα, οὗ καὶ δρᾶμα ὅλον οὕτως ἐπιγέγραπται
Μαμμάκουθοι, ὅ τινες Πλάτωνος λέγουσιν;

ii Hesychius μ 216

μαμμάκυθος· μωρός. ἔστι δὲ καὶ δρᾶμα πεποιημένον
Πλάτωνι.

ΜΕΝΕΛΕΩΣ

Fragments

76 Athenaeus 641b

                              {Α.} εἰπέ μοι,
ὡς ὀλίγα λοιπὰ τῶν ἐπιτραπεζωμάτων.
{Β.} ὁ γὰρ θεοῖσιν ἐχθρὸς αὐτὰ κατέφαγεν.

77 Zenobius *Common Proverbs* 6.17

τί οὐκ ἀπήγξω, ἵνα Θήβησιν ἥρως γένῃ;

Testimonia

i "Dolts": Aristarchus says that it is a made-up name. How then, says Demetrius, unless the term was familiar to them [Athenians]? There is an entire play so titled, *Dolts*, which some say is by Platon.

ii "Dolt": a stupid person. There is also a play written by Platon.

MENELAUS

A comedy about Menelaus could have dealt with anything from his courting of Helen to Paris' "abduction" of his wife to incidents at Troy, or adventures on his return home (cf. Proteus, the satyr play with the Oresteia *in 458). It is impossible to say who "the goddamned fellow" might be, or what the connection (if any) with Thebes might be. V 20 shows a comic scene with a female figure on shipboard, accompanied by a male figure, looking back at another male. The scene has been identified by some as Helen, fleeing with Paris as Menelaus looks on. Platon's* Menelaus *might be the comedy depicted here.*

Fragments

76 (A) Tell me, because there's so little left of the dessert table.
    (B) That goddamned fellow has wolfed it down.

77 Why don't you just hang yourself so that you may become a hero at Thebes?

127

78 Athenaeus 110d

ἀγελαίους ἄρτους

ΜΕΤΟΙΚΟΙ

Fragments

80 Photius (s^z) α 2867

οὐκ ἐμάνθανον
κακῶν μεγίστων ἀρραβῶνα λαμβάνων

81 Pollux 10.24

σημεῖα παρασημεῖα, κλεῖν παρακλείδιον

82 Photius (b, S^z) α 1386

ὧδ᾽ ἀναισχυντοῦντε τὼ μιλτηλιφῆ

78 Ordinary bread loaves.

Brief fragment: (F 79) "blamelessly."

METICS

Crates and Pherecrates are each credited with a Metics, *to which one fragment only is assigned (Crates F 26). In the case of Pherecrates, the source is Apollonius Dyscolus, who cites Pherecrates'* Metics *for the unusual use of* emautos *in the nominative (113.17), but who earlier (69.18) cited* Metics *by Platon (F 83) for the same peculiarity. The safest solution is to recognise one comedy, a* Metics *by Platon.* Metics *(*metoikoi*) were the formally registered non-Athenian residents of Athens, and they were seen as part of the community (see* Acharnians *508). They could certainly have formed an appropriate comic chorus.*

Fragments

80 I did not realise that I was getting a deposit of really bad things.

81 Fake seals, a false key.

82 The pair of you, stained with the red-ochre rope, and unashamed.

Brief fragment: (F 83) "myself."

ΜΥΡΜΗΚΕΣ

NIKAI

Fragments

84 Σ Aristophanes *Lysistrata* 288

τουτὶ προσαναβῆναι τὸ σιμὸν δεῖ.

85 Σ Aristophanes *Birds* 1297

διαβάλλεται δὲ εἴς τε πονηρίαν, ὡς Πλάτων ἐν Νίκαις.

86 Σ (Arethas) Plato *Apology* 19c

κωμῳδεῖται δὲ ‹ὅτι› καὶ τὸ τῆς εἰρήνης κολοσσικὸν ἐξῆρεν ἄγαλμα. Εὔπολις Αὐτολύκῳ, Πλάτων Νίκαις.

87 Pollux 7.40

ἰχθύων δὲ πλύμα

ANTS

An Ants *by Platon is otherwise unknown. Cantharus wrote a comedy with this title, and Pherecrates an* Ant-Men.

VICTORIES

We may consider several possibilities to explain the title, which should refer to the chorus of the comedy: person-ifications of victory in war (Nike), the sculptured victories on the balustrade on the Acropolis, or victories in the thea-tre. The last would fit well with the theatrical themes im-plied by titles such as Laconians *or* Poets, Poet, Stage Properties, Security. *The mention of Meidias (F 85) and of the statue of Peace (F 86) suggests a date in the early 410s.*

Fragments

84 ⟨You?⟩ must get up and over this hill.

85 He [Meidias] is attacked also for wickedness, so Platon in *Victories.*

86 He [Aristophanes] is also made fun of because he set up a huge statue of Peace. Eupolis in *Autolycus* [F 62], Platon in *Victories.*

87 Water used for cleaning fish.

Brief fragment: (F 88) "for the temples."

ΝΥΞ ΜΑΚΡΑ

It is often assumed that the title refers to the conception of Heracles during a "long night," when the Sun at Zeus' request did not take out his horses for three days and thus provided Zeus more time with Amphitryon's wife, Alcmena. See Lucian Dialogues of the Gods *14, where the phrase "long night" occurs at the end of the sketch. Some have seen in Platon's* A Long Night *the original for Plautus'* Amphitryo *and thus identified Alcmena as the speaker of F 89 and related the business about hanging a lamp on someone's forehead (F 90) to Mercury's warning at* Amphitryo *142–45 that the spectators can tell the real Jupiter by a gold brim on his hat. On the same reasoning the angry couple*

Fragments

89 Photius (b, z) α 988

ἀλλ᾽ αὖ γέλοιον ἄνδρα μου μὴ φροντίσαι
μηδέν

90 Athenaeus 700f

ἐνταῦθ᾽ ἐπ᾽ ἄκρων τῶν κροτάφων ἕξει λύχνον
δίμυξον.

91 Athenaeus 699f

ἕξουσιν οἱ πομπεῖς λυχνούχους δηλαδή.

A LONG NIGHT

coming to a reconciliation in F 93 are Amphitryon and Alcmena. But all of this depends on seeing the "long night" of the title as the night during which Heracles was conceived. In F 91 we get a mention of "those in procession"; it is a reasonable conclusion that these formed the chorus.

Archippus wrote a comic Amphitryon, *and for tragedy, both Aeschylus and Ion of Chios composed an* Alcmena, *but we have only the title of each. Euripides wrote an* Alcmena, *of which we do have some remains, enough to tell us that the plot dealt with the consequences of that night, but in a more serious fashion. See the account in Apollodorus (2.4.6–8) and* Euripides VII, *100–13.*

Fragments

89 (WOMAN) But then again it is ridiculous that my husband took no thought at all for me.

90 Here on the side of his forehead he will hang a lamp with two wicks.

91 Those in procession will certainly be carrying lamp holders.

92 Athenaeus 110d

κᾆθ᾽ ἧκεν ἄρτους πριάμενος
μὴ τῶν καθαρύλλων, ἀλλὰ μεγάλους Κιλικίους.

93 Photius (Sᶻ) α 2712

ἥξειν ἀποφλεγμήναντας εἰς διαλλαγάς

ΞΑΝΤΑΙ Η ΚΕΡΚΩΠΕΣ

Fragments

95 Photius p. 583.17

ἦν δὴ θόρυβος τευταζόντων.

92 And then he arrived after buying some loaves of bread, not some of the dainty white ones, but some large Cilician ones.

93 For them to cease being angry and to come to a reconciliation.

Brief fragment: (F 94) "improvisation."

WOOL-CARDERS or CERCOPES

This comedy is cited three, perhaps four, times in addition to its inclusion in the list given in the Suda *(T 1). Of the four times when Platon is named as the author, three call the play* Xantai *or "Wool-carders" [masc.], and one, Hephaestion citing F 96,* Xantriai *or "Women carding wool." A second title,* Cercopes, *is given only in the* Suda *(T 1), but if "men carding wool" refers to Heracles' servitude to Omphale, then an allusion to the Cercopes is not out of place. In some versions the Cercopes are located not in central Greece (see Hermippus'* Cercopes*), but in Asia Minor and form part of the story of Heracles and Omphale (Diodorus of Sicily 4.31.5–8). Lucian (Dialogue of the Gods 15) describes how Heracles wore women's clothes and carded wool for Omphale. Both Achaeus and Ion of Chios wrote satyr plays called* Omphale. *Cercopes were traditionally two in number, but this could have easily been increased to provide a chorus.*

Fragments

95 There was indeed a hubbub of people bustling about.

96 Hephaestion *Handbook* 15.12

χαῖρε παλαιογόνων ἀνδρῶν θεατῶν ξύλλογε
παντοσόφων.

ΠΑΙΔΑΡΙΟΝ

Fragments

98 Σ Aristophanes *Peace* 948b

φέρε τοῦτ᾽ ἐμοὶ
δεῖξον τὸ κανοῦν μοι δεῦρο· πῇ μάχαιρ᾽ ἔνι;

99 Σ Aristophanes *Peace* 734b

εἰ μὲν μὴ λίαν ‹∪ ∪ –› ὦνδρες, ἠναγκαζόμην
στρέψαι δεῦρ᾽, οὐκ ἂν παρέβην εἰς λέξιν τοιάνδ᾽
ἐπῶν.

100 Athenaeus 316c

ὥσπερ τοὺς πουλύποδας πρώτιστά σε

101 Σ Aristophanes *Frogs* 308

διασκώπτειν τοὺς ἀκρωμένους

96 Greetings, gathering of ancient-born spectators, clever in every way.

Brief fragment: (F 97) "in a musical fashion."

THE LITTLE KID

The title might imply that a young child had something to do with the plot, and F 98 might be put in the mouth of an exasperated parent or minder dealing with a domestic situation. F 99 comes very probably from the opening of the parabasis and reminds one of the knights' reluctance to sing the praises of any other poet but Aristophanes (Knights 507–9). We can only guess at the identity of the chorus. Pirrotta (213) dates the comedy to 420–410.

Fragments

98 Bring this basket here to me, show it to me. Where is there a knife in it?

99 Gentlemen, if I were not being so ⟨forcefully?⟩ compelled to turn in this direction, I would not have come forward [*parabainein*] to deliver these lines.[1]

[1] The metre is eupolideans and the context the delivery of the parabasis by the chorus.

100 First of all . . . you [sing.] as octopuses.

101 To make fun of the audience.

ΠΕΙΣΑΝΔΡΟΣ

*Peisander (PAA 771270) was a political figure of consider-
able importance in the 420s and 410s. He originally posi-
tioned himself as a demagogue, especially so during the
scandals of 415, when he was appointed as one of the inves-
tigating commissioners into what he described as "a pre-
lude to the overthrow of the democracy" (Andocides 1.27,
36, 43). In 411 he changed his loyalties and became one of
the leading members of the oligarchic coup that we know as
the Revolution of the 400 (Thucydides 8.49–56, 63–68).
After the collapse of that oligarchic regime, he fled to De-
celeia, which was under Spartan control, and thereafter
vanishes from history.*

*Comedy makes fun of him for a number of reasons: (1)
political malpractice (Aristophanes Lysistrata 489–91, F
84); (2) his alleged cowardice in military service (Birds
1556–58, Eupolis F 35, Phrynichus F 21, and Xenophon
Symposium 2.14 which probably depends on comedy); (3)
his corpulence and repulsive appearance (Eupolis F 195,
Hermippus F 7, Phrynichus F 21); and (4) a gluttonous
appetite (Eupolis F 99.1–4; PCG VIII F 119).*

*This comedy was one of Platon's three demagogue com-
edies, all titled with the name of their target, unlike Knights*

Fragments

102 Athenaeus 385d

{A.} ἤδη φαγών τι πώποθ', οἷα γίγνεται,
ὀψάριον ἔκαμες, καὶ προσέστη τοῦτό σοι;
{B.} ἔγωγε, πέρυσι κάραβον φαγών.

PEISANDER

where Cleon was "disguised" as Paphlagon and Eupolis'
Maricas, which "hid" Hyperbolus. The fragments do not
contribute to seeing how the comedy made fun of Pei-
sander, unless Peisander is debating another glutton about
food in F 102, or embezzling money from the state in F 103,
or displaying his cowardice in war (F 112), "Ares' fledg-
ling" being used ironically of him. The mentions of Anti-
phon (F 110), the principal figure in the coup of 411, and
Euathlus (F 109), and the technical verb in F 111, "to
launch a countersuit," fit nicely with a play with a strong
political theme. Sommerstein suggests that F 105 is spoken
metaphorically of the relationship between Athens and her
allies (cf. Eupolis' Cities).

Jokes at Peisander are found in comedy from 426 to 411,
and this play is usually dated to the mid-410s, when Pei-
sander was most prominent as a political figure of the dem-
agogic sort. Sommerstein has made a strong case, however,
for dating the comedy to the Dionysia of 422 or the Lenaea
of 421; in that case it would have been produced with
Eupolis' Maricas, another demagogue comedy, this one
against Hyperbolus.

Recent bibliography: A. H. Sommerstein, in Rivals 437–51
[439–40].

Fragments

102 (A) Have you ever eaten some fish, and (as often hap-
pens) become ill, when it disagreed with you?

(B) I have, last year after eating crawfish.

103 Σ Aristophanes *Clouds* 249b

χαλεπῶς ἂν οἰκήσαιμεν ἐν Βυζαντίῳ,
ὅπου σιδαρέοισι †νομίσμασι†.

104 Herodian *On Singular Vocabulary* II p. 944.23

ὥσπερ κνεφάλλων ἢ πτίλων σεσαγμένος

105 Photius (b, z) α 782

γυνὴ γάρ, ἢν μὲν αὐτὴν
ἀεὶ κολάζῃς, ἐστὶ πάντων κτημάτων κράτιστον,
ἐὰν δ᾽ ἀνῇς, ὑβριστόν <ἐστι> χρῆμα κἀκόλαστον.

106 Photius (z) α 2817, Eustathius *On the Iliad* p. 302.77

Ἀρκάδας μιμούμενος· παροιμία, ᾗ κέχρηται Πλάτων
ἐν Πεισάνδρῳ, ἐπὶ τῶν ἄλλοις ταλαιπωρούντων· μαχι-
μώτατοι γὰρ ὄντες αὐτοὶ μὲν οὐδέποτε ἰδίαν νίκην
ἐνίκησαν, ἄλλοις δὲ αἴτιοι νίκης πολλοῖς ἐγένοντο.
καὶ ὁ Πλάτων οὖν διὰ τὸ τὰς κωμῳδίας ποιῶν ἄλλοις
παρέχειν διὰ πενίαν Ἀρκάδας μιμεῖσθαι ἔφη.

107 Zenobius 2.78

τετράδι γέγονας

103 We would not live very easily in Byzantium, where ⟨they use⟩ iron as money.

104 A man stuffed full of foam and feathers.

105 For if you are always beating a woman [your wife?], she is the best of all your possessions, but if you let her have her own way, she is an arrogant and undisciplined creature.

106 "Copying the Arcadians": Platon in *Peisander* uses this proverb of those who toil on behalf of others. For although the Arcadians were very warlike and were responsible for the victories of many others, they never won a victory of their own. That is why Platon says that he is "copying the Arcadians" when he writes the comedies himself but because of his poor financial situation hands them over to others.

107 Born on the fourth.[1]

[1] A proverb meaning someone who labours at someone else's command. Originally applied to Heracles, whose Labours were performed for Eurystheus, it was used of Aristophanes, who had his plays produced through other men (Aristonymus F 3, Ameipsias F 27).

108 Σ Aristophanes *Birds* 1556

δύο δέ εἰσι Πείσανδροι, καθάπερ Εὔπολις ἐν Μαρικᾷ
φησιν . . . καὶ Πλάτων ἐν Πεισάνδρῳ περὶ ἀμφοτέρων
λέγει.

109 Σ Aristophanes *Wasps* 592b

Εὔαθλος ῥήτωρ συκοφάντης, οὗ μνημονεύει καὶ ἐν
Ἀχαρνεῦσι καὶ ἐν Ὁλκάσιν . . . μνημονεύει δὲ αὐτοῦ
καὶ Πλάτων ἐν Πεισάνδρῳ καὶ Κρατῖνος ἐν Θρᾴτταις.

110

(a) [Plutarch] *Lives of the Ten Orators* 833c

κεκωμῴδηται δ' εἰς φιλαργυρίαν ὑπὸ Πλάτωνος ἐν
Πεισάνδρῳ.

(b) Philostratus *Lives of the Sophists* 1.15.2

καθάπτεται δὲ ἡ κωμῳδία τοῦ Ἀντιφῶντος ὡς δεινοῦ
τὰ δικανικὰ καὶ λόγους κατὰ τοῦ δικαίου ξυνκειμένους
ἀποδιδομένου πολλῶν χρημάτων αὐτοῖς μάλιστα τοῖς
κινδυνεύουσιν.

108 There are two men named Peisander, as Eupolis says in *Maricas* [F 195] . . . and Platon in *Peisander* speaks about both men.

109 Euathlus was a politician and an informer, whom he [Aristophanes] mentions in *Acharnians* [710] and in *Merchant-Ships* [F 424] . . . Platon mentions him in *Peisander* and Kratinus in *Thracian Women* [F 82].[1]

[1] Euathlus (*PAA* 425665) was a pupil of Protagoras, about whom Aulus Gellius (5.10) tells an anecdote, in which the clever pupil outwits his master.

110

(a) Antiphon has been made fun of for his love of money by Platon in *Peisander*.

(b) Comedy seized on Antiphon for being clever in forensic matters and for selling at a large price speeches that were against the interests of justice, especially to those who were in legal trouble.[1]

[1] If *Peisander* is as early as Sommerstein maintains, then (a) and (b) probably refer to different Antiphons: (b) to the celebrated orator from Rhamnous (*PAA* 138625), and (a) to the man made fun of at *Wasps* 1301–2 (*PAA* 138825), Antiphon the son of Lysonides.

Brief fragments: (F 111) "launch a countersuit," (F 112) "Ares' fledgling," (F 113) "beat one's fellow citizens."

ΠΕΡΙΑΛΓΗΣ

We can say very little for certain about this comedy. The title clearly refers to the situation of the central character, and we can cite Phrynichus' Hermit, Menander's Bad-Tempered Man, Theopompus' Lovejoy, or Pherecrates' Forgetful Man for other examples of a play so named. If the book by Orbilius (a first-century BC scholar at Rome, who taught Horace) has anything to do with Platon's play, then we might conjecture that its central character was a man fond of complaining about his lot and about the wrongs that he had suffered. The term perialgēs *and its cognates are most commonly found in the prose writers of later antiquity and the Byzantine period to express dramatically*

Testimonia

i Photius p. 414.17

περιαλγής· †ὁ σπενήρης† τῷ τόνῳ καὶ τοῦ δράματος τοῦ Πλατωνικου.

ii Suetonius *On Grammarians* 9

librum etiam cui est titulus Perialgos edidit continentem querelas de iniuriis quas professores neglegentia aut ambitione parentum acciperent.

THE ONE IN GREAT PAIN

emotional or physical suffering. We do, however, find ex-
amples twice in Thucydides (4.14.2 of the Spartan reaction
to Pylos, 6.54.3 of Aristogeiton's outrage), but Platon's use
of the term is unique in classical poetry.

*   The play is an earlier comedy by Platon. Leogoras,*
Morychus, and Glaucetes (F 114) are all made fun of in
Aristophanes' plays of 422 and 421. Morychus is found as
early as Acharnians *(887—in 425) and Glaucetes as late as*
*411 (*Thesmophoriazusae *1037). Meidias (F 116) is a comic*
target of the 410s. The claim to have been the first to attack
Cleon (F 115) can certainly have been made after Cleon's
death (cf. Clouds 549, around 418). A date between 420
and 415 would not be far out of place.

Testimonia

i "In great pain": . . . in accent and of the Platonic play.

ii He [Orbilius] produced a book with the title "those in
great pain" containing the complaints about the injuries
which teachers had suffered by the negligence or ambi-
tions of parents.

Fragments

114 Σ Aristophanes *Clouds* 109d

ὦ θεῖε Μόρυχε· πῶς γὰρ οὐ δαίμων ἔφυς;
καὶ Γλαυκέτης ἡ ψῆττα, καὶ Λεωγόρας,
οἳ ζῆτε τερπνῶς οὐδὲν ἐνθυμούμενοι.

115 Priscian *Institutes of Grammar* 18.221

ὃς πρῶτα μὲν Κλέωνι πόλεμον ἠράμην

116 Σ Aristophanes *Birds* 1297

χρηστὸν μὴ κατὰ Μειδίαν ὀρτυγοκόπον

117 Priscian *Institutes of Grammar* 18.275

ἀλλ᾽ ἡγούμεσθ᾽ εὖ κἀνδρείως πολλῷ πάντων
προέχοντες.

ΠΟΙΗΤΗΣ

PLATON

Fragments

114 O divine Morychus—for you must have been born a god—and Glaucetes the flatfish, and Leogoras, who live very pleasantly without a care in the world.[1]

[1] Comedy made fun of all these as gluttons and epicures. For Morychus see *PAA* 658855, for Glaucetes *PAA* 274620, and Leogoras (the father of Andocides) *PAA* 605075.

115 I was the one who first declared war on Cleon.

116 An honest man, not like Meidias the quail tapper.

117 We are well and truly in the lead, way ahead of everyone else.[1]

[1] The metre is anapaestic tetrameter catalectic, used in the agon and in the parabasis proper of Old Comedy. The "we" could be the poet speaking through his chorus about the relative merits of his comedy.

POET

We can say virtually nothing about this comedy. The title suggests a literary or dramatic subject, for which we may find parallels in other comedies by Platon. The most interesting of the few remaining fragments is F 121, where it has been attractively suggested that the speaker is Death—compare Frogs *1392 (= Aeschylus F 161).*

Fragments

118 Athenaeus 375b

τὸν δέλφακα
ἀπῆγε σιγῇ.

119 Athenaeus 657a

δέλφακα δὲ ῥᾴότατον

ῥαιότατον Α, ὡραιότατον Casaubon.

120 Σ Aristophanes *Frogs* 1159

ὁρᾶτε τὸ διῆρες ὑπερῷον.

121 Athenaeus 644a

μόνος δ᾽ ἄγευστος,
ἄσπλαγχνος ἐνιαυτίζομαι, ἀπλάκουντος,
ἀλιβάνωτος.

122 Pollux 10.190

†θαυμάζω τὸν τὴν δαπιθάκνην
πότερ᾽ ὀστρακίνην ἢ βίβλον ἔχων τὴν δήποτε†

123 The Antiatticist p. 116.21

ψήφισμα ἔθηκεν

PLATON

Fragments

118 He led the suckling pig away in silence.

119 A suckling pig in the prime of life.

120 Do you people see the upper floor?

121 The only one who never gets a taste, I go through the whole year without entrails, or any flat-cakes, or incense.

122 I wonder about the man who . . . whether holding a pot or a book . . .

123 He proposed a decree.

125 Σ Aristophanes *Frogs* 427

καὶ Σεβῖνος ἴσως παρὰ τὸ βινεῖν. ἔστι δὲ καὶ Σεβῖνος
ὠνομασμένος παρὰ Πλάτωνι Ποιητῇ.

ΠΡΕΣΒΕΙΣ

*Leucon produced a comedy of this title at the Lenaea of
422, and one recalls the memorable opening scenes in
Acharnians, where Athenian ambassadors return first
from Persia (61–125) and then from Thrace (134–72). Also
at the end of Lysistrata (1072–75) envoys from Sparta are
presented in a somewhat derogatory and stereotypical
fashion. Ambassadors were usually sent out in groups of
three, five, or ten, but the humour may consist of a large
number enjoying the benefits of a cushy position.*

*It is often assumed that the title refers to Epicrates' ac-
tivities as an ambassador (F 27), certainly with Andocides
to Persia in 392/1, and perhaps on earlier occasions. The
comedy would thus have had a strongly political theme.
However, we should not assume that the title refers to an
actual historical embassy; it could have easily featured*

Fragments

127 Athenaeus 229f

κᾆτ' ἔλαβον Ἐπικράτης τε καὶ Φορμίσιος
παρὰ τοῦ βασιλέως πλεῖστα δωροδοκήματα,
ὀξύβαφα χρυσᾶ καὶ πινακίσκους ἀργυροῦς.

125 Sebinus perhaps from *binein* (to fuck). There is also a Sebinus mentioned in Platon's *Poet*.

Brief fragments: (F 124) "chamber pot," (F 126) "crumbling."

ENVOYS

fictional and appropriately comic envoys. The Spartan allusions in F 132 and 134 could very well suggest a chorus of stereotypically dressed Spartans coming to Athens. If there is any truth to the story in Plutarch (Pelopidas 30.7) and Hegesander (ap. Athenaeus 251b) about Epicrates' facetious proposal that instead of nine archons chosen annually by lot the Athenians should choose nine poor men to be envoys to Persia, this might have seemed a suitable theme for a comedy.

Epicrates and Phormisius are kōmōidoumenoi *of the late 400s and 390s. Phormisius is known as early as* Frogs *965–66, while Epicrates disappears after the courts condemned him and Andocides (F 133) for the failure of their embassy to Persia in 392/1. Thus a date in the late 390s seems very likely.*

Fragments

127 Then Epicrates and Phormisius received a very great many bribes from the King, golden vinegar bowls and silver trays.[1]

[1] Epicrates (*PAA* 393945), honoured as a hero of the democratic restoration in 403 (Demosthenes 19.280), was said to have been involved in (and profited from) several embassies of the 390s

128 Athenaeus 424a

κυάθους ὅσους ἐκλέπτεθ' ἑκάστοτε

129 Harpocration p. 46.19

σκευάρια δὴ κλέψας ἀπεκήρυξ' ἐκφέρων

130 Σ Aristophanes *Assembly-Women* 71

ἄναξ ὑπήνης Ἐπίκρατες σακεσφόρε

131 Athenaeus 287d

Ἡράκλεις, τῶν βεμβράδων

132 Anonymous *On Aristotle's Nicomachean Ethics* 4.13

χαίρεις, οἶμαι, μεταπεττεύσας αὐτὸν διακλιμακίσας
   τε,
τὸν ὑπηνόβιον σπαρτιοχαίτην ῥυποκόνδυλον
   ἑλκετρίβωνα.

133 Harpocration p. 144.15

ζητητής· ἀρχή τις Ἀθήνησι κατὰ καιροὺς καθιστα-
μένη, εἴ ποτε τοὺς ἀδικοῦντάς τι δημοσίᾳ δέοι ζητεῖν·
Δημοσθένης ἐν τῷ κατὰ Τιμοκράτους καὶ Ἀνδοκίδης
ἐν τῷ περὶ ἐνδείξεως. οὗτος δὲ ὁ ῥήτωρ καὶ ζητητής
ποτε ἐγένετο, ὥς φησι Λυσίας καὶ Ἰσοκράτης καὶ
Πλάτων ὁ κωμικὸς Πρέσβεσιν.

to Persia and to Sparta. The latter (in 392/1) led to his condemnation in absentia and exile. Both he and Phormisius (*PAA* 962695) were notorious for their long, dark beards (*Ecclesiazusae* 71, 97).

128 All the ladles that you [pl.] stole on every occasion.

129 He stole the dinner things, carried them off and put them up for sale.

130 Epicrates, lord of the moustache, beard bearer.

131 Heracles, the anchovies!

132 You quite enjoy, I expect, putting him in check and knocking him down, that man who with a life-long beard, with hair like rope, filthy knuckles, and a tunic that drags in the dirt.[1]

[1] These qualities seem stereotypically Spartan (see *Birds* 1281–82, *Lysistrata* 279–80), and given Epicrates' Spartan connections and distinctive beard, he may be the man meant here. Note especially "with hair like rope" (*spartiochaitēn*).

133 "Investigator": an official position set up at Athens on certain occasions, whenever it was necessary to seek out criminals publicly, so Demosthenes in his *Against Timocrates* [24.11] and Andocides in his speech about his deposition [1.14, 36, 65]. This man [Andocides] had once been a politician and an inspector, as Lysias tells us [F 431 Carey] and Isocrates and the comic poet Platon in *Envoys*.

Brief fragments: (F 134) "regulators," (F 135) "he opened a vein."

ΡΑΒΔΟΥΧΟΙ

The existence of this comedy was revealed by the publication in 1968 of P. Oxy. 2737 (= Aristophanes F 591). Lines 44–51 (T 8) record that Platon had had early successes with comedies produced through others, but when he produced for the first time on his own, he finished fourth and "was shunted back to the Lenaea." The Greek title is Rhabdouchoi, *literally "staff bearers," the term for officials whose job it was to enforce the rules and keep order at*

ΣΚΕΥΑΙ

Skeuē *is clothing, something one puts on or wears, and is usually translated as "costume" in a play, although Pirrotta (272) argues for "stage properties." At* Frogs *108 Dionysus tells Heracles that he is wearing this get-up "to look like you," and at* Knights *232 and Aristotle* Poetics *1450b20 we hear of the costume maker (skeuopoios), among whose jobs was the making of the masks. In view of the theatrical references in F 136, 138, 140, and 142, we may safely regard this comedy as another play with a theatrical theme. But does the plural title denote the chorus, and what sort of chorus would a collection of "costumes" be? Both F 136*

SECURITY

games and in the theatre. It was also the Greek translation of the formal Roman term, lictor. *Aristophanes at* Peace *734–35 has his chorus say that "any comic poet who comes forward in the anapaests to praise himself should be beaten by the security people." The comedy probably belongs to the early 420s, when the number of comedies produced would have returned to five after the Peace of Nicias. It may be an alternative title for a known comedy. I would suggest* Poet *or possibly* Victories *or* Costumes.

COSTUMES

and 138 suggest a debate over merits of performers. The anapaestic tetrameters of the latter may indicate an agon.

The play can be dated to the last decade of the fifth century. Sthenelus (F 136) is known in comedy from 422 to c. 408, Morsimus from 424 to 405, Melanthius (F 140) from 421 to c. 400. But Agyrrhius and Archinus (F 141) belong to the 400s and 390s, and although they are mentioned as possible candidates for the unnamed politician at Frogs *367, there is no reason why the jokes against them by Platon and Sannyrion (F 9) must be later than* Frogs. *Pirrotta (272) prefers 407–404.*

THE POETS OF OLD COMEDY

Fragments

136 Σ Aristophanes *Wasps* 1312

ἅψαι μόνον σὺ κἂν ἄκρῳ τοῦ Μορσίμου,
ἵνα σου πατήσω τὸν Σθένελον μάλ᾽ αὐτίκα.

137 Photius p. 420.16

καὶ τοῖς τρόποις ἁρμόττον ὥσπερ περὶ πόδα

138 Athenaeus 628d

ὥστ᾽ εἴ τις ὀρχοῖτ᾽ εὖ, θέαμ᾽ ἦν· νῦν δὲ δρῶσιν
   οὐδέν,
ἀλλ᾽ ὥσπερ ἀπόπληκτοι στάδην ἑστῶτες ὠρύονται.

139 Moeris p. 188.14

ἀναβιῶν᾽ ἐκ τῆς νόσου

140 Σ Aristophanes *Birds* 151

Πλάτων δὲ αὐτὸν ἐν Σκευαῖς ὡς λάλον σκώπτει.

141 Σ Aristophanes *Frogs* 367

τοῦτο εἰς Ἀρχῖνον. μήποτε δὲ καὶ εἰς Ἀγύρριον. μέ-
μνηται δὲ τούτων καὶ Πλάτων ἐν Σκευαῖς καὶ Σαννυ-
ρίων ἐν Δανάῃ. οὗτοι γὰρ προϊστάμενοι τῆς δημοσίας
τραπέζης τὸν μισθὸν τῶν κωμῳδῶν ἐμείωσαν κωμῳ-
δηθέντες.

Fragments

136 Touch Morsimus just once with even the tip ‹of your finger›, and I will trample right back all over your Sthenelus.[1]

[1] A pair of uninspiring tragedians. Morsimus in particular (*PAA* 658818; *TrGF* 29) is remembered as "frigid" and "inferior." For Sthenelus (*PAA* 819075; *TrGF* 32) see Platon F 72.

137 And suited to his style like ‹a shoe› on a foot.

138 And so if someone danced well, it was a sight worth watching. But now they don't do anything, but they stand stock still, as if they were paralysed, and howl.

139 To recover from illness.

140 Platon makes fun of him [Melanthius] in *Stage-Properties* as a mouthy sort.

141 This ‹is directed› against Archinus, or perhaps also at Agyrrhius. Platon mentions them in *Costumes* and Sannyrion in *Danae* [F 9]. When they were in charge of the public treasury, they reduced the payments to the comic poets because they had been made fun of.

142 Herodian *On Universal Vocabulary* F 31

Εὐριπίδης δὲ ἐποίησεν ὑδροφοροῦσαν †αὐτήν†
ἐμοὶ δὲ †πυραυνακτιανειησο . . . ον†
καί καινόν, εἰ πύραυνον ὀστράκινον ἔχοι;

ΣΟΦΙΣΤΑΙ

Sophist means more than just a philosopher or an intellectual; it can include musicians or poets as well. "Intellectual specialist" might cover it best. For such a chorus we can cite Amepisias' Connus (D-423), where we either had an individuated chorus or, more likely, various members of the chorus were named at some point. Something similar may have happened with Eupolis' Spongers and Cratinus' All-Seers. F 149 suggests that Platon gave names of real persons to members of his chorus of "experts," in this case Bacchylides the aulos *player and Xenocles (F 143).*

As for the date, Xenocles is made fun of from 422 until 405, but the association with his father, Carcinus, might

142 ⟨Since/if⟩ Euripides again portrayed her [Electra?] carrying water, but ⟨when she serves⟩ for me why is it ⟨too clever⟩ and innovative, if she were to have a clay dish of hot coals?[1]

[1] The text of this fragment is corrupt, especially the second line. I have adopted the interpretation of West (*Maia* 20 [1968] 202) and Hunger (*JŒByzG* 16 [1967] 1–33) that Platon is referring to Euripides' portrayal of Electra carrying water at *Electra* 55.

SOPHISTS

suggest a production closer to the earlier date, since his father is mentioned with him in both Wasps *(1508–15) and* Peace *(782–95). The same adjective "of the sea" is used of Carcinus in F 143 and at* Wasps *1519. Sporgilus is mentioned at* Birds *299, while Dracontides is made fun of at* Wasps *157. Even if he is the same as the Dracontides of the Thirty, Platon's mention of him is not automatically tied to the last years of the century. If Apolexis (F 150) is one of the ten (or thirty) commissioners active in 411—the text of Harpocration reads "fifty"—then a date in the late 410s is indicated.*

Recent bibliography: C. Carey, in Rivals *425–26.*

Fragments

143 Σ Aristophanes *Peace* 792a

Ξενοκλῆς ὁ δωδεκαμήχανος,
ὁ Καρκίνου παῖς τοῦ θαλαττίου

144 Σ Aristophanes *Birds* 299

τὸ Σποργίλου κουρεῖον, ἔχθιστον τέγος

145 Syncellus p. 174.22 Mosshammer

προμηθία γάρ ἐστιν ἀνθρώποις ὁ νοῦς.

146 Athenaeus 312b

κἂν ᾖ γαλεός, κἂν λειόβατος, κἂν ἔγχελυς.

147 Eustathius *On the Odyssey* p. 1403.32

ἐν τρισὶν
πληγαῖς ἀπηδέσθη τὸ ῥάμφος.

148 Σ Aristophanes *Wasps* 157a

πονηρὸς οὗτος καὶ πλείσταις καταδίκαις ἐνεχόμενος,
ὡς Πλάτων ἐν Σοφισταῖς φησίν. Καλλίστρατος δὲ
ἕνα τῶν λ' φησίν, εἰ μὴ ὁμώνυμος.

Fragments

143 Twelve-trick Xenocles, son of Carcinus the sea-
⟨god⟩.

144 The barbershop of Sporgilus, most hateful edifice.

145 For men the mind is something Promethean.

146 Even if it be a sturgeon, or a skate, or an eel.

147 In three strokes the beak was eaten off.

148 This man [Dracontides] was a wicked man and the
subject of numerous lawsuits, as Platon says in *Sophists*.
Callistratus says he was one of the Thirty, unless that is
another man with the same name.[1]

[1] Of the several men named Dracontides in the 5th c., the best
candidates for the *kōmōidoumenos* are the member of the Thirty
(*PAA* 374040, from Aphidna), the accuser of Pericles in the 430s
(374100, of Thorae), or the father of Lysicles (374060, of Bate).

149 Σ Aristophanes *Clouds* 331a

Πλάτων γοῦν ὁ κωμικὸς ἐν δράματι Σοφισταῖς καὶ τὸν
Ὀπούντιον αὐλητὴν Βακχυλίδην εἰς τοὔνομα κατ-
έταξε τῶν σοφιστῶν.

150 Harpocration p. 47.9

Ἀπόληξις· εἷς τῶν ν΄ συγγραφέων, ὃν Πλάτων κωμῳ-
δεῖ ἐν Σοφισταῖς.

151 Pollux 10.167

ὀθόνινον πρόσωπον

ΣΥΜΜΑΧΙΑ

*There was some debate over the authorship of this comedy.
Seven fragments are attributed to an* Alliance *by Platon
(F 162–63, 167–68, 171, 173–74), while five others are
cited as "Platon or Cantharus" (F 164–66, 169, 172). F 170
is cited only as "Cantharus in* Alliance.*" The question is (1)
whether we have two plays with similar titles:* Alliance *by
Platon, and* Alliance(s) *by Cantharus, (2) a single play
about whose authorship there was some confusion, or (3)
Cantharus perhaps acting as producer of this play for
Platon.*

149 At any rate the comic poet Platon in *Sophists* has included the *aulos* player Bacchylides the Opuntian under the designation "sophist."

150 Apolexis: one of the fifty commissioners, whom Platon makes fun of in *Sophists*.

151 Linen mask.

Brief fragments: (F 152) "to recover," (F 153) "tolerable," (F 154) "I welcome gladly," (F 155) "recently," (F 156) "unfiltered" (?), (F 157) "to have had dinner," (F 158) "tails," (F 159) "red stone," (F 160) "square" (military formation), (F 161) "oracular nonsense."

ALLIANCE

Was the "alliance" of the title an allusion to anything in real life, e.g., the four-way alliance of 420 against Sparta, or (fancifully) the collaboration between Nicias and Alcibiades to effect the ostracism of Hyperbolus in 416? The date must remain a mystery despite attempts to place it in the mid-410s on the grounds that the analogy of the "pot sherd" of F 168.4 refers to the ostracism of Hyperbolus. F 167–68 show that there was an agon, in which one speaker is urged on by the chorus in metaphorical terms (boxing) and employs the analogy of a boys' game of ostrakinda *(sherds).*

THE POETS OF OLD COMEDY

Fragments

162 Pollux 2.183

ὠτογλυφίδα λαβοῦσ᾽ ἀνασκαλεύεται.

163 Pollux 6.17

τὸ γὰρ ἔψημά σου
γευόμενος ἔλαθον ἐκροφήσας.

164 Athenaeus 314a

νάρκη γὰρ ἑφθὴ βρῶμα χαρίεν γίγνεται.

165 Priscian *Institutes of Grammar* 18.170

ἐγὼ γὰρ ὑμῖν ἣν φράσω

166 Athenaeus 312c

βατίς τε καὶ σμύραινα πρόσεστι.

167 Photius (z, S^z) α 3353

ἄγε δὴ < > κἀνδρείως ὥσπερ πύκτης ἀφίδρωσον
καὶ πιτύλευσον τὴν ῥῆσιν ὅλην καὶ κίνησον τὸ
θέατρον.

PLATON

Fragments

162 Taking an ear pick she is cleaning out her ears.

163 You didn't notice me [masc.] tasting your boiled wine and then gulping it down.

164 Boiled stingray makes a very pleasant dish.

165 For if I tell you [pl.].

166 In addition there is both a flatfish and a moray eel.

167 Well then . . . and bravely wipe off your [sing.] sweat like a boxer, swing away at the whole speech, and bring down the house.

1 This couplet sounds very much like an encouragement of a competitor in the agon by the chorus.

168 Hermias *On Plato's Phaedrus* 241b

εἴξασιν γὰρ τοῖς παιδαρίοις τούτοις, οἳ ἑκάστοτε
γραμμὴν
ἐν ταῖσιν ὁδοῖς διαγράψαντες, διανειμάμενοι δίχ'
ἑαυτούς,
ἑστᾶσ' αὐτῶν οἱ μὲν ἐκεῖθεν τῆς γραμμῆς, οἱ δ' αὖ
ἐκεῖθεν·
εἷς δ' ἀμφοτέρων ὄστρακον αὐτοῖσιν ἀνίησ' εἰς
μέσον ἑστώς,
5 κἂν μὲν πίπτῃσι τὰ λεύκ' ἐπάνω, φεύγειν ταχὺ τοὺς
ἑτέρους δεῖ,
τοὺς δὲ διώκειν.

169 Athenaeus 68b

ἢ 'ξ Ἀρκαδίας †οὕτω† δριμυτάτην ὀρίγανον

170 Photius p. 404.16

αὐλητρίδα πεζήν

ΣΤΡΦΑΞ

168 For they compared them to these little boys, who all the time draw a line in the streets and divide themselves into two groups, some standing on this side, the others on the other. One boy stands between the two groups and throws a pot sherd, and if the white side falls face up, one group must run away, while the others chase them.

169 Or some very spicy marjoram from Arcadia.

170 A flute-girl from the rank and file.

Brief fragments: (F 171) "empty vessel" [hunger], (F 172) "bird catcher," (F 173) "deposit," (F 174) "to keep a brothel."

RIFF-RAFF

Syrphax *means "sweepings" or "rubbish" and is used at* Wasps *673 to describe how the allies look at the average Athenians, "you and the rest of the riffraff, living off the jury box and dining on nothing." It is possible, however, that it could here be a comic proper name—cf.* ploutax *at Eupolis F 172.9 and Labrax the pimp in Plautus' Rope. F 180 suggests a scene of aggression between two characters. The anapaestic tetrameter is suitable for an agon.*

THE POETS OF OLD COMEDY

Fragments

175 Athenaeus 344d

{A.} ὁδὶ μὲν Ἀναγυράσιος ὀρφώς ἐστί σοι.
{B.} οἶδ᾽, ᾧ φίλος Μυννίσκος ἔσθ᾽ ὁ Χαλκιδεύς.
{A.} καλῶς λέγεις.

176 Σ Aristophanes *Birds* 168

νοεῖ μὲν ἕτερ᾽, ἕτερα δὲ τῇ γλώττῃ λέγει.

177 *Etymologicum Genuinum* AB

δότω τις ἡμῖν μαζονομεῖον ἔνδοθεν.

178 Herodian *On Universal Vocabulary* F 32

καὶ ταῦτα μανάκις, μυριάκις τῆς ἡμέρας

179 Athenaeus 446e

καὶ πίεσθ᾽ ὕδωρ πολύ.

180 Hesychius π 201

σὲ μέν, ὦ μοχθηρέ, παλινδορίαν παίσας αὐτοῦ
καταθήσω.

PLATON

Fragments

175 (A) This is a sea perch from Anagyrus.

(B) I know, of whom Mynniscus of Chalchis is very fond.

(A) You're quite right.[1]

[1] Mynniscus (*PAA* 661940) was a tragic actor, who won a victory at D-422 (*IG* ii² 2325.24), and who is said to have acted as second actor for Aeschylus (*Life of Aeschylus* 15). This would give him a career of at least 465–420.

176 He [Teleas] is thinking one thing, while he says another.[1]

[1] Teleas (*PAA* 878910) was a secretary of the board of stewards of Athena in 415/4. He is made fun of as a glutton at *Peace* 1008, as a *pithēkos* at Phrynichus F 21, and at *Birds* 167–68. Σ *Birds* 167 adds other comic insults.

177 Let someone get us a bread tray from inside.

178 This ‹happens› rarely, about a million times a day.

179 And you [pl.] will drink a lot of water.

180 You wretch, I will lay you out right here after giving you a proper pounding.

Brief fragment: (F 181) "cavalry subsidy."

ΥΠΕΡΒΟΛΟΣ

This was probably the first of Platon's demagogue comedies (but see Sommerstein's dating of Peisander *to 421), all of which did not disguise their target under another name (Kleon-Paphlagon in Aristophanes'* Knights, *Eupolis'* Hyperbolus-Maricas). *If "everyone else" of* Clouds *558 (T 1) includes Platon's* Hyperbolus, *then the comedy belongs to 420 or 419, since the uncompleted revision of* Clouds *belongs to c. 418. It was thus performed before the ostracism of Hyperbolus in 416, and F 203, which refers to his ostracism in the past tense, cannot belong to this play.*

Testimonia

i Aristophanes *Clouds* 558–59

ἄλλοι τ' ἤδη πάντες ἐρείδουσιν εἰς Ὑπέρβολον,
τὰς εἰκοὺς τῶν ἐγχέλεων τὰς ἐμὰς μιμούμενοι.

ii Σ Aristophanes *Clouds* 558–59

καὶ γὰρ Πλάτων ὅλον δρᾶμα ἔγραψεν εἰς Ὑπέρβολον.

iii Plutarch *Alcibiades* 13.4

ἦν δέ τις Ὑπέρβολος Περιθοΐδης, οὗ μέμνηται μὲν ὡς ἀνθρώπου πονηροῦ καὶ Θουκυδίδης, τοῖς δὲ κωμικοῖς ὁμοῦ τι πᾶσι διατριβὴν ἀεὶ σκωπτόμενος ἐν τοῖς θεάτροις παρεῖχεν.

HYPERBOLUS

The few fragments that we possess tells us little about how the play unfolded. F 182 reveals that the stereotypes of the demagogue's questionable citizenship and less than pure Attic Greek were employed. For the latter see F 61 and Frogs 674–85 (of Cleophon) and Eupolis F 99.23–34 (of Hyperbolus?). Whereas Cleophon's foreign associations lie in the North (Thrace), those of Hyperbolus seem to be with the East (the Persian theme in Maricas, Phrygia at Polyzelus F 5, Lydia here at F 185, Syria at Σ Peace 692).

Testimonia

i Then everyone else starts in on Hyperbolus, copying my metaphor of the eels.

ii For Platon wrote an entire play against Hyperbolus.

iii There was a certain Hyperbolus of the deme Perithoidae, whom Thucydides mentions as a base man [8.73.3]; he provided constant material for all the comic poets to make fun of him in the theatre.

THE POETS OF OLD COMEDY

Fragments

182 Σ Aristophanes *Thesmophoriazusae* 808

{A.} εὐτυχεῖς, ὦ δέσποτα.
{B.} τί δ᾽ ἔστι; {A.} βουλεύειν ὀλίγου ᾽λαχες πάνυ.
ἀτὰρ οὐ λαχὼν ὅμως ἔλαχες, ἢν νοῦν ἔχῃς.
{B.} πῶς ἢν ἔχω νοῦν; {A.} ὅτι πονηρῷ καὶ ξένῳ
5   ἐπέλαχες ἀνδρί, †οὐδέπω γὰρ† ἐλευθέρῳ.

{B.} ἄπερρ᾽· ἐγὼ δ᾽ ὑμῖν τὸ πρᾶγμα δὴ φράσω·
Ὑπερβόλῳ βουλῆς γάρ, ἄνδρες, ἐπέλαχον.

183 Herodian *On Singular Vocabulary* II p. 926.3

ὁ δ᾽ οὐ γὰρ ἠττίκιζεν, ὦ Μοῖραι φίλαι,
ἀλλ᾽ ὁπότε μὲν χρείη "διητώμην" λέγειν,
ἔφασκε "δητώμην," ὁπότε δ᾽ εἰπεῖν δέοι
"ὀλίγον," <"ὀλίον"> ἔλεγεν.

184 Σ Aristophanes *Birds* 121

                                    καὶ
τοσοῦτον εὐερίας ἀπολέλαυχ᾽ ὥστε <νῦν>
αὐχμότατός ἐστι.

185 Σ Lucian *Timon* 30

Πολύζηλος δὲ ἐν Δημοτυνδάρεῳ Φρύγα αὐτὸν εἶναι

Fragments

182 (A) Congratulations, master.

(B) For what?

(A) You were selected to serve on the Council, well almost. Though you weren't selected, you were, if you understand.

(B) What do you mean, if I understand?

(A) Because you were chosen as an alternate to a nasty foreign person, not yet a free citizen.

(B) You, get out of here. Gentlemen, I will in fact explain the situation to you people: I am an alternate on the Council to Hyperbolus.

183 O dear Fates, the man [Hyperbolus] just couldn't speak Attic Greek. But when he ought to be saying "I used to live," he would come out with "I use to live," and when he should be saying "just a bit," he would say <"jus' a bit">.[1]

[1] Colvin (*Rivals* 285–98) argues that Hyperbolus' dialect was "low-urban" rather than "barbarian."

184 Also he has enjoyed the cushy life to such an extent that he is <now> very squalid.

185 Polyzelus in his *Demo-Tynadareus*, joking at his for-

φησιν εἰς τὸ βάρβαρον σκώπτων. Πλάτων δὲ ὁ κωμικὸς ἐν Ὑπερβόλῳ Λυδὸν αὐτόν φησιν εἶναι Μίδα γένος.

186 Athenaeus 56f

φύλλιον ἢ ῥαφανίδιον

ΦΑΩΝ

The tale of Phaon occurs variously in Palaephatus, Aelian (Historical Miscellany 12.18) and Servius (On the Aeneid 3.279), but the basic story is that Phaon was a boatman (usually on Lesbos, but Lucian locates him on Chios), who unknowingly ferried the disguised goddess Aphrodite for free and thus earned her gratitude and a reward, which was either to be rejuvenated and thus become the object of all women's sexual advances, or to receive an unguent which, when applied, produced the same results. By the end of the fourth century (Menander Leucadia 10–14), Phaon was connected romantically with Sappho, the great poetess of Lesbos, but when and how that story was developed is unknown. The earliest connection of Phaon with Aphrodite appears to be in Cratinus' comedy Seasons (F 370).

F 188 is spoken by a goddess who calls herself Kourotrophos, *"Nurse of Youths" (7), a title applied to (among others) Hecate, Artemis, Earth, and Aphrodite, as well as to the islands of Ithaca and Delos. Thesmophoriazusae 300 lists "Kourotrophos" as a goddess associated with the*

eign nature, says that he [Hyperbolus] is a Phrygian [F 5].
Platon the comic poet in *Hyperbolus* says that he is "a
Lydian, of the race of Midas."

186 A little leaf or a small radish.

Brief fragment: (F 187) "to eat bread."

PHAON

*Mother and Daughter, who seems to be a separate entity in
her own right. Thus at F 188.7 it could be Aphrodite ask-
ing for a sacrifice "in my capacity as Nurse of Youths," or
it could be this independent deity speaking in her own
name here. We are told that in Aristophanes' lost* Thes-
mophoriazusae *the prologue was spoken by "Fair Birth"
(Kalligeneia), herself mentioned with Nurse of Youths at*
Thesmophoriazusae *299.*

*Whoever the speaker of F 188, it is clear that Phaon in
this play exercised his attractive sexual power over women
(see ll. 5, 20–21). Is he then the speaker of F 189, who is
consulting the newly published* Cook-book *by Philoxenus
of Leucas to find foods that will aid his sexual prowess? Or
could the speaker be the old man of F 195, who is finding it
difficult to perform sexually or to attract women? Did a
scene in the comedy turn on his attempts to emulate, imi-
tate, or steal the magic ornament from Phaon?*

*Recent bibliography: E. Degani, Eikasmos 9 (1998) 81–99;
F. Casolari, in Festschrift H.-D. Blume (2000) 91–102; M.
Pellegrino (Utopie) 237–61; Olson 336–39.*

Testimonium

i Σ Aristophanes *Wealth* 179

Πλάτων ἐν τῷ Φάωνι ἑπτακαιδεκάτῳ ἔτει ὕστερον
διδαχθέντι ἐπὶ Φιλοκλέους

Fragments

188 Athenaeus 441e

εἶεν γυναῖκες <‒ ∪> ὡς ὑμῖν πάλαι
οἶνον γενέσθαι τὴν ἄνοιαν εὔχομαι·
ὑμῖν γὰρ οὐδέν, καθάπερ ἡ παροιμία,
ἐν τῷ καπήλῳ νοῦς ἐνεῖναί μοι δοκεῖ.
5 εἰ γὰρ Φάωνα δεῖσθ᾿ ἰδεῖν, προτέλεια δεῖ
ὑμᾶς ποιῆσαι πολλὰ πρότερον τοιαδί.
πρῶτα μὲν ἐμοὶ γὰρ Κουροτρόφῳ προθύεται
πλακοῦς ἐνόρχης, ἄμυλος ἐγκύμων, κίχλαι
ἐκκαίδεχ᾿ ὁλόκληροι μέλιτι μεμιγμέναι,
10 λαγῷα δώδεκ᾿ ἐπισέληνα. τἆλλα δὲ
ἤδη †ταῦτ᾿ εὐτελέστατα†. ἄκουε δή.
βολβῶν μὲν Ὀρθάννῃ τρί᾿ ἡμιεκτέα,
Κονισάλῳ δὲ καὶ παραστάταιν δυοῖν
μύρτων πινακίσκος χειρὶ παρατετιμένων·
15 λύχνων γὰρ ὀσμὰς οὐ φιλοῦσι δαίμονες.

---

[1] This passage is riddled with sexual double meanings. As sacrifices of animals were often specified to be "with testicles attached" (uncastrated) or "pregnant," here the sacrifical cakes take on these characteristics. The verb "mingled" (with honey) is one

Testimonium

i Platon in his *Phaon* which was performed seventeen years later in the archonship of Philocles [392/1].

Fragments

188 Well then, women, since I have been hoping for a long time that your foolishness would turn into wine. For as the old saying goes, your mind doesn't seem to me to be in the tavern at all. Now if you want to see Phaon, you have to provide the following advance payment:[1] first to me as Tender of Youths an initial sacrifice is to be made, a cake with testicles still attached, a pregnant scone of the finest meal, sixteen immaculate thrushes mingled with honey, twelve hares marked with the moon (?). The rest will not cost much—so listen. For Orthanes three pecks of bulbs, and for Conisalus and his two sidekicks a little dish of myrtle berries plucked by hand, since the gods don't like the stench from lamps.[2] For the Hounds and Hunters a back-

often used of getting together in the sexual sense, while for the twelve hares *episelēna* might mean "with a crescent marking" or "pieces of hare meat shaped into crescents," but the point is a joke on *selēna* as the female genitalia.

[2] Orthanes (from *orthos*—"erect") and Conisalus (an ithyphallic fertility figure—*Lysistrata* 982) are both mentioned at Aristophanes F 325 as minor sexual deities. Conisalus' "sidekicks" are the testicles. Bulbs were a known aphrodisiac (see F 189.9, also Athenaeus 64b) and "myrtle" was a colloquial term for the female pubic region. "Stench of lamps" refers to pubic depilation using lamps (see *Ecclesiazusae* 12–13).

†πύργης τετάρτης† Κυσί τε καὶ Κυνηγέταις,
Λόρδωνι δραχμή, Κυβδάσῳ τριώβολον,
ἥρῳ Κέλητι δέρμα καὶ θυλήματα.
ταῦτ' ἐστὶ τἀναλώματ'. εἰ μὲν οὖν τάδε
20 προσοίσετ', εἰσέλθοιτ' ἄν· εἰ δὲ μή, μάτην
ἔξεστιν ὑμῖν διὰ κενῆς βινητιᾶν.

189 Athenaeus 5b

ἐγὼ δ' ἐνθάδ' ἐν τῇ ἐρημίᾳ
τουτὶ διελθεῖν βούλομαι τὸ βιβλίον
πρὸς ἐμαυτόν. {Β.} ἔστι δ', ἀντιβολῶ σε, τοῦτο τί;
{Α.} Φιλοξένου καινή τις ὀψαρτυσία.
5 {Β.} ἐπίδειξον αὐτὴν ἥτις ἔστ'. {Α.} ἄκουε δή.
ἄρξομαι ἐκ βολβοῖο, τελευτήσω δ' ἐπὶ θύννον.
{Β.} ἐπὶ θύννον; οὐκοῦν †τῆς τελευτ† πολὺ
κράτιστον ἐνταυθὶ τετάχθαι τάξεως.
{Α.} βολβοὺς μὲν σποδιᾷ δαμάσας καταχύσματι
δεύσας
10 ὡς πλείστους διάτρωγε· τὸ γὰρ δέμας ἀνέρος ὀρθοῖ.
καὶ τάδε μὲν δὴ ταῦτα· θαλάσσης δ' ἐς τέκν' ἄνειμι

οὐδὲ λοπὰς κακόν ἐστιν· ἀτὰρ τὸ τάγηνον ἄμεινον,
οἶμαι

---

1 Two poets of the 4th c. were named Philoxenus, one from
Cythera, author of the *Cyclops,* and the other from Leucas, whom
Athenaeus argues is the author of the *Dinner.* At 146f Athenaeus
has another speaker wonder if the author is not in fact the poet

quarter of rump (?), a drachma for Bend-over-Backwards, three obols for Crouch-Forward, and for the hero Upright Rider leather hide and barley cakes.[3] This is what it will cost you. If you were to provide all this, you would get in. But if not, you can be horny all you want, but to no avail.

[3] "Hound and Hunters" are probably the penis plus testicles again; the nature of their offering is lost in a corrupt text. The next three names are comic constructions based on sexual positions. "Leather" (lit. "skin," "hide") may refer to leather dildos (*Lysistrata* 110).

189 (A) Here in solitude I want to read this book to myself.

(B) Please tell me, what is it?

(A) It's a brand-new cookbook by Philoxenus.[1]

(B) Give me a sample of what it's like.

(A) Listen here. "I shall begin with bulb and conclude with tunny fish."[2]

(B) With a tunny fish? In that case . . . it's by far the best thing to be posted here in the last ranks.

(A) "Subdue the bulbs with hot ash, soak them with sauce, and munch down as many as you can, for then a man's body stands straight up. So much for that. I shall now pass on to the children of the sea."

"Not that a stewing dish is bad, but the frying pan is better, in my opinion."

from Cythera. The metre of ll. 6 and 9–22 is the epic dactylic hexameter. [2] Bulbs were served first as an appetiser and the fish as the main course. These were reputed to be an aphrodisiac (see F 188), and the speaker is reading the cookbook with a view to improving his sexual prowess.

ὀρφών αἰολίαν συνόδοντά τε καρχαρίαν τε
15 μὴ τέμνειν, μή σοι νέμεσις θεόθεν καταπνεύσῃ·
ἀλλ' ὅλον ὀπτήσας παράθες· πολλὸν γὰρ ἄμεινον.
πουλύποδος †πλεκτὴ δ', ἂν ἐπιλήψῃ† κατὰ καιρόν,
ἑφθὴ τῆς ὀπτῆς, ἢν ᾖ μείζων, πολὺ κρείττων·
ἢν ὀπταὶ δὲ δύ' ὦσ', ἑφθῇ κλαίειν ἀγόρευω.
20 τρίγλη δ' οὐκ ἐθέλει νεύρων ἐπιήρανος εἶναι·
παρθένου Ἀρτέμιδος γὰρ ἔφυ καὶ στύματα μισεῖ.
σκορπίος αὖ {B.} παίσειέ γέ σου τὸν πρωκτὸν
ὑπελθών.

190 Athenaeus 367d

τὰ δ' ἀλλότρι' ἔσθ' ὅμοια ταῖς παροψίσι·
βραχὺ γάρ <τι> τέρψαντ' ἐξανήλωται ταχύ.

191 Orus *On Orthography* fol. 283[v]

τὸν ἀλεκτρυόνα τὸν ᾠὸν ἀπονίξασά μου

192 Athenaeus 424a

τῷ στόματι τὸν κύαθον ὧδ' εἰληφότες

193 Photius (b, z) α 1507

καὶ τῆς θύρας ἀνακῶς ἔχειν

194 Photius p. 400.1

ὡς καὶ νῦν ἔχομεν παρουσίας

"And do not slice up the sea perch or the speckle fish or sea bream or shark, lest Nemesis from the gods breathe upon you, but roast and serve them whole. They're much better that way. If you . . . of an octopus in the right season, it is much better boiled than roasted, if it's a large one. But if there are two roasted ones, then I say to the boiled one 'get lost.' The red mullet does not tend to be helpful to the penis, for she belongs to the maiden Artemis and hates erections.[3] Now the scorpion fish . . . "

(B) I hope, will creep up and sting you in the ass.

[3] Pirrotta (365) suggests that *triglē* (red mullet") was also the name of a prostitute.

190 Love affairs are like side dishes, a short sweet taste and over quickly.

191 The woman who wrung my rooster's neck.

192 Having taken [pl.] the ladle in their mouth like so.

193 To be careful of the door.

194 As even now we have wealth.

195 Photius γ 148

ὦ χρυσοῦν ἀνάδημα,
ὦ τοῖσιν ἐμοῖς τρυφεροῖσι τρόποις < > ὦ γλυκὺς
ἀγκών.

196 Σ Aristophanes *Wealth* 179

ἐμφαίνει δὲ καὶ Πλάτων ἐν τῷ Φάωνι ἑπτακαιδεκάτῳ
ἔτει ὕστερον διδαχθέντι ἐπὶ Φιλοκλέους, ὡς μηκέτι
αὐτῆς οὔσης. δύναται μέντοι καὶ αὐτῆς ζώσης λέγε-
σθαι.

ΑΔΗΛΩΝ ΔΡΑΜΑΤΩΝ

199 Plutarch *Themistocles* 32.5

ὁ σὸς δὲ τύμβος ἐν καλῷ κεχωσμένος
τοῖς ἐμπόροις πρόσρησις ἔσται πανταχοῦ,
τοὺς ἐκπλέοντάς τ᾽ εἰσπλέοντάς τ᾽ ὄψεται,
χὠπόταν ἅμιλλ᾽ ᾖ τῶν νεῶν θεάσεται.

200 Galen *On the Aphorisms of Hippocrates* 18.1

μετὰ ταῦτα δὲ
† Εὐαγόρου ὁ παῖς ἐκ πλευρίτιδος Κινησίας †
σκελετός, ἄπυγος, καλάμινα σκέλη φορῶν,
φθόης προφήτης, ἐσχάρας κεκαυμένος
5   πλείστας ὑπ᾽ Εὐρυφῶντος ἐν τῷ σώματι.

195 "Sweet treasure in the arm": . . . The comic poet Platon has used this in his *Phaon*. He has an old man on stage in love with an *aulos* girl:

(OLD MAN) My precious crown, . . . to my luxurious ways, sweet treasure in my arm.

196 Platon also implies in *Phaon*, produced sixteen years later in the archonship of Philocles [392/1], that she [Lais] was no longer alive, although this could have been said while she was still living.

Brief fragments: (F 197) "to say no," (F 198) "misfortune."

UNASSIGNED FRAGMENTS

199 Your [Themistokles'] tomb, a mound set in a fair place, will be hailed by travellers from everywhere, will behold those sailing in and those sailing out, and will be watching whenever the warships race.[1]

[1] A tomb for Themistocles was set on a spur of land along the entry to the Peiraeus.

200 And next ⟨there was⟩ Cinesias the son of Euagoras (?) by Pleurisy, thin as a rake, no butt to speak of, walking on legs like reeds, an advertisement for Consumption, with Euryphron's cautery scars all over his body.[1]

[1] On Cinesias see the notes to Strattis' *Cinesias*. "Euagoras" probably hides a "father" for Cinesias equivalent to Pleurisy as his mother. Euryphon is a doctor from Cnidus.

201 Plutarch *Precepts of Statecraft* 801a

Πλάτων ὁ κωμικὸς τὸν Δῆμον αὐτὸν λέγοντα ποιεῖ·

{ΔΗΜΟΣ.} λαβοῦ λαβοῦ τῆς χειρὸς ὡς τάχιστά
   μου·
μέλλω στρατηγὸν χειροτονεῖν Ἀγύρριον.

καὶ πάλιν αἰτοῦντα λεκάνην καὶ πτερόν, ὅπως ἐμέσῃ,
λέγοντα

προσίσταταί μου πρὸς τὸ βῆμα Μαντίας.

βόσκει δυσώδη Κέφαλον, ἐχθίστην νόσον.

202 Stobaeus 2.3.3

          ἢν γὰρ ἀποθάνῃ
εἷς τις πονηρός, δύ᾽ ἀνέφυσαν ῥήτορες·
οὐδεὶς γὰρ ἡμῖν Ἰόλεως ἐν τῇ πόλει,
ὅστις ἐπικαύσει τὰς κεφαλὰς τῶν ῥητόρων.
5 κεκολλόπευκας· τοιγαροῦν ῥήτωρ ἔσῃ.

203 Plutarch *Nicias* 11.6

καίτοι πέπραγε τῶν τρόπων μὲν ἄξια,
αὑτοῦ δὲ καὶ τῶν στιγμάτων ἀνάξια·
οὐ γὰρ τοιούτων οὕνεκ᾽ ὄστραχ᾽ ηὑρέθη.

201 Platon the comic poet makes Demos himself declare:

(DEMOS) Take my hand, take it quickly. I am about to elect Agyrrhius as general.[1]

and again asking for a basin and a feather

Mantias is standing beside my rostrum.[2]

It is nourishing foul-smelling Cephalus, that loathsome plague.[3]

[1] Agyrrhius (*PAA* 107660) was an important political figure from the late 5th c. into the 380s. He may be the politician alluded to at *Frogs* 367, who proposed a reduction in the comic poets' *misthos*. He was elected general in 389/8.   [2] Mantias (*PAA* 632545) was the treasurer of the naval yards in 377/6, and the subject of Demosthenes 39–40.   [3] Cephalus (*PAA* 566650) was a major figure in the first third of the 4th c., regarded with considerable respect by the later orators (Demosthenes 18.219, 251; Aeschines 3.194, Deinarchus 1.38–39).

202 If one wicked person dies, two politicians grow back in his place, for there is no Iolaus in the city who will cauterise the heads of the politicians. You've been buggered, that means you're going to be a politician.

203 What's happened to him [Hyperbolus] suits his character, but not his brand-marks, for it was not for men such as he that ostracism was instituted.

[*Hyperbolus, The Man in Great Pain, Alliance*?]

204 Σ Euripides *Hecuba* 838

{A.} οὗτος, τίς εἶ; λέγε ταχύ· τί σιγᾷς; οὐκ ἐρεῖς;
{B.} Ἑρμῆς ἔγωγε Δαιδάλου φωνὴν ἔχων
ξύλινος βαδίζων αὐτόματος ἐλήλυθα.

205 Athenaeus 783d

λύσας †δὲ ἀργὴν† στάμνον εὐώδους ποτοῦ
ἵησιν εὐθὺς κύλικος εἰς κοῖλον κύτος·
ἔπειτ' ἄκρατον κοὐ τεταργανωμένον
ἔπινε κἀξημύστισεν.

206 Pollux 6.103

φείδεσθε τοὐλαίου σφόδρ'· ἐξ ἀγορᾶς δ' ἐγὼ
ὠνήσομαι στίλβην τιν', ἥτις μὴ πότις.

207 Plutarch *Pericles* 4.1

πρῶτον μὲν οὖν μοι λέξον, ἀντιβολῶ· σὺ γάρ,
ὥς φασι, Χείρων ἐξέθρεψας Περικλέα.

208 Photius (z, Sᶻ) α 3399

οἴμοι τάλας, ἀπολεῖς μ'. Ἀφροδιταρίδιον
γλυκύτατον, ἱκετεύω σε, μή με περιίδῃς.

209 Pollux 4.56

†ὅτι δ' ἂν ᾖ ἡ συβώτρια, μηδ' ἀγαθὴ γένοιτό μοι†.
ἔχειν δοκεῖ μοι δακτύλους αὐλητικούς.

204 (A) Hey you, who are you? Speak quickly. Why are you silent? Aren't you going to say anything?

(B) I am a wooden Hermes by Daedalus. I can talk and I have come here walking on my own.

[*Daedalus, Long Night*?]

205 Then opening . . . a jar of sweet-smelling drink, he poured it into the hollow of an empty cup. Then he put it to his lips and chugged it down unmixed and unadulterated. [*Phaon*?]

206 Be very sparing [pl.] of the oil. I shall be buying a lamp from the agora which isn't a drunkard.

207 [to Damon] First tell me, please. For they say that you, like Chiron, brought Pericles up.[1]

[1] Damon (*PAA* 301540) was remembered as the music teacher and advisor of Pericles.

208 Oh no, you'll be the death of me. Sweetest, dearest Aphrodite, I beg you, don't let me . . .

[*Zeus Badly Treated, Phaon*?]

209 That the woman herding swine might not be good . . . she seems to me to have the fingers of an *aulos* player.

210 Michael of Italy *Letters* 24

οὐδεὶς ὁμαίμου συμπαθέστερος φίλος,
κἂν ᾖ <   > τοῦ γένους μακράν

211 Pollux 6.49

καὶ περιών γ᾽ ἅμα
τιλτὸν τάριχος ἐπριάμην τοῖς οἰκέταις.

212 Photius (z) α 3417

ἐκ Δελφῶν δ᾽ ἔχων
ἥκει τι κακὸν ἄφωνον

213 Photius (z) α 3461

αἰσχύνομαί σε, ὦ ξένε, μακρὰν
ὁδὸν ἀνύσαντα ἄχρηστον ἀπολῦσαι.

214 *PBerlin* 9772

γυναῖκα] κρεῖσσόν ἐστ᾽ ἐν οἰκίᾳ
ἢ φαρμακίτα]ς τῶν παρ᾽ Εὐδήμου τρέφειν.

215 Athenaeus 67c

ἐν σαπρῷ γάρῳ
βάπτοντες ἀποπνίξουσί με.

210 No friend is more sympathetic than a kinsman, even if . . . a distant relationship. [*Phaon*?]

211 As I was making my way around, I bought some scaled salt fish for my servants.

212 He has come from Delphi with a bad and unspeakable ⟨response?⟩.

213 Stranger, I am ashamed to let you go without an answer from the oracle, when you have come such a long way. [*Adonis*?]

214 It is better to have ⟨a woman⟩ in your house ⟨than the magic rings⟩ of Eudemus.

215 They will drown me by dipping me in putrid fish sauce.

216 Etymologicum Genuinum AB

ἵναπερ ποδώκης ἐστ᾽ Ἀχιλλεὺς ὅ τε Μίνων.

217 Photius (b, z) α 472

πατρὶς ‹δ᾽› Ἀθῆναί μοῦστιν ‹αἱ› χρυσάμπυκες.

218 Pollux 7.210

τὰ γραμματεῖα τούς τε χάρτας ἐκφέρων

219 Pollux 2.175

ἔπειτα δ᾽ οὐδείς ἐστ᾽ ἀνὴρ γαστρίστερος.

220 Pollux 6.25

ἀνακογχυλιαστὸν ἐχθοδοπόν τι σκευάσω.

221 Photius p. 420.14

ὡς ἔστι μοι τὸ χρῆμα τοῦτο περὶ πόδα.

222 Pollux 2.9

παῖδες, γέροντες, μειράκια, παλλάκια.

223 Anonymous grammarian

ἐμαυτὸν εἰς ἀπωλίαν οἰχήσομαι.

216 Where swift-footed Achilles is and Minos.

217 My homeland is Athens of the golden diadems.

218 Bringing out the account books and sheets of papyrus.

219 Next there is no man more gluttonous.

[*Peisander*?]

220 I shall prepare something quite unpleasant as a gargle.

221 Since this suits me to a T.

222 Boys, old men, young men, teenagers.

223 I shall leave ‹ . . . ing› myself to certain doom.

224 Photius (z, Sᶻ) α 3482

ὦ τᾶν, ταχὺ τρέχων ἀπωλόμην.

225 *Etymologicum Magnum* p. 106.33

σχοίνους λαβὼν ἄνειρε τὰ κρέα.

226 Photius (b, Sᶻ) α 2098

βόα νῦν ἀντίδουπά μοι.

227

(a) Plato *Alcibiades* I 121cd

ἐπειδὰν δὲ γένηται ὁ παῖς ὁ πρεσβύτατος . . . πρῶτον μὲν ἑορτάζουσι πάντες οἱ ἐν τῇ βασιλέως . . . εἶτα εἰς τὸν ἄλλον χρόνον ταύτῃ τῇ ἡμέρᾳ βασιλέως γενέθλια πᾶσα θύει καὶ ἑορτάζει ἡ Ἀσία· ἡμῶν δὲ γενομένων, τὸ τοῦ κωμῳδοποιοῦ, οὐδ᾽ οἱ γείτονες σφόδρα τι αἰσθάνονται.

(b) Olympiodorus ad loc

Πλάτων γὰρ ὁ κωμικὸς τοῦτο παρατίθεται.

228 Hermann's *Lexicon* 182

χρῆσον <   > μοι τὴν χλαμύδα σου.

224 Mate, I have done myself in by running so fast.

225 Take the wooden spits and put the pieces of meat on.

226 Shout out a reechoing cry for me.

227

(a) [Describing customs in Persia] When the eldest son is born, first everyone in the palace celebrates . . . and then on that day all of Asia makes sacrifice and observes the birthday of the prince. But when we are born, to quote the comic poet, not even the neighbours notice anything very much.

(b) Platon the comic poet makes this observation.

228 Lend me your cloak.

229 *Etymologicum Simeonis*

ἐμαυτὸν οὐ διεχρησάμην

230 Athenaeus 48a

κᾆτ᾽ ἐν κλίναις ἐλεφαντόποσιν καὶ στρώμασι
    πορφυροβάπτοις
κἂν φοινικίσι Σαρδιακαῖσιν κοσμησάμενοι
    κατάκεινται.

231 Eustathius *On the Odyssey* p. 1479.46

σὲ δὲ κοκκύζων < > ἀλέκτωρ προκαλεῖται.

232 Hesychius κ 4141

κριὸς ἀσελγόκερως

δούριον ἵππον

234 Zenobius 2.27

αὐτὸν Μελιτέων, ἀλλ᾽ ἐπὶ τὸν οἶκον

235 Σ Aristophanes *Frogs* 303

τοῦτον δὲ καὶ ὡς ἀτερπῆ τὴν φωνὴν Πλάτων σκώπτει.

236 Σ Aristophanes *Peace* 313a

καὶ Πλάτων δὲ ὁ κωμικὸς Κέρβερον αὐτὸν ὠνόμασεν.

229 I did not do away with myself.

230 Then they lie down on couches with ivory feet and rugs dyed purple, dressing themselves in the crimson-red of Sardis.   [*Envoys*?]

231 A crowing cock is summoning you.

232 A ram with an unbelievable horn . . . a wooden horse.

234 But to the house of the Meliteans.

235 Platon mentions him [Hegelochus] as having an unpleasant voice.

236 The comic poet Platon called him [Cleon] "Cerberus."

237 Plutarch *Antony* 70.1

ὁ δὲ Τίμων ἦν Ἀθηναῖος [ὃς] καὶ γέγονεν ἡλικίᾳ
μάλιστα κατὰ τὸν Πελοποννησιακὸν πόλεμον, ὡς ἐκ
τῶν Ἀριστοφάνους καὶ Πλάτωνος δραμάτων λαβεῖν
ἔστι· κωμῳδεῖται γὰρ ἐν ἐκείνοις ὡς δυσμενὴς καὶ
μισάνθρωπος.

238 Σ Aristophanes *Wealth* 177

Φιλέψιος· οὗτος πένης ὤν, λέγων ἱστορίας ἐτρέφετο.
τερατώδης δὲ καὶ λάλος διαβάλλεται, ὡς ὁ Πλάτων ὁ
κωμικός

239 Sextus Empiricus *Against the Mathematicians* 2.34–
35

ἀλλ᾽ ἥ γε ῥητορικὴ κατὰ τῶν νόμων εἰσκεκύκληται.
τεκμήριον δὲ παμμέγεθες τὸ παρὰ μὲν τοῖς βαρ-
βάροις, παρ᾽ οἷς ἢ οὐδ᾽ ὅλως ἢ σπανίως ἔστι ῥητορι-
κή, τοὺς νόμους ἀσαλεύτους μένειν, παρὰ δὲ τοῖς
προσιεμένοις αὐτὴν ὁσημέραι νεοχμοῦσθαι, ὥσπερ
καὶ παρ᾽ Ἀθηναίοις, καθάπερ καὶ Πλάτων ὁ τῆς ἀρ-
χαίας κωμῳδίας ποιητὴς λέγει· "καὶ γὰρ τρεῖς ἐάν
τις," φησίν, "ἐκδημήσῃ μῆνας, οὐκέτι ἐπιγινώσκειν
τὴν πόλιν, ἀλλὰ παραπλησίως τοῖς νυκτὸς περιπα-
τοῦσι παρὰ τὰ τείχη καθάπερ τινὰς ἀγγάρους κατ-
άγεσθαι, τὸ ὅσον ἐπὶ τοῖς νόμοις μὴ τῆς αὐτῆς οὔσης
πόλεως."

237 Timon was an Athenian, who lived right around the time of the Peloponnesian War, as one can infer from the plays of Aristophanes [*Birds* 1549, *Lysistrata* 809ff.] and Platon. He is made fun in these as a fierce misanthropist.

238 Philepsius [*PAA* 924570] was a poor man, who made a living by telling stories. He is accused of being strange-looking and talkative, as Platon the comic poet ⟨says⟩.

239 Now rhetoric has made its way to the fore to the detriment of the laws. A compelling proof ⟨of this⟩ is that among foreigners, where rhetoric is nonexistent or very rare, laws remain unchanged, but among those who admit it laws change daily, for example at Athens as Platon, the poet of Old Comedy, maintains when he says:

"If someone goes away for three months, he longer recognizes his city, but like those who travel at night, like mounted couriers, pass by the walls, and as far as its laws go it is just not the same city." [*Greece*?]

Brief fragments:

(F 233) *"the feast of Aletis,"* (F 240) *"an unfulled cloak,"* (F 241) *"warps unspun,"* (F 242) *"passage with a harbour at each end,"* (F 243) *"bellies stuffed with dung,"* (F 244) *"I cut the cackle,"* (F 245) [corrupt], (F 246) *"stop beating down the price,"* (F 247) *"face,"* *"of milk,"* (F 248) *"wag the tail,"* (F 249) *"in an unseemly way,"* (F 250) *"auditory."*

(F 251) *"untrained,"* (F 252) *"more absurd, most absurd,"* (F 253) *"wrongful,"* (F 254) *"darkened,"* (F 255) *"a tunic with two sleeves,"* (F 256) *"earflaps,"* (F 257) *"to limber up,"* (F 258) *"filled full of"* [negative sense], (F 259) *"he withered away,"* (F 260) *"you [sing.] will run off."*

(F 261) "oaks," (F 262) "training," (F 263) "song, singing, songlet," (F 264) "fast as lightning," (F 265) "with a squalid life," (F 266) "they released," (F 267) "leather curtain," (F 268) "I desired," (F 269) "carefully combed out," (F 270) "having six feet."

(F 271) "one-fifth," (F 272) "to get up early, to be awake in the evening," (F 273) "kites," (F 274) "smoky" [of wine], (F 275) "to comb down wool," (F 276) "to work the woof," (F 277) "cake cutter," (F 278) "from New City," (F 279) "to be a boy lover," (F 280) "little feet."

(F 281) "stocks," (F 282) "loafers" [type of shoe], (F 283) "cut the spine," (F 284) "scarce," (F 285) "tornado," (F 286) "to tickle," (F 287) "actors' outfits," (F 288) "you tell marvellous stories," (F 289) "three-quarters of an obol," (F 290) "fond of life," (F 291) "crumbling," (F 292) "to swallow cold wine."

ΠΟΛΙΟΧΟΣ

Testimonia

i *IG* ii² 2325.127

Πο[λίοχος] I

ii Lysias 18.13

εὖ δ᾽ οἶδ᾽, ὦ ἄνδρες δικασταί, ὅτι περὶ πλείστου ἂν
ποιήσαιτο Πολίοχος τοῦτον τὸν ἀγῶνα κατορθῶσαι,
ἡγούμενος αὐτῷ καλὴν εἶναι τὴν ἐπίδειξιν καὶ πρὸς
τοὺς πολίτας καὶ τοὺς ξένους, ὅτι Ἀθήνησι τοσοῦτον
δύναται, ὥσθ᾽ ὑμᾶς τοὺς αὐτούς, περὶ ὧν ὅρκους
ὀμωμόκατε, ὑμῖν αὐτοῖς τὰ ἐναντία ποιεῖν ψηφίζε-
σθαι.

200

POLIOCHUS

The name is rare at Athens, with only three documented examples in PAA, two from the early fourth century. Thus it is tempting to identify the comic poet with the prosecutor of Lysias' speech (T 2). Poliochus' name is restored on the list of victors at the Lenaea (T 1) before the names of Metagenes, Theopompus, and a poet for whom we have part of his name Pol[. . . . .]s with four victories. The only other Old Comic poet whose name begins in Pol– is Polyzelus, for whom five plays are attested as opposed to one for Poliochus. Thus Polyzelus is more likely to be the latter poet and this earlier one on the list should be restored as Poliochus, whose only victory at the Lenaea came around 400.

Testimonia

i [On the list of victors at the Lenaea, c. 400]

Po[liochus] 1

ii Men of the jury, I am well aware that Poliochus would consider it a matter of the greatest importance to win this case, believing it to be a fine demonstration both to his fellow citizens and to foreigners, that he has so much power at Athens that he can make you vote to do the opposite of the oaths that you yourselves have sworn.

THE POETS OF OLD COMEDY

Fragment

ΚΟΡΙΝΘΙΑΣΤΗΣ

1 Athenaeus 313c

> ὅπως σε πείσει μηδὲ εἶς, πρὸς τῶν θεῶν,
> τοὺς βόακας, ἄν ποτ᾽ ἔλθῃ, λευκομαινίδας καλεῖν.

ΑΔΗΛΟΥ ΔΡΑΜΑΤΟΣ

2 Athenaeus 60b

> μεμαγμένην
> μικρὰν μελαγχρῆ μᾶζαν ἠχυρωμένην
> ἑκάτερος ἡμῶν εἶχε δὶς τῆς ἡμέρας
> καὶ σῦκα βαιά, καὶ μύκης τις ἐνίοτ᾽ ἂν
> 5 ὤπτᾶτο, καὶ κοχλίας γενομένου ψακαδίου
> ἠγρεύετ᾽ ἄν, καὶ λάχανα τῶν αὐτοχθόνων
> θλαστή τ᾽ ἐλαία, καὶ πιεῖν οἰνάριον ἦν
> ἀμφίβολον.

POLIOCHUS

Fragment

WHORE-MASTER

The actual title is Korinthiastes, *but as the verb* korinthiazesthai *can mean "be a courtesan," the best of which came from Corinth (Wealth 149, Plato Republic 404d, as well as the most famous of all hetaerae, Lais), the title suggests a brothel keeper or pimp. The Middle Comic poet Philetaerus also wrote a comedy with this title.*

1 ⟨Be careful⟩ by the gods, if ever you go there, that no one persuades you to call grunt fish white-sprats.

UNASSIGNED FRAGMENT

2 Twice a day each of us had a tiny dark bran meal bun, and a few figs, and occasionally someone would roast a mushroom or catch a snail when it rained a little. There were vegetables that grew wild and a bruised olive, and to drink there was a "wine" of doubtful quality.

ΠΟΛΥΖΗΛΟΣ

The list of victors at the Lenaea contains two partial names
a few places apart, first a Po[......] with one victory, and
three places later a Pol[....]s with four victories. The
names of the intervening poets, Metagenes and Theopom-
pus, make it clear that we have reached the end of the fifth
century at this point on the list. Two comic poets beginning
with Po– are known for this period of comedy, Poliochus
and Polyzelus. As the latter is known for five plays and
rather more fragments (thirteen as opposed to two), it
would seem logical to identify the second poet as Polyzelus.

Testimonia

i *Suda* π 1961

Πολύζηλος, κωμικός. δράματα αὐτοῦ Νίπτρα, Δημο-
τυνδάρεως, Μουσῶν γοναί, Διονύσου γοναί, Ἀφροδί-
της γοναί.

ii *IG* ii² 2325.130

Πολ[ύζηλο]ς ΙΙΙΙ

POLYZELUS

Apart from Demos-Tyndareus, *which could be a political comedy and belong around 410–406, Polyzelus' plays appear to have been burlesques of myth. He seems to have been especially fond of the "birth comedies," which were in vogue from 405–380, and of which much of the humour probably turned on the placing of divine or heroic births in the mundane context of the "real" world. This is the technique that Lucian would adopt brilliantly in his humorous sketches in the second century AD.*

Recent bibliography: H. Heftner, ZPE 128 (1999) 33–43.

Testimonia

i Polyzelus: comic poet, His plays are *Bath-Scene*, *Demos-Tyndareus*, *Birth of the Muses*, *Birth of Dionysus*, *Birth of Aphrodite*.

ii [From the list of victors at the Lenaea, c. 400]

Pol[yzelu]s 4

THE POETS OF OLD COMEDY

Fragments

ΑΦΡΟΔΙΤΗΣ ΓΟΝΑΙ

Two very different ancient myths recounted the birth of the goddess of love and beauty. In one she is the daughter of Zeus and the minor goddess Dione, born as one of the second generation of Olympians (Iliad 370–430), but in Hesiod (Theogony 190ff.) she is born of the sea from the blood that dripped from the genitals of castrated Uranus—

ΔΗΜΟΤΥΝΔΑΡΕΩΣ

The title of this comedy has curious implications. We do know of other compound titles in Old Comedy, Dionysalexander *by Cratinus, Aristophanes'* Aeolosicon, *Pherecrates'* Heracles the Mortal, *which suggest that the comedy lay in the fusion of two incongruous personalities. But the point is not that easy to see here. Demos is presumably the Athenian people—we get a character of that name in* Knights *and very probably in Eupolis'* Maricas, *also the speaker of Platon F 201—but what is the force of Tyndareus? An obscure entry in the* Suda *(α 1806) records that Aesop was so well loved by the gods that he came back to life, "just like Tyndareus in fact." Scholars have thus concluded that a Demos, "brought back to life" like Tyndareus, alludes to the restoration either after 411 or after the fall of the Thirty (403). But this is a great deal to place on an obscure reference. What sort of story would one naturally associate with Tyndareus? That his wife Leda was seduced by Zeus? That Leda incubated the egg of Nemesis*

POLYZELUS

Fragments

BIRTH OF APHRODITE

Aphrodite means "foam spun." Plato at Symposium *180c1–185c3 has Pausanias expound on the philosophical implications of the two Aphrodites ("celestial" and "common"). We might expect that more dramatic and comic value was to be had from the second version of her birth. Nothing remains of the play except the title.*

DEMOS-TYNDAREUS

that produced Helen—cf. Cratinus' lost comedy Nemesis, *and Tyndareus appearing on vases that display the scene? That he arranged the formal courtship of his daughter Helen by the foremost eligible males of the Greeks? That he attempted to secure the condemnation of his grandchildren for the murder of their mother?*

Much depends on F 3 and 5 which mention Theramenes and Hyperbolus. The former was mentioned in comedy as early as Eupolis' Cities (F 251, usually dated to 422) and was executed by the Thirty in 404. Hyperbolus was killed in 411 but is mentioned as late as Frogs 570 (in 405). What exactly are Theramenes' "three things" of F 3? There was an ancient tradition about "the three ways to die": the sword, hanging, or hemlock (poison). But we seem to be getting here imprisonment, poison, and flight. At Thucydides 8.70.2 we learn that the democracy after the restoration in 411/10 dealt with those involved in the Revolution of 411 by imprisoning some, executing some, and exiling

207

1 Erotianus *Vocabulary of Hippocrates* δ 23

† ἀμαθῶς γὰρ αὐτίτης πᾶσί τε θεοξενίης ἐγίνετο

2 Photius (z) ε 986

ἴξῃ πρὸς Ἐννεάκρουνον, εὔυδρον τόπον.

3 Photius p. 613.4

τριῶν κακῶν γοῦν ἦν ἑλέσθ᾽ αὐτῷ τι πᾶσ᾽ ἀνάγκη,
ἢ ξύλον ἐφέλκειν, ἢ πιεῖν κώνειον, ἢ προδόντα
τὴν ναῦν ὅπως τάχιστα τῶν κακῶν ἀπαλλαγῆναι.
ταῦτ᾽ ἔστι τρία Θηραμένους, ἅ σοι φυλακτέ᾽ ἐστί.

4 Pollux 10.76

† λεκανίῳ γὰρ πρῶτον μὲν ἐναπονίψεις,
ἐνεξεμεῖς, ἐνεκπλυνεῖς, ἐναποβάσεις κυανία. †

5 Σ Lucian *Timon* 30

Πολύζηλος δὲ ἐν Δημοτυνδάρεῳ Φρύγα αὐτὸν εἶναί
φησιν εἰς τὸ βάρβαρον σκώπτων.

some. The scholiast to Frogs *541 takes a similar line: "He [Theramenes] seems to have legislated three punishments: to be imprisoned in the stocks, to drink hemlock, or to go into exile," although his use of "seems" may give one cause to pause. In that case a date around 410 would suit both this explanation and the mention of Hyperbolus in F 5.*

1 For . . . homemade wine for all was (?) of the god of strangers.[1]

[1] The text, cited for the rare word *autitēs* (homemade wine), is heavily corrupt.

2 You [sing.] will come to Nine Fountains, a well-watered place.[1]

[1] Nine Fountains was a spring on the River Ilissus in Athens, where water was drawn for the ritual baths for brides.

3 At any rate his only possibility was to choose from three unpleasant options: (1) to drag a wooden beam about, (2) to drink hemlock, and (3) to give up the ship and get away from all his troubles as quickly as possible. These are the "three alternatives of Theramenes," which you [sing.] must watch out for.

4 First you will wash in a basin, be sick in a basin, clean up in a basin, dye (?) ⟨clothes⟩ blue in a basin.[1]

[1] Reading ἐναποβάψεις for ἐναποβάσεις.

5 Polyzelus in *Demos-Tyndareus* pokes fun at his [Hyperbolus'] foreign birth by saying that he is a Phrygian.

ΔΙΟΝΥΣΟΥ ΓΟΝΑΙ

6 Pollux 10.109

οὗπερ αἱ χύτραι κρέμανται καὶ τὸ φρύγετρόν γε
πρός

7 Photius (b, z) α 1118

ῥήμαθ᾽ ἁμαξιαῖα

ΜΟΥΣΩΝ ΓΟΝΑΙ

8 Photius ε 1323

ἱερῷ γὰρ ἐντετύχηκας Ἐπακρίου Διός.

POLYZELUS

BIRTH OF DIONYSUS

The parodos to Euripides' Bacchae gives a brief account of the strange birth of Dionysus (89–104), while Lucian (Dialogue of the Gods 9) shows how the story can be treated humorously. It is also possible that comedy did something with the story of the eidōlon *that Zeus gave to Hera as a "hostage" (Bacchae 292–94), or the tending of the infant by Silenus and the satyrs—Sophocles' satyr drama,* Little Dionysus, *seems to have proceeded along these lines.*

6 Where the pots hang and the grain roaster as well.

7 Words to fit in wagons.

BIRTH OF THE MUSES

The birth of the Muses, canonically nine but sometimes seven or fewer in early texts (Epicharmus F 39), would have been the archetypal multiple birth, and clearly would have made good comedy, although one wonders how an entire play would have been sustained. Perhaps the story included Zeus' pursuit of Memory or some scenes where some or all of the Muses operated in their own specific area. In F 9 the "us" is very likely Zeus and "the woman" Memory. Zeus is expressing his wonder for the number of children that she is producing.

8 For you have chanced upon the temple of Zeus of the High Places.

211

9 Zenobius *Proverbs* (Ath.) 51

ὥσπερ Χαλκιδικὴ τέτοκεν ἡμῖν ἡ γυνή.

10 Athenaeus 370f

ὑψιπέταλοί τε κράμβαι συχναί

ΝΙΠΤΡΑ

ΑΔΗΛΩΝ ΔΡΑΜΑΤΩΝ

12 Σ Aristophanes *Wealth* 550c

χὠ μαινόμενος ἐκεινοσὶ Διονύσιος
χρυσοῦν ἔχων χλίδωνα καὶ τρυφήματα
ἐν τῷ μύρῳ παρ' Ἀθηναίων βαυκίζεται.

13 Pollux 2.118

ἀλλ' οὐ τρυγεροὺς τὰ φθέγματ' οὐδὲ γλύξιδας.

9 She has borne children for us like a woman from Chalkis.[1]

[1] The point of "a woman from Chalkis" was lost on the commentators who struggle to find an allusion that fits the reference.

10 Lots of high-leafed cabbages.

Brief fragment: (F 11) "fond of women."

BATH-SCENE

*This term is used twice by Aristotle (*Poetics *1454b, 1460a) to denote the scene in* Odyssey *19 where Odysseus is recognized by his old nurse while she is bathing him. Comedy did treat episodes from the* Odyssey—*Cratinus'* Odysseus and Company *(the Cyclops scene), Philyllius'* Nausicaa, *presumably Theopompus'* Penelope—*and it is a reasonable assumption, though not proven, that Polyzelus made a comic drama out of this moment from the* Odyssey. *Apart from the title, nothing remains of the play.*

UNASSIGNED FRAGMENTS

12 And crazy Dionysius over there in the perfume market, wearing a golden bracelet and his finery, courts advances from the Athenians.[1]

[1] This is probably Dionysius of Syracuse, whose support the Athenians had been seeking during the 390s and 380s. The splendour would be that appropriate for a tyrant.

13 Not full of dregs in their words, nor too sweet.

ΣΑΝΝΥΡΙΩΝ

Testimonia

i *Suda* σ 93

Σαννυρίων, Ἀθηναῖος, κωμικός. δράματα αὐτοῦ ἐστι
ταῦτα· Γέλως, Δανάη, Ἰώ, Ψυχασταί· ὡς Ἀθήναιος ἐν
Δειπνοσοφισταῖς.

ii *Suda* δ 1155

Διοκλῆς . . . ἀρχαῖος κωμικός, σύγχρονος Σαννυρίωνι
καὶ Φιλυλλίῳ.

SANNYRION

*A minor comic poet from the end of the fifth century, San-
nyrion is best known for his intertextual activity. He was
made fun of twice by Strattis (T 4) for a thin and emaciated
appearance and once in splendid fashion by Aristophanes
(T 5), and he himself pointed out Hegelochus' slip of the
tongue in Euripides' Orestes (F 8). Since the title Cool-
Seekers, recorded by the Suda (T 1), is attested for Strattis
with six fragments, it should probably be removed from
Sannyrion's list of plays. Confusion arising from the cita-
tion at Athenaeus 551c (Strattis F 57), which mentions
both Sannyrion and Strattis, may be the source of the
misattribution. The only comedy about which we have any
hints is Danae. F 8 reveals that it handled the story of Zeus'
seduction of Acrisius' daughter, Zeus himself appearing as
a character in the play.*

Testimonia

i Sannyrion: of Athens, comic poet. These are his plays:
Laughter, Danae, Io, Cool-Seekers, so Athenaeus in *The
Learned Banqueters* (F 2.3, 11).

ii Diocles: . . . poet of Old Comedy, a contemporary of
Sannyrion and Philyllius.

iii Aelian *Historical Miscellany* 10.6

ἐκωμῳδοῦντο ἐς λεπτότητα Σαννυρίων ὁ κωμῳδίας
ποιητής.

iv

(a) Strattis F 21 (*ap.* Pollux 10.189)

τὸ μὲν δὴ ξύλον ᾧ περιπλάττουσι τὸν πηλὸν οἱ κορο-
πλάθοι, κάναβος καλεῖται· ὅθεν καὶ Στράττις ἐν τῷ
Κινησίᾳ τὸν Σαννυρίωνα διὰ τὴν ἰσχνότητα κάναβον
καλεῖ·

(b) Strattis F 57 (*ap.* Athenaeus 551c)

Σαννυρίωνος σκυτίνην ἐπικουρίαν

v Aristophanes F 156 (*Gerytades*)

{Α.} καὶ τίς νεκρῶν κευθμῶνα καὶ σκότου πύλας
ἔτλη κατελθεῖν; {Β.} ἕνα μὲν ἀφ' ἑκάστης τῆς
    τέχνης
εἱλόμεθα κοινῇ γενομένης ἐκκλησίας,
οὓς ᾖσμεν ὄντας ᾀδοφοίτας καὶ θαμὰ
5 ἐκεῖσε φιλοχωροῦντας. {Α.} εἰσὶ γάρ τινες
ἄνδρες παρ' ὑμῖν ᾀδοφοῖται; {Β.} νὴ Δία
μάλιστά γ'. {Α.} ὥσπερ Θρᾳκοφοῖται; {Β.} πάντ'
    ἔχεις.
{Α.} καὶ τίνες ἂν εἶεν; {Β.} πρῶτα μὲν Σαννυρίων

iii Among those made fun of for being thin are Sannyrion the comic poet etc.

iv

(a) The wooden core around which model makers mould their clay is called a "skeleton." For this reason Strattis in his *Cinesias* calls Sannyrion "a skeleton" because of his leanness.

(b) Sannyrion's leather helper.

v (A) And who has dared descend into the halls of the dead and the gates of darkness?
　(B) At a general meeting of the assembly we chose one man from each poetic genre, men whom we knew to be "Death-Trippers," devotees of things on the other side.
　(A) You actually have "Death-Trippers" among you?
　(B) Yes indeed.
　(A) Like "Thrace-Trippers"?
　(B) Exactly.
　(A) Who would these men be?
　(B) Well, first from the comic poets Sannyrion, from

ἀπὸ τῶν τρυγῳδῶν, ἀπὸ δὲ τῶν τραγικῶν χορῶν
10 Μέλητος, ἀπὸ δὲ τῶν κυκλίων Κινησίας.
{Α.} ὡς σφόδρ᾽ ἐπὶ λεπτῶν ἐλπίδων ὠχεῖσθ᾽ ἄρα.
τούτους γάρ, ἢν πολλῷ ξυνέλθῃ ξυλλαβὼν
ὁ τῆς διαρροίας ποταμὸς οἰχήσεται.

vi Aelian *Historical Miscellany* 13.15

λόγος δέ τις καὶ Σαννυρίωνα τοιοῦτον γενέσθαι, ὃς ἐν
τῇ ληκύθῳ τὴν κλίμακα ἐζήτει. καὶ Κόροιβον δὲ καὶ
Μελιτίδην καὶ ἐκείνους ἀνοήτους φασίν.

Fragments

ΓΕΛΩΣ

1 Harpocration p. 243.7

πέλανον [   ]
ἃ καλεῖτε σεμνῶς ἄλφιθ᾽ ὑμεῖς οἱ βροτοί.

the tragedians Meletus, and from the dithyrambists Cinesias.

(A) You are certainly riding on slender hopes, since if the River Diarrhoea rises in full flood, it will snatch these men and carry them away.

vi There is also a story that Sannyrion was like this too [foolish], "who kept looking for the tempest in the teapot." They say that Coroebus and Melitides were stupid as well.[1]

[1] In the Greek, the phrase "tempest in a teapot" is actually "ladder in a *lecythus*," both words being terms of rhetoric flourish–see Calder, *Philologus* 117 (1973) 141f. There is no guarantee that this is the comic poet.

Fragments

LAUGHTER (LAUGHING-STOCK?)

The title might also mean "laughing stock" or "funny story." Can we imagine a personified figure of Laughter, such as Comedy in Cratinus' Wine-Flask *or Dialogue in Lucian's* Twice Accused? *In F 1 someone is addressing "you mortals"; this implies a divine or semidivine figure. Or could it denote a central character who was the butt of people's jokes? Compare Platon's* Blockhead.

1 "Pelanon" . . . which you mortals solemnly call "barley meal."

2 Athenaeus 551c

Μέλητον τὸν ἀπὸ Ληναίου νεκρόν

3 Athenaeus 286c

ὦ βατίδες, ὦ γλαύκων κάρα

4 Pollux 10.185

κεραμικὴν γαῖαν στρέφων

5 Σ (Arethas) Plato *Apology* 19c

Ἀριστώνυμος δ᾽ ἐν Ἡλίῳ ῥηγοῦντι καὶ Σαννυρίων ἐν
Γέλωτι "τετράδι" φασὶν αὐτὸν "γενέσθαι," διὸ‹τι› τὸν
βίον κατέτριψεν ἑτέροις πονῶν.

ΔΑΝΑΗ

*The dramatists found the story of Danae a popular one.
Euripides' Danae dealt with the pregnancy of Danae and
the reaction by her father, Acrisius, so too Sophocles'
Acrisius and Danae (the two may be the same play).
Aeschylus' satyr play Net-Haulers showed the discovery
on Seriphus of the floating chest in which Danae and her
baby son, Perseus, were imprisoned, while Euripides'*

2 Meletus, that corpse from the Lenaeum.[1]

[1] A tragic poet of the late 5th and early 4th c. (*TrGF* 47). On the various men named Meletus at this time, see D. MacDowell, *Andokides. On the Mysteries* (Oxford 1962) 208–10.

3 O skates, O heads of dogfish.

4 Turning the potter's earth.

5 Aristonymus in his *The Sun is Cold* [F 4] and Sannyrion in his *Laughter* says that he [Aristophanes] was "born on the fourth," because he had spent his life toiling for others.[1]

[1] "Toiling for others" refers to the fact that Aristophanes had many of his plays produced through others, such as Callistratus and Philonides.

Brief fragments: (F 6) "ship owner," (F 7) "playing to the citizens."

DANAE

Dictys handled the later threat from the king of Seriphus to Danae. As F 8 must be Zeus contemplating how to penetrate the tower in which Danae has been put away, this comedy dealt with the actual seduction of Danae by Zeus (in the form of a golden shower of rain—see Menander Samian Woman 589–91), although subsequent events may have also been part of the action.

8 Σ Euripides *Orestes* 279

τί οὖν γενόμενος εἰς ὀπὴν ἐνδύσομαι;
ζητητέον· φέρ' εἰ γενοίμην ⟨ ⟩ γαλῆ·
ἀλλ' Ἡγέλοχος ⟨εὐθύς⟩ με μηνύσειεν ⟨ἂν⟩
ὁ τραγικὸς ἀνακράγοι τ' ἂν εἰσιδὼν μέγα
5 "ἐκ κυμάτων γὰρ αὖθις αὖ γαλῆν ὁρῶ."

9 Σ Aristophanes *Frogs* 367

τοῦτο εἰς Ἀρχῖνον. μήποτε δὲ καὶ εἰς Ἀγύρριον. μέ-
μνηται δὲ τούτων καὶ Πλάτων ἐν Σκευαῖς καὶ Σαννυ-
ρίων ἐν Δανάῃ. οὗτοι γὰρ προϊστάμενοι τῆς δημοσίας
τραπέζης τὸν μισθὸν τῶν κωμῳδῶν ἐμείωσαν κωμῳ-
δηθέντες.

10 Photius (b, Sᶻ) α 2058

ἀνταυγὲς κάλλος

ΙΩ

11 Athenaeus 261f

φθείρεσθ' ἐπίτριπτοι ψωμοκόλακες.

ΑΔΗΛΩΝ ΔΡΑΜΑΤΩΝ

8 What should I turn myself into and sneak in through the chimney? Let me think. Suppose I became a ferret? But Hegelochus the tragic actor would ⟨immediately⟩ give me away. When he saw me, he'd shout in a loud voice, "For now after the storm I see it's ferret again."[1]

[1] Hegelochus was the actor who at Euripides' *Orestes* 279 mispronounced *galén'* (fair out) as *galên* (ferret). His faux pas was also made fun of twice by Strattis (F 1, 63) and at *Frogs* 303–4.

9 This ⟨is directed⟩ against Archinus, and perhaps also at Agyrrhius. Platon mentions them in *Costumes* [F 141] and Sannyrion in *Danae*. They were in charge of the public finances and reduced the pay for the comic poets because they had been made fun of.

10 Sparkling beauty.

IO

Platon also wrote an Old Comedy with this title, while Io appears as a character in Prometheus *with horns denoting the heifer into which she has been transformed.*

11 Get lost, you damned bread spongers.

UNASSIGNED FRAGMENTS

Brief fragments: (F 12) "to have come back to life," (F 13) "without sleep."

ΣΤΡΑΤΤΙΣ

No reference in the surviving fragments of Strattis needs to be earlier than 410, and as certain of the plays parodied by him belong around 410 (Philoctetes, Orestes, Phoenician Women, Chrysippus, Hypsipyle), we should set the beginning of his career around that time. His career certainly lasted into the 380s. The latest reference would appear to be that in F 3, to Isocrates and his mistress Lagisce.

While the other poets of Old Comedy do mention, cite from, and parody the tragedians, Strattis and Aristophanes are the principal poets to engage in a major way with tragedy, especially with Euripides. The first attested instance of the verb paratragōiden *occurs at F 50. In F 1 the speaker is referring to the archon or the* chorēgos *who hired Hegelochus as the lead actor in Orestes—and thus "ruined Euripides' most clever play." Several of his comedies suggest a direct parody of well-known tragedies of the late fifth century:* Troilus *of Sophocles'* Troilus *(418?);* Philoctetes *of Sophocles' extant play of 409;* Medea *probably of Euripides' play of 431;* Chrysippus *of Euripides' late tragedy,* Lemnomeda, *a combination of* Andromeda *and* Hypsipyle; *and* Phoenician Women, *with two direct allusions to Euripides' play (F 47–48) but with opening lines taken from* Hypsipyle. *The mysteriously titled* Orestes the Mortal *and* Atalantos *(a male Atalanta?) may depend to*

STRATTIS

some extent on Euripides' late plays *Orestes* and *Meleager*. Callippides *must be about the popular tragic actor of the time, and while* Cinesias *is about a dithyrambic poet, and not a dramatist, both continue Strattis' (and his audience's) interest in the public entertainment of Athens in the late fifth century. F 71, an ode to leek bugs, is a parody of a tragic lyric rather like Aristophanes' parody of a Euripidean monody at* Frogs *1309–22.*

There are allusions also to comic poets, to Philyllius at F 38 and to Sannyrion (F 21, 57), and Strattis does make jokes about various prominent figures of the day: Isocrates (F 3), Epicrates (F 10), Laispodias (F 19), and perhaps Thrasybulus (F 20). But none of these jokes is political; rather, they are aimed more at their personal lives. This is very much in the spirit of later comedy. There are also references to Lais the famous hetaera (F 27), Megallus and Deinias the perfume sellers (F 34), and an unknown Phormion (F 6).

Recent bibliography: F. Cannata, QS 24 (1998) 195–210; Storey & Allan 208; S. Miles, Strattis, Tragedy, and Comedy (diss. Nottingham 2009); C. Orth, Strattis. Die Fragmente (Berlin 2009).

THE POETS OF OLD COMEDY

Testimonia

i *Suda* σ 1178

Στράττις, Ἀθηναῖος, κωμικός. τῶν δραμάτων αὐτοῦ ἐστι ταῦτα· Ἀνθρωπορέστης, Ἀταλάντη, Ἀγαθοὶ ἤτοι Ἀργυρίου ἀφανισμός, Ἰφιγέρων, Καλλιππίδης, Κινησίας, Λιμνομέδων, Μακεδόνες, Μήδεια, Τρωΐλος, Φοίνισσαι, Φιλοκτήτης, Χρύσιππος, Παυσανίας, Ψυχασταί· ὥς φησιν Ἀθήναιος ἐν τῷ β΄ βιβλίῳ τῶν Δειπνοσοφιστῶν.

τραγικός AGM, στρατηγὸς τραγικός V, στρατηγός, τρυγικός F; κωμικός Reinesius.

ii The Names and Plays of the Poets of Old Comedy (Koster VIII.2)

Στράττιδος δράματα ις΄

iii Athenaeus 453c

ὁ δὲ Ἀθηναῖος Καλλίας . . . μικρὸν ἔμπροσθεν γενόμενος τοῖς χρόνοις Στράττιδος.

iv *IG* ii² 2325.138

Στράττι]ς Ι

ΑΓΑΘΟΙ ΗΤΟΙ ΑΡΓΥΡΙΟΥ
ΑΦΑΝΙΣΜΟΣ

Testimonia

i Strattis: of Athens, comic poet. These are his plays: *Orestes the Mortal, Atalanta, Good Men* or *The Money Vanishes, Iphigeron, Callippides, Cinesias, Limnomedon, Macedonians, Medea, Troilus, Phoenician Women, Philoctetes, Chrysippus, Pausanias, Chill-Seekers,* as Athenaeus says in Book 2 of *The Learned Banqueters*.

ii The plays of Strattis, 16.

iii Callias the Athenian . . . who was a bit earlier in time than Strattis.

iv [From the list of victors at the Lenaea, after 400]

Stratti]s 1

GOOD MEN or THE MONEY VANISHES

The comedy is cited five times as "Good Men," three times by Athenaeus as the work of "Pherecrates or Strattis," and twice by Pollux as the work of Pherecrates (q.v.). The alternative title "The Money Vanishes" is provided only by the Suda (T 1), but may give us a clue to the plot: good men becoming rich (in the manner of Aristophanes' Wealth—see l. 495) and then quickly going through their newly acquired wealth. The title "The Money Vanishes" is found three times in Middle Comedy.

ΑΝΘΡΩΠΟΡΕΣΤΗΣ

There are a number of compound titles in Old Comedy: Aristophanes' Aeolosicon, Polyzelus' Demos-Tyndareus, and closest to this title, Pherecrates' Heracles the Mortal. But assuming that the Orestes of the title is the son of Agamemnon, supported by the reference to Euripides' play of 408 of that title, what is the point of his being "mortal"? Orth (44) suggests that the sense is "Orestes as an ordinary mortal." Some have adopted the variant reading in the scholiast, Anthroporaistes, "Man-Destroyer," with no reference to the son of Agamemnon. Another possibility is to

Fragments

1 Σ Euripides *Orestes* 279

καὶ τῶν μὲν ἄλλων οὐκ ἐμέλησέ μοι μελῶν,
Εὐριπίδου δὲ δρᾶμα δεξιώτατον
διέκναισ' Ὀρέστην, Ἡγέλοχον τὸν Κυντάρου
μισθωσάμενος τὰ πρῶτα τῶν ἐπῶν λέγειν.

Κυντάρου codd., Κιννάρου Bentley.

2 Athenaeus 127c

τῶν δὲ διδύμων ἐκγόνων σεμιδάλιδος

ORESTES THE MORTAL

*take Anthropos as a proper name, or to consider Orestes as
the Athenian clothes thief of that name (Acharnians 1166–
70, Birds 712, 1490–93). There is some dispute in F 1
whether in line 3 the elided verb form is first or third per-
son. If third, then the speaker could be Tragedy or Poetry
or a Muse; if first, either the archon in charge of the festival
or the* chorēgus.

Recent bibliography: A. Meriani, in Scritti I. Gallo *(2002)
405–28.*

Fragments

1 Now I didn't care about the other songs, but he ruined
Orestes, Euripides' most clever play, by hiring Hegelo-
chus, the son of Artichoke (?), to play the leading role.[1]

[1] The reading of the scholion, Κυντάρου, is not a known Athe-
nian name. I suspect that we have a false patronymic (cf. "Amynias
the son Sellus" at *Wasps* 1267, to denote a boaster, or "Antimachus
the son of Spit" at *Acharnians* 1251). Bentley's reading relates the
patronymic to the *kinara* (artichoke), which Borthwick (*CQ* 1967)
151–52 shows was considered injurious to the voice. See Platon F
235 for the "unpleasant voice" of Hegelochus.

2 From the twin offspring of the fine flour.

ΑΤΑΛΑΝΤΟΣ

Testimonium

i Σ Aristophanes *Frogs* 146

πολλῷ γὰρ ὕστερον τῶν Βατράχων δεδίδακται ὁ Ἀτά-
λαντος Στράττιδος.

Fragments

3 Zosimus *Life of Isocrates* p. 102.19 Dindorf

καὶ τὴν Λαγίσκαν τὴν Ἰσοκράτους παλλακὴν
εὑρεῖν με συκάζουσαν εὐναίαν ἔτι
τὸν τ᾽ αὐλοτρύπην αὐτόν εἶθ᾽ ἥκειν ταχύ.

---

¹ "Plucking figs" (*sykazousan*) should bear a sexual connotation. Can *me* be construed as the object of *sykazousan* and thus turn the speaker's dream into an erotic fantasy?

ATALANTUS

*Ancient sources were not certain whether the title of
Strattis' comedy was* Atalanta *(T 1) or* Atalantus *(T 2) or
even* Atalantai *(Photius δ 672). If it were* Atalantus, *we
may compare Aristophanes'* Dramata *or* Niobus, *where F
294 shows that the comedy at some point mentioned the
story of the children of Niobe. Thus* Atalantus *may have
been a male version of the famous huntress. Tragic influ-
ences might be Aeschylus'* Atalanta *or Euripides'* Meleager
(for the latter see Frogs *864, 1240–41, 1402). This was
a popular subject in Old and Middle Comedy—of Old
Comic poets we may cite an* Atalanta *by Callias, Euthycles,
and Philyllius.*

*F 3 refers to Lagisce, a hetaera who was at one point
in her life the mistress of Isocrates "as he grew older"
(Plutarch* Moralia *839b). This would date her liaison with
Isocrates and thus Strattis' comedy to the fourth century.
Athenaeus (586e) cites Lysias' lost* Against Laïs *for the
inclusion of Lagisce among a list of known hetaerae.*

Testimonium

i For Strattis' *Atalantus* was produced much later than
Frogs [L-405].

Fragments

3 And ‹I dreamt› I found Isocrates' mistress, Lagisce,
still in bed, plucking figs,[1] and then the flute maker himself
came in quickly.

231

THE POETS OF OLD COMEDY

4 P. Oxy. 2742

ἀπὸ τῆς κράδης, ἤδη γὰρ ἰσχὰς γίν[ομαι
ὁ μηχανοποιός μ' ὡς τάχιστα καθελέτω.

5 Athenaeus 302d

ὑπογάστριον θύννου τι κἀκροκώλιον
δραχμῆς ὕειον

6 Σ Aristophanes *Peace* 348e

ὁ δὲ δεύτερος ἦν κωφός· † μέμνηται καὶ Στράττις.
τρίτος μοιχός· Κρατῖνος Ἀταλάντῃ.† τέταρτος Κρο-
τωνιάτης ἀρχαῖος· Κρατῖνος Τροφωνίῳ.

ΖΩΠΥΡΟΣ ΠΕΡΙΚΑΙΟΜΕΝΟΣ

*Zopyrus is a common name in Athens at all periods, but the
most prominent fifth-century holder of the name was an el-
derly Thracian slave whom Pericles made the* paedagogus
*of Alcibiades (PAA 465118). This is possibly the same man
as the physiognomist known from Plato (Alcibiades I 122a)
and the subject of a lost work by Phaedo of Elis. Comedy
could make fun of Connus, the music teacher of Socrates,*

4 Let the crane man get me down from the branch as quickly as possible, for I am turning into a fig already.[1]

[1] This is one of a number of comic instances where a character on the *mēchanē* calls attention to his situation (Aristophanes *Peace* 174, F 160; Strattis F 46).

5 An under slice of tunny fish and a drachma's worth of pigs' trotters.

6 The second ⟨Phormion⟩ was deaf. Strattis mentions him. The third was an adulterer—Cratinus in *Atalanta*. The fourth was a man of ancient times from Croton—Cratinus in *Trophonius*.[1]

[1] Since Cratinus did not write an *Atalanta*, there seems to be some confusion in the scholion.

Brief fragments: (F 7) "couch bearers," (F 8) "dung."

THE BURNING OF ZOPYRUS

and Damon the music teacher of Pericles (Platon F 201). Since the tragedian Spintharus (TrGF I 40) wrote a play The Burning of Heracles, *Meineke and others have considered Strattis' comedy as a parody of that tragedy. Cratinus (F 187) mentions "the talents of Zopyrus," a reference to a Persian known from Herodotus (3.153–60). The meaning of the title and the theme of the comedy remain mysterious.*

Fragments

9 *Etymologicum Genuinum* A

ἀλλ' εἰ μέλλεις ἀνδρείως
φῴζειν ὥσπερ μύστακα σαυτόν

10 Hesychius o 1764

τῶν οὐ μάλα τέθηκα κεκυκκᾶν Ἐπικράτη

ΙΦΙΓΕΡΩΝ

Fragments

9 But if you are going to sear yourself manfully like you would a moustache.

10 Of these I have not considered Epicrates worth a pip.

MIGHTY OLD MAN

The scholiast to Peace *542 assigns a fragment to a play of this title by Apollophanes (F 3), while Harpocration attributes the verb "to treat like a brother" to the* Mighty Old Man *by "Strattis or Apollophanes" (F 4). We have either one play of disputed authorship or two comedies with this unusual title. The compound title (cf.* Orestes the Mortal, Lemnomeda*) might favour an authorship by Strattis. The first part "Iphi" might suggest a connection with the story of Agamemnon's daughter (variously called Iphigenia, Iphimede, and Iphianassa), but that seems a lot to build on a single prefix. An old man named "Iphis," for instance, appears in Euripides'* Suppliant Women. *Might we not look there for a link to tragedy? Or as one of the leading political and military figures from the late 390s on, was* Iphicrates *the son of Timotheus (PAA 542925), perhaps a comedy whose title began with Iphi– might have brought his name to mind, especially as he was a young man in the late 390s, hence a play on* gerōn?

ΚΑΛΛΙΠΠΙΔΗΣ

The subject of this comedy should be the well-known tragic actor of the late fifth and early fourth centuries (PAA 558950) who was victorious in the actors' competition at L-418 (IG ii² 2319) and the subject of several anecdotes preserved by Athenaeus and Plutarch. Xenophon and Aristotle describe Callippides' highly emotional style of performance, the latter adding that Mynniscus, an actor of an earlier period (see Platon F 175), called Callippides "an ape," for his lack of restraint in playing dramatic roles. If we take "in Callippides" (T 1) as meaning "in <Strattis' play> Callippides, a reasonable inference since "at Cal-

Testimonium

i Aristophanes F 490 (*Women Claiming Tent-Sites*)

ὥσπερ ἐν Καλλιππίδῃ
ἐπὶ τοῦ κορήματος καθέζομαι χαμαί.

Fragments

11 Photius (b, Sᶻ) α 1285

δὸς νῦν τὸν ἄμυλον πρῶτον αὐτῷ τουτονί

12 Athenaeus 656b

αὐτίκα δ' ἥρπασε τεμάχη
θερμάς τε κάπρου φλογίδας ἔβρυχέ τε πάνθ' ἅμα.

CALLIPPIDES

lippides' ⟨house⟩" would be en Kallippidou, *then there
was a scene in which a character was depicted sitting
among the rubbish, perhaps that left after the party im-
plied by the extant fragments. Aristophanes' comedy,*
Women Claiming Tent-Sites, *belongs to the later part of
his career but gives no real help in dating Strattis' play.
Orth (93) prefers around 399.*

*The three fragments we have all concern food. F 12
implies that Heracles was a character in the comedy. For
this we can compare Platon F 46, where Heracles appears
in the context of a dinner party at a brothel.*

Recent bibliography: D. Braund, in Rivals *151–61; E.
Csapo, in Easterling & Hall 127–47.*

Testimonium

i Just as in *Callippides* I am sitting on the ground in rub-
bish.

Fragments

11 Now first give him this fine-flour cake.

12 Straightaway he [Heracles] seized slices and hot boar
steaks and chomped them all down together.

Brief fragment: (F 13) "small tunny fish."

ΚΙΝΗΣΙΑΣ

Cinesias (PAA 569985) is the dithyrambic poet, best known from his scene in Aristophanes' Birds (1372–1409) and the complaint made against him and other musicians by Music at Pherecrates F 155.8–12. He served in politics as a bouleutēs in 394/3 (IG ii² 18) and was the object of two speeches by Lysias (F 85–86 Carey). Comedy made fun of his thin and emaciated appearance, an embarrassing public attack of diarrhoea, his alleged impiety, and his new style of music. F 15–17 suggest that the comedy may have been a parody of the story of Achilles' withdrawal from the war at Troy. Some have seen Strattis' Cinesias and his Myr-

Testimonia

i Athenaeus 551d

ὁ Κινησίας, εἰς ὃν καὶ ὅλον δρᾶμα γέγραφεν Στράττις.

ii Harpocration p. 178.2

οὗτος ὁ διθυραμβοποιός, οὗ μέμνηνται πολλάκις οἱ κωμικοὶ καὶ Στράττις ὅλον δρᾶμα ποιήσας εἰς αὐτόν, ὅπερ ἐπεγράφη Κινησίας.

CINESIAS

midons *as the same play. The vocative "Achilles of Phthia"
(F 17) has been seen by some as a pun on* phthisis *(wasting
away), alluding to Cinesias' poor physical condition.*

*The comedy could be dated anywhere after 410—
Laispodias (F 19) vanishes from history after his involve-
ment with the coup in 411, but he is made fun of by Theo-
pompus (F 40) and Philyllius (F 8), who belong rather
later. Sommerstein argues for a date of 411–408; the* opinio
communis *favours shortly after the democratic restoration
in 403.*

Recent bibliography: A. Meriani, in I. Gallo (ed.), Seconda
miscellanea filologica *(1995) 21–45.*

Testimonia

i Cinesias, against whom Strattis even wrote an entire
play.

ii This would be the dithyrambic poet, whom the comic
poets mention many times; Strattis wrote an entire play
against him, which is titled "Cinesias."

Fragments

14 Pollux 4.168–69

{A.} τὰ δ᾽ ἄλφιθ᾽ ὑμῖν πῶς ἐπώλουν; {B.} τεττάρων
δραχμῶν μάλιστα τὸν κόφινον. {A.} τί λέγεις;
  μέτρῳ
ἐχρῶντο κοφίνῳ; {B.} † ἢ <   > τοῦτ᾽ αὖθ᾽ ὅτι
οἴνου κόφινος, δυνάμενος τρεῖς χοᾶς
πυρρῶν ταῖς κοφίναις ταὐτὰ ταῦτα δυνάμενος†

15 Pollux 10.169

                    ἁλμυρόν θ᾽ ὕδωρ,
ἕτερόν τε λεπτὸν ἐν ἁλίᾳ κεκομμένον.

16 Σ Aristophanes *Frogs* 405

σκηνῇ μὲν <   > τοῦ χοροκτόνου Κινησίου.

17 Athenaeus 551d

Φθιῶτ᾽ Ἀχιλλεῦ

18 Harpocration p. 177.16

Κινησίας· Λυσίου β᾽ λόγοι εἰσὶ πρὸς Κινησίαν, ἐν οἷς
πολλάκις μνημονεύει τἀνδρὸς, λέγων ὡς ἀσεβέστατος
εἴη καὶ παρανομώτατος, καὶ ὅτι καὶ οἱ κωμῳδοδι-
δάσκαλοι καθ᾽ ἕκαστον ἐνιαυτὸν γράφουσιν εἰς αὐτόν.

Fragments

14 (A) How did they [the Boeotians] sell grain to you?

(B) Usually a basket for four drachmas.

(A) What are you saying? They used a basket as a measurement?

(B) . . . just the same, that a basket of wine holds three *choes*, and in the same amount for baskets of wheat.

15 Salt water, and another thing finely pounded out in a salt grinder.

16 ⟨This is⟩ the tent of the chorus-killing Cinesias.

17 Achilles of Phthia.

18 Cinesias: there are two speeches of Lysias against Cinesias, in which he mentions the man many times, alleging that he was a very impious and lawless person, and that the comic poets wrote about him every year. This would

εἴη δ᾽ ἂν οὗτος ὁ διθυραμβοποιός, οὗ μέμνηνται πολ-
λάκις οἱ κωμικοὶ καὶ Στράττις ὅλον δρᾶμα ποιήσας
εἰς αὐτόν, ὅπερ ἐπεγράφη Κινησίας, ἐν ᾧ καὶ τὴν
ἀσέβειαν αὐτοῦ κωμῳδεῖ.

19 Σ Aristophanes *Birds* 1569

εἶχε δὲ καὶ περὶ τὰς κνήμας αἰτίας τινάς, ὥς φησι
Στράττις ἐν Κινησίᾳ.

20 Σ Aristophanes *Wealth* 550c

μήποτε ὁ μὲν ἀξιωματικὸς καὶ αὐθάδης, ὡς Στράττις
ἐν τῷ Κινησίᾳ.

21 Pollux 10.189

τὸ μὲν δὴ ξύλον ᾧ περιπλάττουσι τὸν πηλὸν οἱ κορο-
πλάθοι, κάναβος καλεῖται· ὅθεν καὶ Στράττις ἐν τῷ
Κινησίᾳ τὸν Σαννυρίωνα διὰ τὴν ἰσχνότητα κάναβον
καλεῖ

ΛΗΜΝΟΜΕΔΑ

be the dithyrambic poet, whom the comic poets mention many times; Strattis wrote an entire play against him, which is entitled "Cinesias," in which he also makes fun of his impiety.

19 He [Laespodias] also had some problems with his legs, as Strattis says in *Cinesias*.

20 [Thrasybulus]: Perhaps "self-important" or "daring," as Strattis in *Cinesias*.

21 The wooden core around which image makers mould their clay is called a "skeleton." For this reason Strattis in his *Cinesias* calls Sannyrion "a skeleton" because of his leanness.

Brief fragment: (F 22) "with aconite."

LEMNOMEDA

The title of this comedy is variously given as "Limnome-don" (T 1), "Limnopedai" (Arethas on Plato Lysis *206e, citing F 24), and "Lemnomeda" (Athenaeus, citing F 23 and 25; and Harpocration, citing F 26). It is generally agreed that the name is a comic compound derived from two plays by Euripides, his* Hypsipyle *(about the best-known "woman of Lemnos") and his* Andromeda *(D-412). Dramas about the encounter between Jason and the Argonauts and the women of Lemnos are frequent in Greek drama: a possible Lemnos trilogy by Aeschylus, his satyric* Rowers *or* Argonauts, *Sophocles'* Lemnian Women, *and comedies of that title by Nicochares and Aristophanes. Two*

Fragments

23 Athenaeus 473c

Ἑρμῆς, ὃν ἕλκουσ' οἱ μὲν ἐκ προχοιδίου,
οἱ δ' ἐκ καδίσκου ⟨γ'⟩ ἴσον ἴσῳ κεκραμένον.

24 Σ (Arethas) Plato *Lysis* 206e

Χῖος παραστὰς Κῷον οὐκ ἐᾷ λέγειν.

25 Harpocration p. 45.1

ὑποδήματα
σαυτῷ πρίασθαι τῶν ἁπλῶν.

26 Athenaeus 327e

πολλοὺς ἤδη μεγάλους τε φάγρους ἐγκάψας

tragedies about Andromeda are known, an earlier one by Sophocles (before 450?) and the celebrated version of 412 by Euripides that inspired the brilliant parody in Thesmophoriazuse. Phrynichus had also written a comedy "with an old woman set out to be devoured by the sea monster," a parody of the story of Andromeda. Given Strattis' fondness for paratragedy, a comic merging of the two themes is certainly a possibility. Both stories depict a woman who falls in love with a hero from abroad. The few fragments that we have tell us nothing about the plot. It has been suggested that a comedy about Lemnos coupled with the mention of Chios and Cos (F 24) may allude to Athenian activities in the Aegean in the mid-390s and thus imply a date for the comedy around 392. But the usual practice is to date the comedy in the 410s, close in time after the Euripidean originals.

Fragments

23 The Hermes-drink, which some men take from the jug, and others from the cup, mixed in equal parts.

24 A Chian stands by and shuts the Coan up.[1]

[1] The metaphor is one from dice: the "Chian" is a one and the "Coan" a six, but together they produce only an average score, wasting or "shutting up" the Coan.

25 To buy some of the sandals with a single sole.

26 After he gobbled up many large sea bream.

THE POETS OF OLD COMEDY

ΜΑΚΕΔΟΝΕΣ Η ΠΑΥΣΑΝΙΑΣ

Fragments

27 Athenaeus 589a

{A.} εἰσὶν δὲ πόθεν αἱ παῖδες αὗται καὶ τίνες;
{B.} νυνὶ μὲν ἥκουσιν Μεγαρόθεν, εἰσὶ δὲ
Κορίνθιαι· Λαΐς μὲν † ᾗ μέγα κλεος ἰδί.

28 Athenaeus 654f

πολλῶν φλυάρων καὶ ταῶν ἀντάξια,
οὓς βόσκεθ' ὑμεῖς ἕνεκα τῶν ὠκυπτέρων.

29 Athenaeus 323b

{A.} ἡ σφύραινα δ' ἐστὶ τίς;
{B.} κέστραν μὲν ὕμμες ὤττικοὶ κικλήσκετε.

MACEDONIANS or PAUSANIAS

Do we have one or two comedies here? The Suda *(T 1) lists them separately, although* Pausanias *is alphabetically out of place at the end of the list. Athenaeus twice cites a "Macedonians" (citing F 29, 32), once a "Pausanias" (F 28), once a "Macedonians or Pausanias" (F 27), and once a "Macedonians or Cinesias" (F 30)—"Cinesias" is probably an error for "Pausanias." Harpocration, citing F 31, and the Anti-Atticist (on F 33) record a "Macedonians" by Strattis. Orth (144) argues that* Macedonians *is the original title, with* Pausanias *the name of a character in the play.*

Pausanias has been identified with the lover of Agathon and a character in Plato's Symposium, *who according to Aelian (Historical Miscellany 2.21) went with Agathon to Macedon. But he seems an unlikely person on which to build a whole play, and there are other possibilities: the king of Macedon in the mid-390s, or the man from Thessaly known to have been a lover of Lais (see F 27).*

Fragments

27 (A) Who are these girls and where do they come from?

(B) They have come just now from Megara, but they are Corinthian. In fact this one is Lais, of great renown (?).

28 Worth all that silly nonsense and the peacocks which you people raise because of their tail feathers.

29 (ATHENIAN) And what's a pike fish?

(B) You Attic folk call it a spet.

30 Athenaeus 396a

πνικτόν τι τοίνυν ‹– ∪› ἔστω σοι συχνὸν
τοιοῦτον.

31 Harpocration p. 290.5

τὸν πέπλον δὲ τοῦτον
ἕλκουσ᾽ ὀνεύοντες τοπείοις ἄνδρες ἀναρίθμητοι
εἰς ἄκρον ὥσπερ ἱστίον τὸν ἱστόν.

32 Athenaeus 302e

ὑπογάστριά θ᾽ ἡδέα θύννων

ΜΗΔΕΙΑ

Fragments

34 Athenaeus 690f

καὶ λέγ᾽ ὅτι φέρεις αὐτῇ μύρον
τοιοῦτον, οἷον οὐ Μέγαλλος πώποτε
ἥψησεν, οὐδὲ Δεινίας Αἰγύπτιος
οὔτ᾽ εἶδεν οὔτ᾽ ἐκτήσατο.

---

[1] Megallus was a Sicilian reputed to have invented a perfume
called the "Megallion" (Athenaeus 690f). He is mentioned by
late 5th and 4th c. comedy (Aristophanes F 549, Pherecrates F
149). Athenaeus (552f–53a) mentions Deinias as a perfume seller,
whose indulgence in scent led to disaster.

30 May you [sing.] have some smothered meat like this, and lots of it.

31 It takes countless men to hoist this robe to the top, hauling on ropes like sails on a mast.[1]

1 This refers to the new *peplos,* prepared every four years at the Panathenaia, for the statue of Athena in the Parthenon.

32 And a delicious undercut of tunny fish.

Brief fragment: (F 33) "the woman from Macedon."

MEDEA

The most famous dramatic representation of Medea is Euripides' great tragedy of 431, but we know also of versions by Neophron and Melanthius (the latter parodied at Peace 1013–14), and of a comedy by Cantharus (D-422?). Epicharmus' earlier Medea *is known only for its title. F 34 must be from Medea's instructions to a servant carrying not a poisoned robe, but a poisoned ointment. F 35 shows that, as in Euripides' play, Creon was a character, but the speakers are likely a pair of cheeky servants, rather than Medea herself.*

Fragments

34 And say that you [sing.] are bringing her a scented ointment, better than anything Megallus ever made, or Deinias of Egypt ever saw or owned.[1]

35 Athenaeus 467e

{A.} οἶσθ' ᾧ προσέοικεν, ὦ Κρέων, τὸ βρέγμα σου;
{B.} ἐγᾦδα· δίνῳ περικάτω τετραμμένῳ.

36 Harpocration p. 209.6

Μυσῶν λείαν

ΜΥΡΜΙΔΟΝΕΣ

35 (A) Do you know, Creon, what the front of your head looks like?

(B) I know, like a *dinos* jar turned upside down.[1]

1 K.-A. assign the fragment to one speaker only. I follow Meineke and Kaibel in giving the second line to a *bōmolochos* figure.

36 A raid by the Mysians.

MYRMIDONS

The Myrmidons were the soldiers who accompanied Achilles to Troy. In legend they came from a race of "ant-men," created by Zeus to repopulate a plague-stricken Aegina (Hesiod F 205, Ovid Metamorphoses *7.615–60; cf. Pherecrates'* Ant-Men*). Aeschylus wrote a celebrated tragedy with this name, recalled by Aristophanes at* Frogs *911–13, 1264, and Strattis' penchant for comedy with literary themes might suggest a paratragedy with this theme. Orth (175–76) reargues Breitenbach's conjecture (1908) that* Myrmidons *is an alternative title for* Cinesias.

Ingenious but unconvincing is Kock's argument that because Alcibiades' victorious troops in 410 kept themselves arrogantly apart from other forces in the Hellespont (Plutarch Alcibiades *29.1), they were called "Myrmidons" after Achilles' troops who had withdrawn from the Trojan conflict. Since F 37 refers to the iron coinage of Byzantium, successfully captured by Alcibiades in 410, the comedy would, on this explanation, have had a contemporary theme, Alcibiades' "Myrmidons" being the chorus of Strattis' comedy.*

Fragment

37 Pollux 9.78

ἐν τοῖς βαλανείοις προῖκ' ἐλοῦθ' ὁσημέραι
ἁπαξάπασα † γῆ στρατιαὶ σιδαρέων.

ΠΟΤΑΜΙΟΙ

Testimonium

i Σ Aristophanes *Wealth* 1194

ἀλλὰ γὰρ Στράττις πρὸ ἀμφοτέρων τούτων τοὺς Πο-
ταμίους διδάσκων.

Fragments

38 Σ Aristophanes *Wealth* 1194

ὑμεῖς τε πάντες ἔξιτ' ἐπὶ τὸ Πύθιον
ὅσοι πάρεστε, μὴ λαβόντες λαμπάδας
μηδ' ἄλλο μηδὲν ἐχόμενον Φιλυλλίου.

Fragment

37 Every day the entire army would get washed in the bathhouses freely . . . with the payment of iron coins.

POTAMIANS

There were two Athenian demes with this name, the Upper and Lower Potamians. A plural title should designate the chorus, and if so, this would have been a deme comedy with a distinctive group as the chorus—cf. Acharnians and Eupolis' Prospaltians. Harpocration (p. 255.7) and Hesychius (δ 2415) record that the Potamians "were made fun of as readily accepting illegally registered men." The scholiast to Wealth 1194 (quoting F 38) dates the play before Assembly-Women and Wealth. A date in the 390s seems indicated.

Testimonium

i But Strattis, producing his *Potamians* before both of these plays [*Assembly-Women, Wealth*].

Fragments

38 All of you here present, go away, off to the shrine of Pythian Apollo, taking no lamps or anything else that belongs to Philyllius.[1]

[1] The shrine of Pythian Apollo was located to the southeast of the Acropolis, between the Temple of Olympian Zeus and the Ilissus River. It was one of the building projects of the tyrants (Thucydides 6.54).

39 Σ Plato *Euthydemus* 298c

οὐ λίνον λίνῳ συνάπτεις.

40 Athenaeus 299b

ἐγχέλεων ἀνεψιός

ΠΥΤΙΣΟΣ

Fragment

41 Σ Aristophanes *Wasps* 1346a

† ἐγῶδα τοὐπίνικος ὀργισθεὶς ἔφη,
τῷ στόματι δράσω τοῦθ᾽ ὅπερ

ΤΡΩΙΛΟΣ

39 You [sing.] don't tie linen thread to linen thread.[1]

[1] "To tie linen thread to linen thread" was a proverb for always doing the same thing.

40 First cousin to the eels.

PYTISUS (?)

The scholiast to Wasps *1346, commenting on the use of* lesbiazein *("to suck off"), cites the mention of the people of Lesbos at Theopompus F 36 and Strattis F 42 and contin- ues "and in* Pytisos"—*F 41 follows. None of the known titles for Strattis suggests itself as a convenient emenda- tion—Dindorf proposed* Cinesias *and* Pausanias. *Options are to posit an otherwise unknown play title by Strattis, emend the title to a known play by Strattis, assume that the scholiast has omitted the real name of the poet (from Cra- tinus'* Pytine?), *or take "in Pytisos" as part of the quotation (reading* ἦν δὲ πυτίσω *"and if I spit out"), thus continuing the citation from Strattis'* Troilus.

Fragment

41 "I know" . . . he said in anger. "I will do with my mouth what ‹the people of Lesbos do› (?)."

TROILUS

At Iliad *24.257 Priam mentions Troilus "who delighted in horses" as one more son whom "War has destroyed." In the art and literature of the Archaic period, Achilles is shown*

*on vases pursuing and killing a boy, rather than a young
warrior. Achilles is said to have ambushed Troilus at a
fountain house, while the latter was riding with his sister
Polyxena outside the city. Plautus (Bacchides 953–54) tells
of an oracular prediction that Troy would not fall if Troilus
reached the age of manhood. If an ancient tradition, it
would explain Achilles' brutal attack on a young boy. An-*

Fragments

42 Σ Aristophanes *Wasps* 1346a

ἦ μήποτ᾽, ὦ παῖ Ζηνός, ἐς ταὐτὸν μόλῃς,
ἀλλὰ παραδοὺς τοῖς Λεσβίοις χαίρειν ἔα.

43 Athenaeus 76e

   ἐρινὸν οὖν τιν᾽ αὐτῆς πλησίον
νενόηκας ὄντα;

ΦΙΛΟΚΤΗΤΗΣ

Fragments

44 Pollux 7.134

οὐδ᾽ ἐν κοπρίᾳ θησαυρὸν ἐκβεβλημένον

other tradition relates Achilles' anger and the brutality of his treatment of Troilus to his unreciprocated passion for the young Trojan prince. If Strattis knew and parodied this version, we may compare his treatment of a similar theme in Chrysippus. *The most obvious influence on Strattis' comedy would be Sophocles' tragedy* Troilus, *probably produced in 418.*

Fragments

42 May you never get together with her, O son of Zeus, but hand ⟨her⟩ over to the men of Lesbos and say good riddance.[1]

[1] Is the son of Zeus Apollo, and the woman Cassandra?

43 Have you ever noticed a wild fig tree close to it?

PHILOCTETES

Dion of Prusa 52 and 59 gives us details of the three versions of the story of Philoctetes by each of the great tragic poets, but plays with this title are known also for Philocles and Achaeus in the fifth century. Sophocles' play (409) would have been the most recent and perhaps the most suitable for parody by Strattis. The treasure of F 44 abandoned on a dung heap could be made to suit the case of Philoctetes.

Fragments

44 Nor a treasure thrown away on a dung heap.

45 Athenaeus 327e

κᾆτ᾽ εἰς ἀγορὰν ἐλθόντες ἁδροὺς
ὀψωνοῦσιν μεγάλους τε φάγρους
καὶ Κωπᾴδων ἁπαλῶν τεμάχη
στρογγυλοπλεύρων.

ΦΟΙΝΙΣΣΑΙ

Fragments

46 P. Oxy. 2742

Διόνυσος ὃς θύρσοισιν † αὐληταὶ δει·λ
κω[. . .] ἐνέχομαι δι᾽ ἑτέρων μοχθ[ηρ]ίαν
ἥκω κρεμάμενος ὥσπερ ἰσχὰς ἐπὶ κράδης

47 Athenaeus 160b

παραινέσαι δὲ σφῷν τι βούλομαι σοφόν·
ὅταν φακῆν ἕψητε, μὴ ᾽πιχεῖν μύρον.

---

[1] "Perfume on lentils" was a proverbial expression for an incongruous pairing.

45 And then they come into the marketplace and buy large juicy sea bream and slices of tender round-sided Copaic eels.

PHOENICIAN WOMEN

The tragic original of this comedy was clearly Euripides' extant tragedy, dated to 410–408. F 47.1 corresponds word for word with Euripides' Phoenician Women 460, for which Athenaeus (160b) confirms that the comic speaker was also Jocasta. Here Strattis replaces her serious appeal to her two sons to resolve their differences with a piece of comic culinary advice. In F 48 Strattis turns Jocasta's analogy (PW 546) of Night and Day to an anecdote about a child's game. But Strattis does considerably more with his Euripidean original. F 46 is spoken by Dionysus, who has no role in PW, but who enters metatheatrically on the mēchanē, parodying the opening of Euripides' Hypsipyle (F 752). F 49 has an Athenian criticising Thebans for their linguistic peculiarities. Even if spoken in the mythological context, it does have the effect of jerking the play into the modern world

Fragments

46 I am Dionysus, involved with thyrsuses, *aulos* players, and revelries (?). Here I am, trapped by the wickedness of others, hanging on a branch like a fig.

47 (JOCASTE) I wish to give the pair of you sound advice: when you are boiling lentil soup, don't pour in any perfume.[1]

259

48 Pollux 9.123

εἶθ' ἥλιος μὲν πείθεται τοῖς παιδίοις
ὅταν λέγωσιν "ἔξεχ' ὦ φίλ' ἥλιε."

49 Athenaeus 621f

ξυνίετ' οὐδὲν πᾶσα Θηβαίων πόλις·
οὐδέν ποτ' ἄλλ'. οἱ πρῶτα μὲν τὴν σηπίαν
ὀπιτθοτίλαν, ὡς λέγουσ', ὀνομάζετε,
τὸν ἀλεκτρυόνα δ' † ὀρτάλιχον, τὸν ἰατρὸν δὲ †
5 σάκταν, βέφυραν τὴν γέφυραν, τῦκα δὲ
τὰ σῦκα, κωτιλάδας δὲ τὰς χελιδόνας,
τὴν ἔνθεσιν δ' ἄκολον, τὸ γελᾶν δὲ κριδδέμεν,
νεασπάτωτον δ', ἤν τι νεοκάττυτον ᾖ.

50 Orus *On Orthography* fol. 282ᵛ 3

ἐγὼ γὰρ αὐτὸν παρατραγῳδῆσαί τι μοι

51 Pollux 10.183

– ∪ οὐδὲ σχοινί' οὐδὲ στραγγαλίδες εἰσί ∪ –

ΧΡΥΣΙΠΠΟΣ

48 And so the sun listens to the little children when they say, "Come out, dear Sun."

49 You the entire city of Thebes, understand nothing, nothing at all. First, as they tell me, you call the cuttlefish a "rear-squirter," the rooster a "chicken," the doctor a "bagman"; for "bridge" you say "gridge," "tigs" for "figs," and for swallows "twitterers." You call a morsel of food "a bite," and for to laugh you say "to screech." If something is newly stitched, it is "new-leathered."

50 For I ⟨asked?⟩ him to do some paratragedy for me.

51 They are not ropes or binding cords.

Brief fragments: (F 52) "snake's slough," (F 53) "torch."

CHRYSIPPUS

Strattis very likely based his comedy on Euripides' late play, Chrysippus, *which dramatised the ill-fated passion of Laius for Chrysippus, the young son of Pelops. In myth Chrysippus, abducted by Laius, kills himself (or is killed) because of the shame incurred. Both fragments below could be applied to the young Chrysippus, the first portraying the boy as heavily overprotected by his father and the latter as a young colt. In myth Laius abducted Chrysippus ("golden horse") in a horse-drawn chariot, and in early poetry the image of the young beloved as a colt or filly is well documented (Anacreon F 72, Theognis 1249–52, 1267–70, Hippolytus 545).*

Fragments

54 Athenaeus 169a

εἰ μηδὲ χέσαι γ᾽ αὐτῷ σχολὴ γενήσεται,
μηδ᾽ εἰς ἀσωτεῖον τραπέσθαι, μηδ᾽ ἐὰν
αὐτῷ ξυναντᾷ τις, λαλῆσαι μηδενί.

55 Pollux 10.55

    πρόσαγε τὸν πῶλον ἀτρέμα, προσλαβὼν
τὸν ἀγωγέα βραχύτερον· οὐχ ὁρᾷς ὅτι
<ἔτ᾽> ἄβολος ἐστί;

ΨΥΧΑΣΤΑΙ

Testimonium

i Pseudo-Herodian *Philetaerus* 223

ψυχάσαι καὶ ἀναψῦξαι. καὶ Ψυχασταὶ δρᾶμα Στράτ-
τιδος, οἷον ἀναψύχοντες.

Fragments

54 If he won't even have the time to take a shit or visit a house of a man free with money or to even have a conversation with anyone he should meet.

55 Lead the colt gently, taking a shorter halter. Don't you [sing.] see that he ⟨still⟩ has his first teeth.

Brief fragment: (F 56) "butt cheeks."

CHILL-SEEKERS

The title suggests that the chorus was composed of men who spent their time avoiding the heat of the day by seeking a shady and breezy environment. For such unusual occupations we may compare the Dyers *of Eupolis, the* Broilers *of Aristophanes, or the* Poofters *of Cratinus. Orth (237) speculates that Strattis may be exaggerating some current theory in medicine or natural history. The only clue to dating the comedy is the mention of Sannyrion (F 57), who is a comic poet of the very late fifth century. F 62 may well describe a symposium where guests steal from their host—cf. Eupolis F 395 and Hermippus F 38. Are the chill-seekers professional spongers of the same sort as the* kolakes *in Eupolis?*

Testimonium

i "To relax in the shade and to cool off": also "chill-seekers," a play by Strattis, meaning "those who cool off."

THE POETS OF OLD COMEDY

Fragments

57 Athenaeus 551c

Σαννυρίωνος σκυτίνην ἐπικουρίαν

58 Pollux 10.100–101

πῶς ἂν κομίσειέ μοι τις <
> θυμαλώπων ὧδε μεστὴν ἐσχάραν;

59 Pollux 10.127

ῥιπίδα εἴτε σκιάδειον

60 Athenaeus 124c

οἶνον γὰρ πιεῖν
οὐδ᾽ ἂν εἷς δέξαιτο θερμόν, ἀλλὰ πολὺ τοὐναντίον
ψυχόμενον ἐν τῷ φρέατι <καὶ > χιόνι μεμιγμένον.

61 Athenaeus 373ef

αἱ δ᾽ ἀλεκτρυόνες ἅπασαι
καὶ τὰ χοιρίδια τέθνηκε
καὶ τὰ μίκρ᾽ ὀρνίθια.

Fragments

57 Sannyrion's leather helper.

58 How might someone provide for me . . . a pan so full of burning charcoal?

59 A fan or a parasol.

60 No one would accept warmed wine to drink, but just the opposite, cooled in the well and mixed with snow.

61 All the hens and piglets are dead, and the little chicks as well.

62 Athenaeus 502e

ὁ δέ τις ψυκτῆρ᾽, ὁ δέ τις κύαθον
χαλκοῦν κλέψας ἀπορῶν κεῖται,
  κοτύλη δ᾽ ἀνὰ χοίνικα μάττει.

3 μάττει codd., μετρεῖ Capps.

ΑΔΗΛΩΝ ΔΡΑΜΑΤΩΝ

63 Σ Euripides *Orestes* 279

{A.} γαλῆν᾽ ὁρῶ. {B.} ποῖ, πρὸς θεῶν, ποῖ ποῖ γαλῆν;
{A.} γαληνά. {B.} ἐγὼ δ᾽ ᾤμην σε "γαλῆν" λέγειν
  "ὁρῶ."

64 Athenaeus 30f

οἶνος κοχύζει τοῖς ὁδοιπόροις πιεῖν
μέλας Σκιάθιος, ἴσον ἴσῳ κεκραμένος.

65 Pollux 2.172–73

                    τὰ θυγάτρια
περὶ τὴν λεκάνην ἅπαντα περιπεπλιγμένα

66 Photius (b, z) α 1211

Ἀμμὼν ὁ κριοῦ δέρμα καὶ κέρατ᾽ ἔχων

62 One person stealing a wine cooler, another a bronze bowl and is left there with no idea of what to do, while the cup kneads by the *choinix*.[1]

[1] The sense is obscure, especially the third line which Olson thinks may be a proverb. Capps' proposed μετρεῖ certainly helps.

UNASSIGNED FRAGMENTS

63 (A) I see a ferret.
  (B) Where, by the gods, a ferret, where?
  (A) It's fair out.
  (B) I thought you said "I see a ferret."

64 Dark wine from Sciathus gushes out for travellers to drink, mixed in equal parts.

65 All his little daughters squatting round the basin.

66 Ammon with the hide and horns of a ram.

67 Pollux 3.146

ὥσπερ οἱ σταδιοδρόμοι προανίστασαι

68 Photius (b, Sᶻ) α 2169

ἀνωφέλητος καὶ θεοῖς ἐχθρός

69 Photius (b, z) α 2239

ἀπάλλαξόν με φροντίδων

70 Hesychius κ 3323

ποῦ ᾿στιν; οὐκ ἄξει τις ἔξω τὴν ἀποῦσαν μητέρα
τῶν διδύμων † κολέκαν λέγων †;

71 Athenaeus 69a

πρασοκουρίδες, αἱ καταφύλλους
ἀνὰ κήπους πεντήκοντα ποδῶν
ἴχνεσι βαίνετ᾽, ἐφαπτόμεναι
ποδοῖν σατυριδίων μακροκέρκων,
5 χοροὺς ἑλίσσουσαι παρ᾽ ὠκίμων
πέταλα καὶ θριδακινίδων
εὐόσμων τε σελίνων.

72 Hesychius β 978

βοῦς ἐμβαίη μέγας

67 Just as the runners in the stadium beat the start.

68 A useless man and hated by the gods.

69 Take my cares away.

70 Where is she? Will someone please bring out the absent (?) mother of the twins ... ?   [*Cinesias*?]

71 Leek bugs, who make your way through leafy gardens on tracks of fifty feet, clamping your feet onto little orchids with long stalks, winding your dances among the leaves of basil and lettuce and sweet-smelling celery.[1]

  [1] In l. 4 *satyridia* might mean "little satyrs with long tails," either actual revellers or garden statues.

72 May a large ox tread upon.

73 Σ Euripides *Hecuba* 467

ὅτι δὲ κρόκινός ἐστι καὶ ὑακίνθινος καὶ τοὺς Γίγαντας
ἐμπεποίκιλται, δηλοῖ Στράττις.

74 Zenobius 5.35

ὁ σκνὶψ ἐν χώρᾳ

75 Zenobius 3.139

γαλῆ χιτώνιον

73 Strattis makes it clear that it [the robe of Athena] was purple and yellow and embroidered with Giants.

74 The flea stays still.

75 Ferret and a short cloak.

Brief fragments: (F 76) "fishing net," (F 77) "lack of money," (F 78) "North Wind," (F 79) "you made a good defence," (F 80) "to play knuckle-bones," (F 81) "single-footedly," (F 82) "improviser," (F 83) "laughable," (F 84) "with her crotch exposed," (F 85) "dissimilar," (F 86) "to take out," (F 87) "baked," (F 88) "of the same plumage," (F 89) "stepdaughter," (F 90) "weevils."

ΣΟΤΣΑΡΙΩΝ

When Aristotle begins his account of the history of comedy at Poetics 1448a34, he names Chionides and Magnes as the earliest comic poets. Similarly the Suda reports that "they say Chionides was the first comic poet" (Chionides T 1). But a more anecdotal tradition claims Susarion as "the inventor of comedy," and an easy distinction could be made between Chionides the first poet to win at a state-sanctioned festival and Susarion, who wrote in the period when comedy was performed by "volunteers." This is certainly the line taken in the Glossary of Ansileubus (T 6), and by Norwood who sees Susarion as a "literary forerunner of comedy." Others have not been so sure of his existence at all—Körte, Pickard-Cambridge, and Breitholz all dismiss

Testimonia

i Marmor Parium 239 A 39

ἀφ᾽ οὗ ἐν ᾿Αθ[ήν]αις κωμῳ[δῶν χο]ρ[ὸς ἐτ]έθη, [στη]σάν[των πρώ]των ᾿Ικαριέων, εὑρόντος Σουσαρίωνος, καὶ ἆθλον ἐτέθη πρῶτον ἰσχάδω[ν] ἄρσιχο[ς] καὶ οἴνου με[τ]ρητής.

SUSARION

the ancient testimony as a fiction made up to connect Athenian comic drama from that shadowy entity known as Megarian comedy (see Wasps *54ff., Ecphantides F 3, Eupolis F 261, and Myrtilus F 1).*

The one alleged fragment (F 1) has been suspected for its second line, which seems to have been inserted to confirm a Megarian origin for its author, for its good Attic Greek with none of the Doricisms we would expect from a Megarian, and for its use of the dēmotai *(townsfolk). Aristotle (*Poetics *1448a36–37) cites those who see the etymology of comedy from* kōmē *(the Dorian word for "village," as opposed to the Attic* dēmos*). Women as a proverbial evil was a commonplace of early Greek poetry; see especially Semonides 1. It will recur as the underlying theme of* Thesmophoriazusae *786–99.*

Testimonia

i From the time when a chorus of comic players was instituted at Athens, the people of Icaria being first to do so, the inventor being Susarion, and a prize was established, at first a basket of figs and a quantity of wine.

273

ii Clement of Alexandria *Miscellanies* 1.79.1

ἴαμβον μὲν ἐπενόησεν Ἀρχίλοχος ὁ Πάριος, χωλὸν
δὲ ἴαμβον Ἱππῶναξ ὁ Ἐφέσιος, καὶ τραγῳδίαν μὲν
Θέσπις ὁ Ἀθηναῖος, κωμῳδίαν δὲ Σουσαρίων ὁ Ἰκα-
ριεύς.

iii Anonymous *On Comedy* (Koster III.1)

τὴν κωμῳδίαν ηὑρῆσθαί φασιν ὑπὸ Σουσαρίωνος.

iv Anonymous *On Comedy* (Koster V)

τῆς κωμῳδίας τὸ μέν ἐστιν ἀρχαῖον, τὸ δὲ νέον, τὸ δὲ
μέσον . . . καὶ αὐτὴ δὲ ἡ παλαιὰ ἑαυτῆς διαφέρει. καὶ
γὰρ οἱ ἐν Ἀττικῇ πρῶτον συστησάμενοι τὸ ἐπιτήδευ-
μα τῆς κωμῳδίας—ἦσαν δὲ οἱ περὶ Σαννυρίωνα[1]—καὶ
τὰ πρόσωπα εἰσῆγον ἀτάκτως, καὶ μόνος ἦν γέλως
τὸ κατασκευαζόμενον.

---

[1] Σαννυρίωνα is clearly an error for Σουσαρίωνα.

v Diomedes *Art of Grammar* (Koster XXIV 2.46)

poetae primi comici fuerunt Susarion, Mullus et Magnes.
hi veteris disciplinae iocularia quaedam minus scite ac
venuste pronuntiabant.

vi *The Glossary of Ansileubus* (Koster XXVII.3.8–13)

sed prior ac vetus comoedia ridicularis extitit; postea civi-

ii Archilochus of Paros developed the iambus, Hipponax of Ephesus the limping iamb, Thespis of Athens tragedy, Susarion of Icaria comedy.

iii They say that comedy was invented by Susarion.

iv There is Old Comedy, New Comedy, and Middle Comedy . . . Old Comedy has differences within itself. For those at Athens who first put together the business of comedy—these were Susarion and his people—would bring characters on haphazardly and the humour lay in the performance.

v The first comic poets were Susarion, Myllus, and Magnes. They were of the old style and delivered their jokes rather less skilfully and elegantly.

vi But Old Comedy first began as something silly, but

les vel privates adgressa materias in dictis atque gestu
universorum delicta corripiens in scaenam proferebat,
nec vetabatur poetae pessimum quemque describere vel
cuiuslibet peccata moresque reprehendere. auctor eius
Susarion traditur; sed in fabulas primi eam contulerunt
Magnes *** ita, ut non excederent in singulis versus tre-
centos.

vii John the Deacon on Hermogenes *On the Method of
Force* (Koster XIXa.3–18)

μετὰ γοῦν τὸν ἀνήμερον βίον μεταβολῆς ἐπὶ τὸ βέλ-
τιον γενομένης ἀπαλλαγέντες οἱ ἄνθρωποι τῆς βαλα-
νοφαγίας καὶ ἐπὶ γεωργίαν τραπόμενοι ἀπαρχὴν τῶν
γινομένων καρπῶν τοῖς θεοῖς ἀνετίθεντο, ἡμέρας
αὐτοῖς εἰς πανηγύρεις καὶ ἑορτὰς ἀπονείμαντες· καὶ ἐν
ταύταις ἄνδρες σοφοὶ τὸ τῆς ἀνέσεως ἄλογον ἐπι-
κόπτοντες καὶ βουλόμενοι τὰς πανηγύρεις λογικῆς
παιδιᾶς μετέχειν τὴν κωμῳδίαν ἐφεῦρον, ἧς λόγος
πρῶτον κατάρξαι τὸν Σουσαρίωνα ἔμμετρον αὐτὴν
συστησάμενον. ἐνστῆναι μὲν γὰρ κατὰ τὸ σύνηθες τὰ
Διονύσια, ἐν τούτῳ δὲ τῷ καίρῳ τὴν γυναῖκα τούτου
μεταλλάξαι τὸν βίον· καὶ τοὺς μὲν θεατὰς ἐπιζητεῖν
αὐτὸν ὡς πρὸς τὰς τοιαύτας ἐπιδείξεις εὐφυᾶ, τὸν δὲ
παρελθόντα λέγειν τὴν αἰτίαν καὶ ἀπολογούμενον
εἰπεῖν ταῦτα . . . καὶ εἰπόντος τάδε εὐδοκιμῆσαι παρὰ
τοῖς ἀκούουσι.

later moved on to public and private themes in word and deed, and seizing upon the shortcomings of everybody would bring them on stage as his subjects. A poet was not forbidden to portray anyone in a very bad light or to find fault with the misdeeds or character of anybody he wanted. The founder of this is said to be Susarion, but Magnes ⟨and . . . ⟩ were the first ⟨to put it⟩ into dramatic form, such that they did not exceed three hundred lines at a time.

vii At any rate after a life of savagery a change for the better took place and men abandoned a life of gathering and turned to farming. They began to dedicate a portion of their harvests to the gods, determining certain occasions as all-night festivals and celebrations for them. On these occasions some clever individuals, finding fault with the irrational abandon and wanting the festivals to possess some ordered fun, invented comedy. The story is that the first person to put this into a metrical form was Susarion. The Dionysia was happening at its usual time, and at that time Susarion's wife had died, and when the spectators were expecting him because he was clever at such performances, and he came forward and explained the circumstances and said the following as an explanation [F 1] . . . and when he had said this, he was well received by the audience.

THE POETS OF OLD COMEDY

(a) Tzetzes *Proem* (Koster XIa I.78)

τῆς οὖν κωμῳδίας τῆς καλουμένης πρώτης πρῶτος καὶ
εὑρετὴς γέγονεν ὁ Μεγαρεὺς Σουσαρίων ὁ Τριπο-
δίσκιος, υἱὸς ὢν Φιλίννου, ὃς φαύλῃ γυναικὶ συνοικῶν
ἀπολιπούσῃ αὐτὸν Διονυσίων ἠγμένων εἰσελθὼν εἰς
τὸ θέατρον τὰ τέσσαρα ἰαμβεῖα ταυτὶ ἀνεφθέγξατο, ἃ
μόνα τῶν ἐκείνου συγγραμμάτων ἐφεύρηνται τῶν ἄλ-
λων ἁπάντων ἠφανισμένων·

(b) Tzetzes *Distinctions among Poets* (Koster XXIa 80)

πρώτης μὲν ἦν ἴδιον ἐμφανὲς ψόγος,
ἧς ἦν κατάρξας εὑρετὴς Σουσαρίων.

ix Σ Tzetzes *Distinctions among Poets* 81.

Σουσαρίων οὗτος ὁ κωμικὸς φαύλης τῆς γυναικὸς
τούτου φανείσης καὶ τοῦτον ἀπολειπούσης εἰσελθὼν
ἐν τῷ θεάτρῳ ἐφθέγξατο ταδί· . . . ἰστέον δὲ, ὡς τῶν
Σουσαρίωνος τούτου ποιημάτων μόνα ταῦτα κατ-
ελείφθη τὰ τέσσαρα ἰαμβεῖα· ἡ δὲ λέξις ἡ λέγουσα
"Τριποδίσκος" τοῦ, φησίν, ἀπὸ πόλεως Τριποδίσκης,
μιᾶς τῶν Μεγαρικῶν πόλεων.

viii

(a) The man who first practised and invented what is called "First Comedy" was a Megarian, Susarion of Tripodisce, the son of Philinnus. He was living with a worthless woman who had left him, and at the time that the Dionysia was being held, so he went into the theatre and uttered these four iambic lines, which are the only extant lines of his, all the rest having disappeared [F 1].

(b) Direct insult was characteristic of First ‹Comedy›; the man who originated it was its inventor Susarion.

ix The wife of this Susarion, the comic poet, was known to be a worthless woman who left him, so he went into the theatre and uttered the following [F 1] . . . It must be understood that these four iambic lines are all that is left of Susarion's works. The reference to being a Tripodiscian is from the town of Tripodisce, one of the communities of Megara.

(a) Σ Dionysius Thrax (Koster XVIIIa 19–25)

πρῶτος οὖν Σουσαρίων τις τῆς ἐμμέτρου κωμῳδίας
ἀρχηγὸς ἐγένετο, οὗ τὰ μὲν δράματα λήθη κατέλαβε,
δύο δὲ ἢ τρεῖς ἴαμβοι τοῦ πρώτου δράματος αὐτοῦ ἐπὶ
μνήμῃ φέρονται· εἰσὶ δὲ οὗτοι

(b) Σ Dionysius Thrax (Koster XVIIIb 3.12–14)

καὶ εὑρέθη ἡ μὲν τραγῳδία ὑπὸ Θέσπιδός τινος Ἀθη-
ναίου, ἡ δὲ κωμῳδία ὑπὸ Ἐπιχάρμου ἐν Σικελίᾳ, καὶ ὁ
ἴαμβος ὑπὸ Σουσαρίωνος.

(c) Σ Dionysius Thrax *GrGr* I 3 p. 306.9

ἄρξασθαι δὲ αὐτῆς Ἀριστοτέλης Σουσαρίωνά φησι.

xi Anonymous commentator on Aristotle's *Nicomachean
Ethics* 4.6

διασύρονται γὰρ οἱ Μεγαρεῖς ἐν κωμῳδίᾳ, ἐπεὶ καὶ
ἀντιποιοῦνται αὐτῆς ὡς παρ᾽ αὐτοῖς πρῶτον εὑρεθεί-
σης, εἴ γε καὶ Σουσαρίων ὁ κατάρξας κωμῳδίας
Μεγαρεύς.

xii Marius Plotius Sacerdos *Art of Grammar* III.11

compositum susarionium fit quattuor pedibus trochaicis
praepositis et suniuncto penthemimero dactylico.

x

(a) A certain Susarion was the first creator of comedy in verse form. His plays are lost in oblivion, but two or three iambic lines from his first play are preserved, which are [F 1].

(b) Tragedy was invented by a certain Thespis of Athens, comedy by Epicharmus in Sicily and iambic by Susarion.

(c) Aristotle says that it [tragedy] was created by Susarion.

xi The Megarians are made fun of in comedy, since they claim that it was first invented among their people, because Susarion, the man who invented comedy, was from Megara.

xii The Susarionian is made up of four trochaic feet and a dactylic penthemimer.

xiii Libanius *Letters* 355 (Courtonne)

πάτερ, οὐκ ἐδίδαξας· Ὅμηρος οὗτος ἀνήρ, ἀλλὰ Πλά-
των, ἀλλ᾽ Ἀριστοτέλης, ἀλλὰ Σουσαρίων ὁ τὰ πάντα
ἐπιστάμενος.

Fragment

1 Stobaeus 4.22c.68–69 [ll. 1, 3–5], John the Deacon [T 7,
ll. 1–4]

ἀκούετε λεώ· Σουσαρίων λέγει τάδε,
υἱὸς Φιλίνου Μεγαρόθεν Τριποδίσκιος.
κακὸν γυναῖκες· ἀλλ᾽ ὅμως, ὦ δημόται,
οὐκ ἔστιν οἰκεῖν οἰκίαν ἄνευ κακοῦ.
5 καὶ γὰρ τὸ γῆμαι καὶ τὸ μὴ γῆμαι κακόν.

xiii "Father, you never taught me ‹this›. That man over there, it's Homer; so too for Plato, for Aristotle, for Susarion who understands everything."

Fragment

1 Listen, people, Susarion has this to say, the son of Philinus, from Tripodisce in Megara: women are a bad thing, but nevertheless, my townsfolk, you cannot have a home without a bad thing. Both to marry and not to marry is a bad thing.

ΤΕΛΕΚΛΕΙΔΗΣ

We are particularly poorly informed about Teleclides. Athenaeus (T 1) names only three comedies, although he does cite from Hesiods elsewhere, while the Roman inscription (T 5) gives two new titles, one beginning in Symp– and the other ending in –iōtai, for which Stratiōtai (Soldiers) or Nesiōtai (Islanders) or Sikeliōtai (Men of Sicily) have been suggested. T 2 gives him a total of seven plays, but the lists (T 3, 4) record the impressive total of eight victories, suggesting a rather higher number of comedies for him. That his authorship was doubted in some cases (see F 12, 58) and that the Roman inscription (T 5) includes the description "extant" shows that the ancients had lost considerable knowledge about Teleclides' works.

Teleclides, with his eight victories, was a part of that successful generation of comic poets immediately preceding the advent of Aristophanes and Eupolis. His career probably dates back to the late 440s and runs into the early 420s, since F 44 mentions Nicias, whose political career seems to have begun after the death of Pericles (see Plutarch Nicias 2). If Nicias' four minas (F 44) have anything to do with his passing of the generalship on to Cleon in 425, then Teleclides' play belongs in the late 420s. But Plutarch, who cites the fragment, is not reporting it in the context of Pylos. Some have seen the man coming from Aegina "with a

TELECLIDES

face like a boil" (F 46) as Aristophanes; if so, this too would indicate a date for a play after 427. On the Roman inscription (T 5) epa– in line 1 might indicate the archonship of Epameinon (429/8) and in line 3 "–pi Eud–" has been restored as "epi Eu⟨thy⟩dēmou" (in the archonship of Euthydemus [431/0]). If in line 5 "an–" is correctly supplemented as "anedidaxe" (re-performed), then Rigid Ones was staged on a second occasion. F 44 refers also to Charicles, a politician of the 410s and 400s, and might suggest at least one comedy by him in the 410s.

The fragments show a poet very much in the style and manner of Aristophanes. Of the seventy-three fragments nearly twenty contain personal jokes, some in the familiar political style. F 45 and 47 made fun of Pericles, the latter fastening on his distinctive head. Like Aristophanes, Teleclides found other dramatists a source of humour. F 41–42 turn on the alleged link between Euripides and Socrates (cf. Aristophanes F 392), and if the chervil reference in F 40 is to Euripides and his mother, Aristophanes may not have been the one to have pioneered that joke. The text of F 15 is corrupt but enough survives to show that a female speaker has a fault to find with Philocles, the tragic poet and nephew of Aeschylus. Other poets who caught Teleclides' attention were Nothippus (F 17) and Gnesippus

285

Testimonia

i *Suda* τ 488

Τηλεκλείδης, Ἀθηναῖος, κωμικός. τῶν δραμάτων αὐτοῦ ἐστιν Ἀμφικτύονες καὶ Πρυτάνεις καὶ Στερροί· ὡς Ἀθήναιος λέγει ἐν τοῖς Δειπνοσοφισταῖς.

ii *The Names and Plays of the Poets of Old Comedy* (Koster VIII)

Τηλεκλείδου δράματα ϛ´

iii *IG* ii² 2325.54

Τηλεκλείδ]ης III

iv *IG* ii² 2325.119

Τηλεκλείδης Π

(F 36), and we should not miss the implications of the title Hesiods. *He does not seem to have written the mythological burlesque popular with Cratinus and Hermippus, and while F 1 is a striking expression of the ideal existence, the setting seems to be the modern world, the speaker describing the "life I used to provide."*

Recent bibliography: R. Pietro, GFF *12 (1989) 23–26.*

Testimonia

i Teleclides: of Athens, comic poet. His plays are *Amphictyons* and *Magistrates* and *Rigid Ones,* as Athenaeus says in *The Learned Banqueters.*

ii Plays of Teleclides, 6.

iii [From the list of victors at the Dionysia, from the late 440s or early 430s]

Telecli]des 3

iv [From the list of victors at the Lenaea, c. 440]

Teleclides 5

v *IG Urb. Rom.* 215

```
- - - - - - - - ]επα[- - - - - - - -
- - - - - - - - ]Συμπ[- - - - - - - -
- - - - - - ἐ]πὶ Εὐδ[- - - - - -
- - - - - - ]αι Λήναια[- - - - - -
```
5
```
- - - - Στε]ρροὺς ἀν[εδίδαξε- - - -
- - - - - - ]τέταρτος [- - - - - -
- - - - ῾Ησ]ιόδοις σῴ[ῳ- - - -
- - - - - - ]ιώταις
```

Fragments

ΑΜΦΙΚΤΥΟΝΕΣ

In the classical period "amphictyons" was a technical term for delegates to a league of neighbouring states, most notably that based at Delphi in central Greece, but it can in poetry mean "neighbours," although geitones *would be the usual word in Attic comedy. It is possible that the title denotes a group of such league delegates. More likely it is an allusion to an early king of Attica, Amphictyon son of Deucalion who survived the Flood and was a character in Pherecrates'* Ant-Men. *Thus the title might mean "Amphictyon and his followers." He has been suggested as the speaker of F 1, although he is a shadowy figure in myth and why he should have been the one to provide an ideal life is not clear. Others have suggested Deucalion himself, Dionysus whom Philochorus (*FGrHist *328 F) records as hav-*

v [From a Roman inscription listing the results for a comic poet]

>] in the archonship of A[[1]
>] *Symp*[
>] in the archonship of Eud[
>] at the Lenaea [
>] he re-performed (?) the *Rigid Ones* [
>] fourth place [
>] with *Hesiods*, extant [
>] with . . . *–ers* [

[1] Or "in the archonship of] Epa[meinon," that is 429/8.

Fragments

AMPHICTYONS

ing come to Attica and taught Amphictyon how to mix wine), or Cronus. There was perhaps some connection with Cratinus' Wealth-Gods, where figures from the mythical past come to Athens in the present day.

Diopeithes, mentioned as a "crazy" political figure in F 7, is known to have been active from the late 430s until 390s, but particularly for a decree aimed at "those who do believe in the divine or who teach about celestial objects" (Plutarch Pericles 32.2). As this was an attack on Pericles through his friend Anaxagoras, the decree (and the comedy) should be dated to the late 430s.

Recent bibliography: I. Ruffell, in Rivals *473–506; M. Pellegrino (*Utopie*) 71–84; Olson 75–76, 101–3, 427–28.*

THE POETS OF OLD COMEDY

1 Athenaeus 268a–d

λέξω τοίνυν βίον ἐξ ἀρχῆς ὃν ἐγὼ θνητοῖσι
  παρεῖχον.
εἰρήνη μὲν πρῶτον ἁπάντων ἦν ὥσπερ ὕδωρ κατὰ
  χειρός.
ἡ γῆ δ᾽ ἔφερ᾽ οὐ δέος οὐδὲ νόσους, ἀλλ᾽ αὐτόματ᾽
  ἦν τὰ δέοντα·
οἴνῳ γὰρ ἅπασ᾽ ἔρρει χαράδρα, μᾶζαι δ᾽ ἄρτοις
  ἐμάχοντο
5 περὶ τοῖς στόμασιν τῶν ἀνθρώπων ἱκετεύουσαι
  καταπίνειν,
εἴ τι φιλοῖεν, τὰς λευκοτάτας. οἱ δ᾽ ἰχθύες οἴκαδ᾽
  ἰόντες
ἐξοπτῶντες σφᾶς αὐτοὺς ἂν παρέκειντ᾽ ἐπὶ ταῖσι
  τραπέζαις.
ζωμοῦ δ᾽ ἔρρει παρὰ τὰς κλίνας ποταμὸς κρέα
  θερμὰ κυλίνδων,
ὑποτριμμάτων δ᾽ ὀχετοὶ τούτων τοῖς βουλομένοισι
  παρῆσαν,
10 ὥστ᾽ ἀφθονία τὴν ἔνθεσιν ἦν ἄρδονθ᾽ ἁπαλὴν
  καταπίνειν.
λεκανίσκαισιν δ᾽ † ἀνάπαιστα † παρῆν ἡδυσματίοις
  κατάπαστα.
ὀπταὶ δὲ κίχλαι μετ᾽ ἀμητίσκων εἰς τὸν φάρυγ᾽
  εἰσεπέτοντο·
τῶν δὲ πλακούντων ὠστιζομένων περὶ τὴν γνάθον
  ἦν ἀλαλητός.

1 So then I shall describe the sort of life that I provided for mankind in the days of old. First of all, there was peace, as ready to hand as water for washing. The earth produced nothing fearful, no diseases, and everything you needed came of its own accord. Every creek bed flowed with wine, barley loaves would fight with wheat breads about the lips of men begging them to gulp down the whitest loaves, if you please. Fish would come into your house, grill themselves, and then lie down on your tables. A river of broth flowed by the couches, carrying pieces of hot meat, while channels of sauces were there for those who wanted any— and no one would object when you dipped your morsel 'til it was soft and gulped it down. On side plates there were . . . (?) sprinkled with seasonings.[1] Roasted thrushes with pastry would fly down your gullet, while about your jaws the jostling flat-buns made quite a din. Boys would

---

[1] The reading in A, ἀνάπαιστα (anapaests), makes no sense. Suggestions include Dindorf's ἀνάβραστα (roasted), Meineke's ἂν ψαιστὰ (honey cakes), and Casaubon's ἀλίπαστα (salt-dusted).

μήτρας δὲ τόμοις καὶ χναυματίοις οἱ παῖδες ἂν
   ἠστραγάλιζον.
15 οἱ δ᾽ ἄνθρωποι πίονες ἦσαν τότε καὶ μέγα χρῆμα
   γιγάντων.

2 Photius p. 504.25

ἀλλ᾽ ὦ πάντων ἀστῶν λῷστοι σεῖσαι καὶ
   προσκαλέσασθαι,
παύσασθε δικῶν ἀλληλοφάγων.

3 Pollux 10.164

δουλοπόνηρον ῥυπαρὸν σκόλυθρον

4 Athenaeus 82b

ὦ τὰ μὲν κομψοί, τὰ δὲ φαυλότεροι
φαυλίων μήλων.

5 Photius (b, z) α 2025

ἀνακλαύσομαί τε μεγάλα κἀνοιμώξομαι.

6 Athenaeus 75c

ὡς καλοὶ καὶ φιβάλεῳ

7 Σ Aristophanes *Birds* 988

Σύμμαχος· ὅτι Διοπείθης ὁ ῥήτωρ ὑπομανιώδης ἦν,
ὡς Τελεκλείδης ἐν Ἀμφικτύοσι δῆλον ποιεῖ.

be playing knuckle-bones with slices of sow's womb and scraps of meat. Men of that time were fat, the stuff of giants.

2 O best of all citizens at shakedowns and lawsuits, stop your legal actions that devour one another.

3 Slave-poor, filthy, shabby.

4 You people so clever in some things, and in others inferior to crab apples.

5 I shall give out a great shout and wail of lamentation.

6 How fine and Phibalean.

7 Symmachus ⟨says⟩ that Diopeithes the politician was crazy, as Teleclides makes clear in *Amphictyons*.

8 Athenaeus 619a

καὶ τῶν μισθωτῶν δέ τις ἦν ᾠδὴ τῶν ἐς τοὺς ἀγροὺς φοιτώντων, ὡς Τηλεκλείδης φησὶν ἐν Ἀμφικτύοσιν.

ΑΨΕΥΔΕΙΣ

11 Pollux 10.98

τὰ δὲ τήγανα ζέοντά σοι μολύνεται.

12 Σ Aristophanes *Wasps* 506c

ζῆν βίον γενναῖον· πρὸς τοὺς τοὺς Ἀψευδεῖς ποιήσαντας, ὅτι τὸν Μόρυχον τῶν πολιτικῶν †πεποίηκε πραγμάτων† ἀγνοήσαντες, ὅτι τρυφερὸς καὶ ἡδύβιος κωμῳδεῖται· ἢ καὶ νῦν ἐν εἰρωνείᾳ.

TELECLIDES

8 There was also a song of the hired men going off to the fields, as Teleclides says in *Amphictyons*.

Brief fragments: (F 9) "Ichthyon" [proper name], (F 10) "homemade wine."

TRUTH-TELLERS

The scholiast who cites F 12 seems not to know the author-ship of Truth-Tellers *(not mentioned by Athenaeus [T 1]), but Pollux appears to have had no problem with assigning it to Teleclides. As the word* apseudēs *is usually applied to oracles and seers, we might imagine a chorus of ever-accurate seers. At Euripides* Suppliant Women *869, how-ever, it is applied to the "ever-truthful character" of one of the Seven. The comedy would then turn on men who were never wrong or could not tell a lie.*

11 Your frying pans are getting stained with boiling.

12 "To live the good life ⟨like Morychus⟩": against those who wrote *Truth-Tellers* because he has made Morychus ⟨take part⟩ in politics, not realizing that he is made fun of as a luxurious lover of the sweet life. Or in irony.

Brief fragments: (F 13) "mouth to mouth" [type of kiss], (F 14) "plucked" [type of kiss].

ΗΣΙΟΔΟΙ

Cratinus' Archilochuses, if in fact the earlier play, may have been the model for Teleclides' Hesiods. The title could mean "Hesiod and his friends or followers" or "poets like Hesiod." Three of the fragments contain allusions to other poets (F 15—Philocles; F 17—Nothippus; F 18—Ion of Chios), suggesting that it was a comedy with a literary or poetic theme, perhaps with a contest between rival poets.

15 Σ Aristophanes *Thesmophoriazusae* 168

ἀλλ' ἡ τάλαινα Φιλοκλέα † βδελλ ...... οθεν οὖν †·
εἰ δ' ἐστὶν Αἰσχύλου φρόνημ' ἔχων.

16 Σ Aristophanes *Wasps* 1187a

Ἀνδροκλέα δὲ Κρατῖνος Σεριφίοις φησὶ δοῦλον καὶ
πτωχόν, ἐν δὲ Ὥραις ἡταιρηκότα, <εἰ> ἄρα τὸν αὐτόν·
Τηλεκλείδης δὲ ἐν Ἡσιόδοις καὶ Ἐκφαντίδης βαλ-
λαντιοτόμον.

17 Athenaeus 344d

ὅτι δὲ οὗτός ἐστιν ὁ ποιητὴς σαφῶς παρίστησι Τη-
λεκλείδης ἐν Ἡσιόδοις.

HESIODS

Is the speaker of F 15 a Muse or Poetry or Tragedy? F 18
mentions Pericles' love for Chrysilla of Corinth, imply-
ing (but not conclusively so) that the comedy was writ-
ten during the lifetime of Pericles. Other kōmōidoumenoi
(Philocles, Nothippus, Androcles) would belong easily in a
comedy of the 430s. Only Proxenides (F 19) seems to be a
later comic target, mentioned at Wasps *325–26 and* Birds
1126.

15 Oh I [fem.] am wretched, Philocles makes me sick (?),
even if he does have the mind of Aeschylus.

16 Androcles: Cratinus in *Men of Seriphus* [F 223] says
that he was a slave and a beggar, and in *Seasons* [F 281]
that he was a sexual pervert, if in fact ⟨he means⟩ the same
man. Teleclides in *Hesiods* and Ecphantides [F 5] ⟨call
him⟩ a pickpocket.

17 Teleclides in *Hesiods* shows clearly that this man
[Nothippus] was a poet.[1]

   [1] A tragic poet (*TrGF* 26).

18 Athenaeus 436f

Βάτων δ' ὁ Σινωπεὺς ἐν τοῖς περὶ Ἴωνος τοῦ ποιητοῦ
φιλοπότην φησὶ γενέσθαι καὶ ἐρωτικώτατον τὸν
Ἴωνα. καὶ αὐτὸς δὲ ἐν τοῖς ἐλεγείοις ἐρᾶν μὲν ὁμο-
λογεῖ Χρυσίλλης τῆς Κορινθίας, Τελέου δὲ θυγατρός·
ἧς καὶ Περικλέα τὸν Ὀλύμπιον ἐρᾶν φησι Τηλεκλεί-
δης ἐν Ἡσιόδοις.

19 Σ Aristophanes *Birds* 1126

Τηλεκλείδης δὲ ἐν Ἡσιόδοις ὡς παρειμένον τῷ σώ-
ματι κωμῳδεῖ αὐτόν.

20 Athenaeus 87a

κόγχῃ διελεῖν

ΝΗΣ]ΙΩΤΑΙ

ΠΡΥΤΑΝΕΙΣ

The Athenian boulē *(Council) consisted of fifty members
from each of the ten tribes of Athens. Each group was in
charge of the Council for one month; when in office these
were the* prytaneis *(magistrates). They are mentioned sev-
eral times in the parody of the assembly in the opening
scene of* Acharnians, *perhaps as a visible entity, but Aris-
tophanes probably had his actor refer to the actual magis-
trates seated separately in the* theatron. *At* Knights 624–82

18 Baton of Sinope says in his work on the poet Ion [F 6] that Ion was fond of drinking and a very amorous man. He himself in his elegiac poems [F 31 West] admits that he was in love with Chrysilla of Corinth, the daughter of Teleas, with whom Teleclides in *Hesiods* says that Pericles the Olympian was in love.

19 Teleclides makes fun of him [Proxenides] in his *Hesiods* as neglectful of his body.

20 To break open a mussel shell.

Brief fragments: (F 21) "a pair of amphoras," (F 22) "to contend with," (F 23) "infrequent," (F 24) "nowhere."

ISLAND]ERS

A possible restoration of the partially preserved title on the Roman inscription (T 5, l. 8).

MAGISTRATES

a meeting of the Council is described, including the roles of the magistrates and the "archers" (the "police"). At Thesmophoriazusae 929 a prytanis appears to inquire into the case against Euripides' kinsman. On occasion a character calls upon or threatens another with "the magistrates" (Thesmophoriazusae 654, 1084). It would seem, then, to have been a comedy with a political theme.

25 Athenaeus 553e

καὶ τὸν ἐπὶ Θεμιστοκλέους δὲ βίον Τηλεκλείδης ἐν Πρυτάνεσιν ἁβρὸν ὄντα παραδίδωσι.

26 Σ Aristophanes *Wasps* 836c

ἀλλ᾽ ἔοικεν ὁ Λάβης ὠνοματοπεποιῆσθαι ἁπλῶς, καθάπερ ὁ Δάκης ὁ παρὰ Τηλεκλείδῃ ἐν Πρυτάνεσιν·

Δάκης τις ἐστιν ὅντιν᾽ ἀνθρώπων ὁρᾷς.

27 Athenaeus 485f

καὶ μελιχρὸν οἶνον ἕλκειν
ἐξ ἡδύπνου λεπαστῆς,
τυρίον ἐπεσθίοντα.

28 Pollux 7.135

εὐχροεῖν, ὀρνιθοθηρᾶν, σωφρονεῖν

ΣΙΚΕΛ]ΙΩΤΑΙ

ΣΤΕΡΡΟΙ

33 Athenaeus 399c

ὡς οὖσα θῆλυς εἰκότως οὖθαρ φορῶ.

25 Teleclides in *Magistrates* describes the life in the time of Themistocles as "soft."

26 "Labes" seems just to be a comic coinage, like Daces ["Biter"] in Teleclides' *Magistrates*:

There is a Biter, whom you see among men.

27 And to draw honey-sweet wine from a fragrant limpet cup, while eating a bit of cheese.

28 To look well, go bird hunting, to be wise.

Brief fragments: (F 29) "yes, by the cabbages," (F 30) "all day long," (F 31) "spear-slaying," (F 32) "violent."

MEN [OF SICILY]

A possible restoration of the partially preserved title on the Roman inscription (T 5, l. 8).

RIGID ONES

In fifth-century poetry the adjective sterros *can mean "hard" (of a spear), or "stiff with age" (of an old man's leg—Acharnians 218), or "obstinate" (of one's soul—Clouds 420), or "unbending" (of Necessity or Justice). The mention of Hermes (F 35) could imply a divine context. We would seem to have a chorus of men (deities?) with a rigid or unbending temperament.*

33 Of course I have a breast—I'm a woman.

THE POETS OF OLD COMEDY

34 Athenaeus 648e

φιλῶ πλακοῦντα θερμόν, ἀχράδας οὐ φιλῶ,
χαίρω λαγῴοις ἐπ᾽ ἀμύλῳ καθημένοις.

35 Σ Aristophanes *Peace* 1040

ὦ δέσποθ᾽ Ἑρμῆ, κάπτε τῶν θυλημάτων.

36 Athenaeus 639a

Τηλεκλείδης δὲ ἐν τοῖς Στερροῖς καὶ περὶ μοιχείας
ἀναστρέφεσθαί φησιν αὐτόν.

ΣΤΡΑΤ]ΙΩΤΑΙ

ΣΥΜΠ[

ΑΔΗΛΩΝ ΔΡΑΜΑΤΩΝ

37 Phrynichus *Selection* 353

τίς ἥδε κραυγὴ καὶ δόμων περίστασις;

38 Photius p. 583.21

πάντες δὲ τευτάζουσιν οἱ διάκονοι.

34 I do like a warm flat-bun, I don't like wild pears, I do enjoy hare's meat resting on a fine meal cake.

35 Lord Hermes, gobble up the sacrificial offerings.

36 Teleclides in *Rigid Ones* says that he [Gnesippus] was given to adultery.

SOLDI]ERS

A possible restoration of the partially preserved title on the Roman inscription (T 5, l. 8). Hermippus wrote a play with this title.

SYMP[

The Roman inscription (l. 2) preserves this beginning of a comic title. Perhaps restore as Sympotai *(Party-Goers) or* Sympaizontes *(Revellers)?*

UNASSIGNED FRAGMENTS

37 What means this uproar and thronging about the house?

38 All the servants are bustling about.

39 Bachmann's *Lexicon* p. 114.3

σὺ δὲ φρόνιμος αὐτὸς ὢν
ἀπαρτὶ ταύτης τῆς τέχνης.

40 Athenaeus 56d

ξυγγενέσθαι διὰ χρόνου † λιπαρείτω με
δρυπεπέσι μάζαις καὶ διασκανδικίσαι †

41 *Life of Euripides* 2

Μνησίλοχός ἐστ᾽ ἐκεῖνος, ⟨ὃς⟩ φρύγει τι δρᾶμα
    καινόν
Εὐριπίδῃ, καὶ Σωκράτης τὰ φρύγαν᾽ ὑποτίθησιν.

42 Diogenes Laertius 2.18

Εὐριπίδης σωκρατογόμφους

43 *Lexicon Vindobonense* II D 29

τὸν ὑπερβόρεόν τε δρῦν

44 Plutarch *Nicias* 4.3

Χαρικλέης μὲν οὖν ἔδωκε μνᾶν, ἵν᾽ αὐτὸν μὴ λέγῃ
ὡς ἔφυ τῇ μητρὶ παίδων πρῶτος ἐκ βαλλαντίου·
τέτταρας δὲ μνᾶς ἔδωκε Νικίας Νικηράτου·
ὧν δ᾽ ἕκατι τοῦτ᾽ ἔδωκε, καίπερ εὖ εἰδὼς ἐγὼ
5 οὐκ ἐρῶ, φίλος γὰρ ἀνήρ, σωφρονεῖν δέ μοι δοκεῖ.

39 You, being yourself a completely knowledgeable man about this craft.

40 Let him beg me (?) in time to get together with tree-ripened barley cakes and to munch chervil (?).[1]

1 The reference to chervil may be another of the jokes at Euripides for his mother's alleged occupation as a vegetable seller.

41 Mnesilochus is the man ‹who› is roasting [*phrygei*] a new play for Euripides, and Socrates is laying down the kindling [*phrygana*].[1]

1 Mnesilochus, according to *The Life of Euripides*, was Euripides' father-in-law and the name given to Euripides' kinsman in *Thesmophoriazusae*. Diogenes Laertius (2.18) finds a third play on words, naming the "new play" as *Phrygians,* a title not attested, however, for Euripides.

42 Euripides bolted together with Socrates.

43 The oak tree of the far North.

44 [against an informer] Did Charicles not pay a mina, so that he [the informer] wouldn't say of him that he was his mother's firstborn child, from her money purse? And Nicias, the son of Niceratus, paid up four minas. Now although I know very well for what reason he gave this money, I won't say, because he is a friend of mine and seems a sensible man to me.[1]

1 The most prominent Charicles of the late 5th c. (*PAA* 982980) was active from 415, when he was a commissioner investigating the scandal over the Herms, to 404, when he was one of the Thirty.

45 Plutarch *Pericles* 16.2

ὁ δὲ Τηλεκλείδης παραδεδωκέναι φησὶν αὐτῷ τοὺς
Ἀθηναίους

πόλεών τε φόρους αὐτάς τε πόλεις τὰς μὲν δεῖν τάς
    τ' ἀναλύειν,
λάινα τείχη τὰ μὲν οἰκοδομεῖν † τὰ δὲ αὐτὰ † πάλιν
    καταβάλλειν,
σπονδάς, δύναμιν, κράτος, εἰρήνην, πλοῦτόν τ'
    εὐδαιμονίαν τε.

46 Herodian *Singular Vocabulary* II p. 923.11

ὁ δ' ἀπ' Αἰγίνης νήσου χωρεῖ δοθιῆνος ἔχων τὸ
    πρόσωπον.

47 Plutarch *Pericles* 3.6

Τηλεκλείδης δὲ ποτὲ μὲν ὑπὸ τῶν πραγμάτων ἠπορη-
μένον καθῆσθαί φησιν αὐτὸν ἐν τῇ πόλει καρηβα-
ροῦντα, ποτὲ δὲ μόνον ἐκ κεφαλῆς ἑνδεκακλίνου θόρυ-
βον πολὺν ἐξανατέλλειν.

48 PBerlin 13 360

ἀ]σπιδοφεγγὴς στρ[ατὸς ἐκνεφί]ας ἐγ χειρὶ
    κεραυνο[

45 Teleclides says that the Athenians have handed over to him [Pericles]:

the tribute from the cities, and the cities themselves, to bind some and destroy others, to build up walls of stone and again to pull them down, treaties, power, the military, peace, wealth, and prosperity.   [*Hesiods* ?]

46 He comes from the island of Aegina with a face like a boil.

47 Teleclides once said that confounded by events he [Pericles] sat on the Acropolis with heavy head, and again that alone he caused a great uproar to spring from a head that could fit eleven couches.[1]

  [1] It is possible that Pericles "with heavy head" is meant to allude to Zeus' head pregnant with Athena. Some would regard the "uproar" as the War.

48 An army, shield-gleaming tempest, lightning bolt in hand.

49 Photius p. 565.8

τῶν δυνατῶν τι κέλευ'· οὐ γὰρ παρὰ Κενταύροισιν.

50 Σ Aristophanes *Birds* 17

τὸν μὲν Θαρρελείδου τουτονί· Σύμμαχος Ἀσωπόδω-
ρον. καὶ γὰρ οὗτος ἐπὶ σμικρότητι ὑπὸ Τηλεκλείδου
κεκωμῴδηται.

51 Photius (b,z) α 858

ἀκροκώλια δίεφθα

52 Pollux 3.70

παιδοφίλης, παιδέρως Ζεύς

53 Σ Aristophanes *Acharnians* 860

τραχήλου τύλαν

58 Phrynichus *Selection* 255

βρέχει ἐπὶ τοῦ ὕει· ἔν τινι κωμῳδίᾳ ἀρχαίᾳ προσ-
τιθεμένῃ Τηλεκλείδῃ τῷ κωμῳδῷ ἐστιν οὕτως εἰρη-
μένον, ὅπερ, εἰ καὶ γνήσιον ἦν τὸ δρᾶμα, τῷ ἅπαξ
εἰρῆσθαι ἐφυλαξάμεθ' ἄν.

73 P. Oxy. 2740.41

τούτου μνη[μονεύει] καὶ Τηλεκλεί[δης . . . .] ὡς λω-
πο[δύτου.

49 Command something that is feasible—⟨we're⟩ not among the Centaurs.[1]

[1] Being "among the Centaurs" seems to have been proverbial for an impossible situation.

50 "This son of Tharreleides": Symmachus ⟨identifies him as⟩ Asopodorus, because this man was made fun of by Teleclides for his small stature.

51 Boiled pig's trotters.

52 Paedophile . . . Zeus the kid-lover.

53 The swell of the neck [Doric dialect].

58 "It teems," instead of "it rains." This is found in a certain Old Comedy attributed to Teleclides the comic poet, which, if the play is authentic, we would avoid as a *hapax legomenon*.

73 Teleclides mentions this man as a clothes thief.
[cf. Eupolis F 268]

Brief fragments: (F 54) "of shopping," (F 55) "he would ask a question," (F 56) "he will cheat," (F 57) "stoppered," (F 59) "frights," (F 60) "Bromius," (F 61) "altar thieves," (F 62) "contractors," (F 63) "people of Eutresis," (F 64) "loudly," (F 65) "I shall sit down," (F 66) "have a heavy head" [= F 47], (F 67) "lamp-lighting," (F 68) "blame" [mempheiran], (F 69) "blame" [momphin], (F 70) "female genitalia," (F 71) "sonny," (F 72) "crotch-delight."

ΤΕΛΕΣΤΗΣ

Testimonia

i *Suda* τ 265

Τελέστης, κωμικός. τούτου δράματά ἐστιν Ἀργὼ καὶ
Ἀσκληπιός, ὥς φησιν Ἀθήναιος ἐν τῷ ιδ΄ τῶν Δειπνο-
σοφιστῶν.

ii Marmor Parium

ἀφ᾽ οὗ Τελέστης Σελινούντιος ἐνίκησεν Ἀθήνησιν,
ἔτη ΗΔΔΔΠΙΙΙΙ, ἄρχοντος Ἀθήνησιν Μίκωνος.

TELESTES

At first glance the testimony of the Suda (*T 1*) and the jok-
ing aside at Telestes by Theopompus (*T 3*) might suggest
one comic poet making fun of another. But the other refer-
ences to Telestes (*T 4–5*; Athenaeus 616f, 637a; *PMG F
929*) associate him with the dithyramb, and in particu-
lar with the "new poets" of the late fifth and early fourth
centuries. The fragments we have from his Argo and his
Asclepius (*PMG F 805–6*) are Doricised lyric rather than
Attic comedy. Athenaeus (637a) cites four lines from a
dithyramb called Hymenaeus (*F 808*), and Philodemus a
work which seems to be Birth of Zeus. The last recalls the
birth comedies of the early fourth century (cf. Polyzelus),
and the story of Argo does turn up in comedy and satyr
play. This may explain the Suda's misidentification of
Telestes as a comic poet. See Campbell GL V 122–33.

Testimonia

i Telestes: comic poet. His plays include *Argo* and
Asclepius, as Athenaeus says in Book 14 of *The Learned
Banqueters* [616f–17b].

ii From the time when Telestes of Selinus won a victory
at Athens, 139 years—the archon at Athens was Micon
[402/1].

311

iii Theopompus F 4 (*Althaea*)

λαβοῦσα πλήρη χρυσέαν μεσόμφαλον
φιάλην· Τελέστης δ᾽ ἄκατον ὠνόμαζέ νιν.

iv Plutarch *Alexander* 8.3

τῶν δ᾽ ἄλλων βιβλίων οὐκ εὐπορῶν ἐν τοῖς ἄνω
τόποις, Ἅρπαλον ἐκέλευσε πέμψαι, κἀκεῖνος ἔπεμψεν
αὐτῷ τάς τε Φιλίστου βίβλους καὶ τῶν Εὐριπίδου καὶ
Σοφοκλέους καὶ Αἰσχύλου τραγῳδιῶν συχνάς, καὶ
Τελέστου καὶ Φιλοξένου διθυράμβους.

v Dionysius of Halicarnassus *On Literary Composition* 19

καὶ τοῖς ῥυθμοῖς κατὰ πολλὴν ἄδειαν ἐνεξουσιάζοντες
διετέλουν, οἵ γε δὴ κατὰ Φιλόξενον καὶ Τιμόθεον καὶ
Τελεστήν, ἐπεὶ παρά γε τοῖς ἀρχαίοις τεταγμένος ἦν
καὶ ὁ διθύραμβος.

iii She took a full golden navel cup—Telestes used to call it a "schooner."

iv When he was running out of books while in the back country, he [Alexander] ordered Harpalus to send some. Harpalus sent him the works of Philistus, many of the tragedies of Euripides and Sophocles, and the dithyrambs of Telestes and Philoxenus.

v In the matter of rhythm they continued to employ great freedom, I mean the poets such as Philoxenus and Timotheus and Telestes, for among the older poets the dithyramb also had been a very ordered form.

ΘΕΟΠΟΜΠΟΣ

With seventeen or twenty-four plays attributed to him (T 1, 3), Theopompus is more than a minor player in the latter years of Old Comedy. On the victors' lists his name appears among poets of the late fifth or early fourth century. Some of the references to people and events show him active as early as the late 410s (F 25—Leotrophides, F 40—Laespodias, F 61—Acestor), while the allusions to Peron (F 1, 17) and Callistratus (F 31) belong after 380, and in the case of Callistratus perhaps later. We should be safe with dates of c. 410 to c. 380. His father's name is variously given as Theodectas or Theodorus (T 1) and Teisamenus (T 2).

The titles suggest first of all a poet of mythological burlesque. We may cite Admetus, Althaea, Aphrodite, Theseus (where F 18 suggests a journey to Persia), Odysseus, Penelope (one of which may have dramatised their meeting at the end of the Odyssey—see F 34), Sirens, Phineus. But in most cases we have no way of knowing what aspect of a particular myth was stressed. Some titles suggest comedies about women, Batyle, Barmaids, Pamphile and Nemea (or Nemeas), perhaps also Aphrodite. In the fragments we hear of a woman with a full golden cup (F 4), eating seafood (F 6), having a lover "Attis" (F 28), flirting with a fellow slave (F 33), drinking and misbehaving (F 42–43,

314

THEOPOMPUS

80), learning something from her great-grandmother (F 44), playing old tunes (F 51), twisting her neck to drink from a misshapen vessel (F 55), serving in the army (F 56–57, 82), and being described as ripe as a melon (F 76).

But personal jokes are not absent from his comedy. Of the ninety or so fragments, at least fifteen contain allusions to real persons, some of them casual (F 1, 17 to Peron the perfumer; F 4 to Telestes the poet), but others more overtly political, such as Callistratus bribing "the sons of the Achaeans" (F 31) and the mentions of Philonides (F 5), Isaeus (F 19), Anytus (F 58), and Laespodias (F 40). We get allusions to the tragic poets Euripides (F 35) and Acestor (F 61), and perhaps the first mention of Plato in comedy (F 16). The title, Callaeschrus, might refer to one of the known men of that name, but could equally well be a made-up compound ("fine" + "disgusting"), while Teisamenos might refer to the legal commissioner of the late fifth century, in which case we might have a political comedy named after its target, or to the son of Orestes in myth. But Peace and She-Soldiers seem like comedies of the familiar Aristophanic sort—see F 8 (Peace) in particular, and F 57 for a woman in command. Unfortunately we cannot date either comedy, nor do we know what "peace" the former comedy may have referred to, if in fact to any specific event.

THE POETS OF OLD COMEDY

Testimonia

i *Suda* θ 171

Θεόπομπος, Θεοδέκτου ἢ Θεοδώρου, Ἀθηναῖος, κωμικός. ἐδίδαξε δράματα κδʹ. ἔστι δὲ τῆς ἀρχαίας κωμῳδίας κατὰ Ἀριστοφάνην. δράματα δὲ αὐτοῦ εἰσὶ . . . καὶ ἄλλα πολλά.

ii Aelian F 99

Ἀσκληπιὸς καὶ τῶν ἐν παιδείᾳ ἦν προμηθής. φθόη γοῦν Θεόπομπον ῥινώμενόν τε καὶ λειβόμενον ἰάσατο καὶ κωμῳδίας αὖθις διδάσκειν ἐπῆρεν, ὁλόκληρόν τε καὶ σῶν καὶ ἀρτεμῆ ἐργασάμενος. καὶ δείκνυται καὶ νῦν ὑπὸ λίθῳ Θεοπόμπου (πατρόθεν ὁμολογοῦντος αὐτὸν τοῦ ἐπιγράμματος· Τισαμενοῦ γὰρ ἦν υἱός) εἴδωλον Παρίας λίθου. καὶ ἔστι τὸ ἴνδαλμα τοῦ πάθους μάλα ἐναργές. κλίνη καὶ αὐτὴ λίθου. ἐπʼ αὐτῆς κεῖται νοσοῦν τὸ ἐκείνου φάσμα, χειρουργίᾳ φιλοτέχνῳ· παρέστηκε δὲ ὁ θεὸς καὶ ὀρέγει οἱ τὴν παιώνιον χεῖρα, καὶ παῖς νεαρὸς ὑπομειδιῶν καὶ οὗτος. τί δὲ ἄρα νοεῖ ὁ παῖς; ἐγὼ συνίημι, τοῦ φιλοπαίστην ποιητὴν ὑποδηλοῦν.

iii *The Names and Plays of the Poets of Old Comedy* (Koster VIII.1)

Θεοπόμπου δράματα ιζʹ.

THEOPOMPUS

Recent bibliography: J. L. Sanchis Llopis, in Homenaje a
P. A. Gainzáráin *(2002) 115–25.*

Testimonia

i Theopompus: son of Theodectus or of Theodorus, of
Athens, comic poet. He produced twenty-four plays. He
belongs to Old Comedy along with Aristophanes. His play
are . . . and many others.

ii Asclepius was also concerned for those involved in the
arts. At any rate he did cure Theopompus who was sick
and wasting away with consumption and encouraged him
to put on plays again, by making him hale and hearty and
whole again. Even now can be seen beneath the stone (?) a
likeness of Theopompus in Parian marble, the inscription
confirming his patronymic, for he was the son of Teisame-
nus. The representation of his ailment is quite clear: a bed,
itself also in marble, on it lies the image of the sick man
made with a master's skill. The god stands by and extends a
healing hand to him, and there is a young child smiling as
well. What is the significance of the child? I take it as
showing that the poet is fond of fun.

iii The plays of Theopompus, 17.

iv *IG* ii² 2325.68

Θεόπομπ[ος

v *IG* ii² 2325.129

Θεό[πομπ]ος II

vi Hephaestion *Handbook* 13.2

ἐπιτηδεύουσι δὲ ἔνιοι τῶν ποιητῶν τοὺς πρώτους κα-
λουμένους παιῶνας παραλαμβάνειν πλὴν τῆς τελευ-
ταίας χώρας, εἰς ἣν τὸν κρητικὸν παραλαμβάνουσιν
. . . ᾧ δὴ ἔφαμεν τρόπῳ συνεχῶς κεχρῆσθαι αὐτοὺς
ἐπὶ τοῦ τετραμέτρου, ὥστε τοῖς τρισὶ παιῶσι τοῖς
πρώτοις ἐπάγειν κρητικόν, τούτῳ καὶ ἐπὶ τοῦ πεντα-
μέτρου Θεόπομπος ὁ κωμικὸς ἐχρήσατο ἐν Παισίν,
ἀφ' οὗ καὶ Θεοπόμπειον καλεῖται.

Fragments

ΑΔΜΗΤΟΣ

318

iv [From the list of victors at the Dionysia, from the late fifth century]

Theopomp[us

v [From the list of victors at the Lenaea, from the early fourth century]

Theo[pomp]us 2

vi Some of the poets manage to employ the so-called first paeonics, except for the last foot where they use a cretic ... in the same manner in which we said that they employ continuously for the tetrameter (that is, three first paeonics followed by a cretic), Theopompus the comic poet uses this for the pentameter also, for which reason it is called the Theopompean [F 39 follows].

Fragments

ADMETUS

Aristomenes produced an Admetus *in 388, and the reference to Peron, made fun of by the Middle Comic poet Antiphanes (F 37), suggests a late date for this comedy. Why a play called "Ademtus" and not "Alcestis," the titles of plays by Phrynichus (tragedian) and Euripides, unless the comedy concerned another aspect of the myth of Admetus? We might consider his presence on the Argo, Apollo's year of servitude to Admetus, the wooing of Alcestis, or possibly the account of Apollo's romantic relationship with Admetus (Callimachus 2.47–49).*

319

1 Athenaeus 690a

μνημονεύει τοῦ μυροπώλου τούτου τοῦ Πέρωνος καὶ
Θεόπομπος ἐν Ἀδμήτῳ καὶ Ἡδυχάρει.

ΑΛΘΑΙΑ

3 Pollux 10.180

τὴν οἰκίαν γὰρ ηὗρον εἰσελθὼν ὅλην
κίστην γεγονυῖαν φαρμακοπώλου Μεγαρικοῦ.

4 Athenaeus 501f

λαβοῦσα πλήρη χρυσέαν μεσόμφαλον
φιάλην· Τελέστης δ᾽ ἄκατον ὠνόμαζέ νιν.

ΑΦΡΟΔΙΤΗ

This is a particularly mysterious comedy. We know of several comedies from Old and Middle Comedy called "Birth of Aphrodite," but what aspect of the many myths of Aph-

1 Theopompus also mentions this perfume seller, Peron, in *Admetus* and in his *Lovejoy* [F 17].

Brief fragment: (F 2) "funerary vessel."

ALTHAEA

Althaea is the wife of Oeneus and mother of Meleager and a major character in the myth of Atalanta and the boar of Calydon. Details vary in the early tradition, but essentially she brings about her son's death to avenge her two brothers whom Meleager has killed in a dispute between two neighbouring cities over the hide of the boar. In one version (Bacchylides 5.93ff., Aeschylus Libation-Bearers 602–11), Althaea kills her son through sympathetic magic, by thrusting into the fire the piece of wood to which her son's life is attached. In the fragments we may notice a house that looks like a pharmacist's shop (F 3) and a woman who takes a cup full (of what?) in F 4.

3 When I [masc.] went into the house, I found it had become one whole medicine chest belonging to a pharmacist from Megara.

4 She took a full navel cup, made of gold—Telestes used to call it a "schooner."

APHRODITE

rodite would have made for comedy is uncertain. One of the sources for F 4, the Aldine, reads Aphrodisia *("feast of Aphrodite" or "pleasures of Love") for* Aphrodite.

5 Σ Aristophanes *Wealth* 179b

ὧν εἷς μὲν ὀγκάς ὁ Μελιτεὺς Φιλωνίδης,
ὄνῳ μιγείσης μητρὸς ἔβλαστ᾽ ἐν πόλει.

6 Athenaeus 324b

ἀλλ᾽ ἔντραγε
τὴν σηπίαν τηνδὶ λαβοῦσα καὶ τοδὶ
τὸ πουλυπόδειον.

ΒΑΤΤΛΗ

ΕΙΡΗΝΗ

Aristophanes' extant comedy (D-421) was named for the goddess Peace, whose mute statue serves us a symbol for the larger theme, the end of the Archidamian War. If a real occasion lies behind the play, then the end of the War in

5 One of whom a brayer, Philonides from Melite, was born on the Acropolis after his mother had sex with a donkey.[1]

[1] Philonides (*PAA* 957480), son of Onetor, hence his nickname Onos (ass), was a large, awkward, not very bright, but rich Athenian, said to be the lover of the hetaera Nais. See *Wealth* 179, 303, Nicochares F 4, Theopompus F 5, and the comedy *Philonides* by the Middle Comic poet Aristophon.

6 But take [fem. sing.] and eat this cuttlefish and this little bit of octopus.

BATYLE

This comedy is known only from the scholion to Wealth *1011, where the Aristophanic text itself is in some doubt. The scholiast, followed by the* Suda *(ν 430), comments on what he finds as* βάτιον *in the text: "They call small females 'batylai,' and there is a play by Theopompus,* Batyle." *It is not sure what the "small females" are. The word* batis *can mean both "skate" and "songbird." Kaibel made the attractive suggestion that Batyle was the name of a hetaera, an appropriate name in the sense of "bird." Batyllis occurs as a woman's name at Herodas 5.70.*

PEACE

405/4 or the Peace of Antalcidas in 386 might be considered. But the comedy may just be a bit of wish fulfilment in the unstable atmosphere of the early fourth century. F 8 does recall passages in Acharnians *and* Peace, *where the freedom from the implements of war is celebrated.*

7 Photius (b, z) α 563

ἔπειτα κἂν Δελφοῖσιν ἀνετεθῇ γραφείς·
ἀεὶ γεωργὸς †ὅτι χρηστὸς ἦν
πρῶτον πολὺ τὸν λιμὸν ἀποφεύγων.

8 Pollux 10.118

ἡμᾶς δ' ἀπαλλαχθέντας ἐπ' ἀγαθαῖς τύχαις
ὀβελισκολυχνίου καὶ ξιφομαχαίρας πικρᾶς.

9 Athenaeus 368c

ὁ μὲν ἄρτος ἡδύ, τὸ δὲ φενακίζειν προσὸν
ἔμβαμμα τοῖς ἄρτοις πονηρὸν γίγνεται.

10 Athenaeus 374b

ἄχθομαι δ' ἀπολωλεκὼς
ἀλεκτρυόνα τίκτουσαν ᾠὰ πάγκαλα.

11 Pollux 10.123–24

χλαῖναν <δέ> σοι
λαβὼν παχεῖαν ἐπιβαλῶ Λακωνικήν.

12 Athenaeus 652f

μᾶζαι, πλακοῦντες, ἰσχάδες Τειθράσιαι

ΗΔΥΧΑΡΗΣ

7 Then at Delphi the inscription may be set up: "The good farmer is always the one who first flees hunger . . ."[1]

> [1] There seems to have been a proverb: "Though newly wealthy, he is always a farmer."

8 Us, thanks to luck, now freed from the candle spit and the hateful dagger-sword.

9 Bread is a delicious thing, but deceit added is a very nasty dip for bread.

10 I [masc.] am cross that I have lost a hen that lays very fine eggs.

11 I [masc.] shall take a thick Laconian cloak and put it around you.

12 Barley buns, flat-cakes, Teithrasian figs.

Brief fragment: (F 13) "stepfather."

LOVEJOY

Theopompus seems to have created this compound name, probably for the main character of his comedy (cf. Phryni-chus' Hermit *or Menander's* Bad-Tempered Man *or Pla-ton's* The Man in Great Pain*). The mention of "Plato" in F 16 has led some to identify Plato as the "lovejoy" of the title, an ironic usage based on what Diogenes Laertius says of him (3.26). As Peron the perfume man (F 17) was made fun of in Middle Comedy (Antiphanes F 37), this play should*

14 Athenaeus 308a

καὶ στῆτ᾽ ἐφεξῆς κεστρέων νῆστις χορὸς
λαχάνοισιν ὥσπερ χῆνες ἐξενισμένοι.

15 Σ Aristophanes *Wealth* 768

{Α.} φέρε σὺ τὰ καταχύσματα
ταχέως κατάχει τοῦ νυμφίου καὶ τῆς κόρης.
{Β.} εὖ πάνυ λέγεις.

16 Diogenes Laertius 3.26

ἓν γάρ ἐστιν οὐδὲ ἕν,
τὼ δὲ δύο μόλις ἕν ἐστιν, ὥς φησιν Πλάτων.

17 Athenaeus 690a

μνημονεύει τοῦ μυροπώλου τούτου τοῦ Πέρωνος καὶ
Θεόπομπος ἐν Ἀδμήτῳ καὶ Ἡδυχάρει.

ΘΗΣΕΥΣ

18 Photius (b, z) α 66

ἵξει δὲ Μήδων γαῖαν, ἔνθα καρδάμων
πλείστων ποιεῖται καὶ πράσων ἀβυρτάκη.

*be dated later in Theopompus' career (after 380). The busi-
ness in F 16 about "one not being one" is generally agreed
to refer to Platon Phaedo 96e (dated in the late 380s).*

14 Stand in a row, you starving chorus of mullets, feasted
on greens like geese.

15 (A) Here, quickly pour the nuts over the bride and
groom.
  (B) What a good idea!

16 For there is no one thing that is one, and two is barely
one, or so says Plato.

17 This perfume seller, Peron, is mentioned by Theo-
pompus in *Admetus* [F 1] and in his *Lovejoy*.

THESEUS

*Theseus, as one would expect, was an extremely popular
subject in Athenian drama. Tragedies with this title are
known for Sophocles, Euripides, and Achaeus, a comedy
by Aristonymos, and he appears in two odes by Bacchyli-
des (17, 18), Sophocles' Oedipus at Colonus, Euripides'
Suppliant Women, his lost Aegeus, and the Pirithous at-
tributed to Critias. As the career of Isaeus (F 19) is usually
put c. 390–345, this comedy belongs to Theopompus' later
period. In F 18 someone (Theseus?) is being given direc-
tions, which include the land of the Medes.*

18 You [sing.] will come to the land of the Medes, where
they make a sour sauce of many cardamon seeds and leeks.

19 [Plutarch] *Lives of the Ten Orators* 839f

μνημονεύει δ' αὐτοῦ Θεόπομπος ὁ κωμικὸς ἐν τῷ
Θησεῖ.

ΚΑΛΛΑΙΣΧΡΟΣ

22 Pollux 9.59

οὖ φησιν εἶναι τῶν ἑταιρῶν τὰς μέσας
στατηριαίας.

23 Athenaeus 423a

ἠρίσταμεν· δεῖ γὰρ συνάπτειν τὸν λόγον.

24 Athenaeus 302e

ἰχθύων δὲ δὴ
ὑπογάστρι', ὦ Δάματερ.

19 Theopompus the comic poet mentions him [Isaeus] in *Theseus*.

Brief fragments: (F 20) "crab apples," (F 21) "self-harmer."

CALLAESCHRUS

Callaeschrus is a well-documented Athenian name, with forty entries in PAA, including a member of the coup in 411 (552220), a man for whom Lysias wrote a speech (555195), and the father of the tyrant Critias (552225). Pherecrates (F 46) mentions a Callaeschrus "sitting in the temple of Theseus." Thus it is possible that Theopompus has written a comedy named after a real person, cf. the demagogue plays of Platon and Archippus' Rhinon. An alternative explanation of the title is that Theopompus has created a central character who is both kalos *(attractive) and* aischros *(disgusting). All three fragments are concerned with an entertainment (girls, food, talk).*

22 Where he says there are girls of the second rank who charge a stater.

23 We have had our meal; now we must begin the discussion.

24 Undercuts of fish, indeed, O Demeter.[1]

    1 The dialect of "Demeter" is Doric.

ΚΑΠΗΛΙΔΕΣ

25 Σ Aristophanes *Birds* 1406

Λεωτροφίδης ὁ τρίμετρος ὡς † λεόντινος †
εὔχρως † τε φάναι † καὶ χαρίεις ὥσπερ νεκρός.

26 Pollux 7.158

ἐλεφαντοκώπους ξιφομαχαίρας καὶ δόρη

27 Σ Aristophanes *Acharnians* 1021a

ἢ μετάδος ἢ μέτρησον ἢ τιμὴν λαβέ.

28 Photius (z) α 3131

κολάσομαί σ᾽ ἐγὼ
καὶ τὸν σὸν Ἄττιν.

29 Zenobius 4.44

Ἑστίᾳ θύεις

330

BARMAIDS

As Leotrophides seems to be a kōmōidoumenos *of the 410s
and 400s (see* Birds *1406, Hermippus F 36), Barmaids is
probably one of Theopompus' earliest plays. Such women
would have made for a natural comic chorus. At* Thes-
mophoriazusae *347–48 and* Wealth *435–36, the local bar-
maid serves short measures, and at* Wealth *1120 Hermes
used to receive dainties from the barmaids. F 28 could have
been spoken by a woman angry at another with a hand-
some young lover—cf. the scenes with the old women in*
Assembly-Women *and* Wealth.

25 Leotrophides the triple . . . as an attractive and pleas-
ant corpse for Leontius (?) to look at.[1]

[1] Leotrophides (*PAA* 607070) is made fun of in comedy (*Birds*
1406, Hermippus F 36) as a lean and emaciated looking man. As
the name is rare, he is probably the same as a general in 409
(607065). The text of the first line is corrupt and numerous at-
tempts have been made to make sense of *trimetros* and *leontinos*.
At *Republic* 439e Plato tells of a Leontius who was attracted by the
sight of dead bodies (*nekroi*).

26 Dagger-swords with ivory hilts and spears.

27 Either give me a share or make a loan to me or take
payment.

28 I shall punish you and your Attis.

29 You are sacrificing to Hestia.

ΜΗΔΟΣ

30 Σ Pindar *Pythians* 2.78a

χαρίζεσθαι γὰρ κυρίως λέγεται τὸ συνουσιάζειν,
ὥσπερ Θεόπομπος ἐν Μήδῳ εἰσάγει τὸν Λυκαβηττὸν
λέγοντα·

  παρ' ἐμοὶ τὰ λίαν μειράκια χαρίζεται
  τοῖς ἡλικιώταις.

31 Athenaeus 485c

ὥς ποτ' ἐκήλησεν Καλλίστρατος υἷας Ἀχαιῶν,
κέρμα φίλον διαδούς, ὅτε συμμαχίαν ἐρέεινεν·
οἷον δ' οὐ κήλησε δέμας λεπτὸν Ῥαδάμανθυν,
Λύσανδρον κώθωνι, πρὶν αὐτῷ δῶκε λεπαστήν.

NEMEA

Nemea *was the title of a play by Aeschylus, sometimes
regarded as the satyr play of a trilogy about the Seven
against Thebes, but nothing has survived from the play.*
Nemea *could be the mother of Archemorus, the child in
whose memory the Nemean Games were founded (*Simo-

THE MEDE

The reference to Callistratus "seeking an alliance"(F 31) has been identified with the alliance negotiated by Callistratus in 378 (IG² ii 43), but the identity of Lysander (Rhadamanthus) is unknown. The significance of the title also remains a mystery. For Mount Lycabettus as a speaking character [F 30], compare the appearance of Cyllene in Sophocles' Trackers.

30 "To do favours" really means "to have sex with," as Theopompus in *The Mede* brings on Lycabettus saying:

My place is where the very youthful youths do favours for their friends.

31 As once Callistratus charmed "the sons of the Achaeans" by handing out some very welcome cash, when he was seeking an alliance. But one alone he did not charm with only a canteen, Lysander, that Rhadamanthus of slender build, until he gave him a limpet cup.

Brief fragment: (F 32) "cup without handles."

NEMEA (NEMEAS?)

nides F 553, Bacchylides 9.10–20), and the play thus a mythically based comedy. But Athenaeus (587c) cites Hypereides (F 142) for the existence of a well-known hetaera named Nemeas. If Nemea(s) is a well-off hetaera, F 33 may be set in her household, featuring a couple of her slaves.

33 Athenaeus 470f

{ΣΠΙΝΘΗΡ.} χώρει σὺ δεῦρο, Θηρικλέους πιστὸν
τέκνον·
γενναῖον εἶδος· ὄνομά σοι τί θώμεθα;
ἆρ᾽ εἶ κάτοπτρον φύσεος, ἢν πλῆρες δοθῇς;
οὐδέν ποτ᾽ ἄλλο. δεῦρο δή, γεμίσω σ᾽ ἐγώ.
γραῦ Θεολύτη, γραῦ. {ΘΕΟΛΥΤΗ.} τί με καλεῖς σύ;
5   {ΣΠ.} φιλτάτη,
ἵν᾽ ἀσπάσωμαι· δεῦρο παρ᾽ ἐμέ, Θεολύτη,
παρὰ τὸν νέον ξύνδουλον. οὑτωσὶ καλῶς.
{ΘΕ.} Σπινθὴρ τάλας, πειρᾷς με; {ΣΠ.} ναί, τοιοῦτό
τι·
φιλοτησίαν δὲ <τήνδε> σοι προπίομαι·
10   δέξαι, πιοῦσα δ᾽ ὁπόσον ἄν σοι θυμὸς ᾖ,
ἐμοὶ παράδος τὸ πρῶτον.

ΟΔΥΣΣΕΙΣ

33 (SPINTHER) Come here now, trusty child of Thericles[1], of noble aspect. What name shall I give you? Are you "the mirror of nature," if handed over full? That's certainly the case. Now then, I shall fill you up. Old woman, Theolyte, old woman.

(THEOLYTE) Why are you calling me?

(SPINTHER) So I may kiss you, my dear. Come here beside me, beside your new fellow slave. That's right.

(THEOLYTE) Spinther, you wretch, are you trying to seduce me?

(SPINTHER) Yes, something like that. I shall drink this toast to you. Here take it, and when you have drunk as much as your heart desires, hand it right back.

[1] Athenaeus tells us that Thericles was a Corinthian potter responsible for a certain type of *kylix*.

ODYSSEUS

Comic and satyric drama were very fond of themes and characters from the Odyssey. *Epicharmus wrote several comedies about Odysseus, Cratinus parodied the encounter with the Cyclops in* Odysseus and Company, *which Euripides would turn into the subject of his* Cyclops. *Diocles and Callias wrote* Cyclopes, *and we find Theopompus writing an* Odysseus, *a* Penelope, *and a* Sirens. *See the introduction to Cratinus'* Odysseus and Company *for Sommerstein's theory that Platonius (AOC 3) confused that comedy with Theopompus'* Odysseus *in his history of Greek Comedy.*

34 Eustathius *On the Odyssey* p. 1863.50

<blockquote>
χιτῶνά μοι
φέρων δέδωκας δαιδάλεον, ὃν ἤκασεν
ἄρισθ᾿ Ὅμηρος κρομμύου λεπυχάνῳ.
</blockquote>

35 Athenaeus 165b

<blockquote>
Εὐριπίδου τἄριστον οὐ κακῶς ἔχον,
τἀλλότρια δειπνεῖν τὸν καλῶς εὐδαίμονα.
</blockquote>

36 Σ Aristophanes *Wasps* 1346a

<blockquote>
ἵνα μὴ τὸ παλαιὸν τοῦτο καὶ θρυλούμενον
δι᾿ ἡμετέρων στομάτων <   >
εἴπω σόφισμ᾿, ὅ φασι παῖδας Λεσβίων
εὑρεῖν.
</blockquote>

37 Pollux 7.74

<blockquote>
λάσιον ἐπιβεβλημένος
</blockquote>

ΠΑΙΔΕΣ

38 Pollux 7.66

<blockquote>
τηνδὶ περιζωσάμενος ᾦαν λουτρίδα
κατάδεσμον ἥβης περιπέτασον.
</blockquote>

34 You have brought and given to me a marvellous tunic, which Homer likened very aptly to the skin of an onion.[1]

[1] Eustathius tells us that the speaker was Odysseus. The comparison of a cloak to an onionskin is taken from *Odyssey* 19.232–33 (the cloak that Penelope had given Odysseus). Since Eustathius does not indicate which play by Theopompus, it is possible that this fragment might belong to his *Penelope*.

35 That excellent line of Euripides, very well put, that the truly happy man dines off someone else.

36 So that I may not mention that celebrated old trick of our lips, which they say the girls of Lesbos invented.

37 Having put on a woollen cloth.

BOYS (SLAVES?)

F 39 claims that an association with the speaker has resulted in "all good things for men." From this we might infer a comedy about the education of the young, and compare the extant version of Clouds *and Cratinus'* Chirons. *It is possible that the title could mean "slaves," however.*

38 Throw this bathing cloth about yourself, wrap it round you to cover your privates.

39 Hephaestion *Handbook* 13.2

πάντ᾽ ἀγαθὰ δὴ γέγονεν ἀνδράσιν ἐμῆς ἀπὸ
συνουσίας.

40 Σ Aristophanes *Birds* 1569

εἶχε δὲ καὶ περὶ τὰς κνήμας αἰτίας τινὰς . . . διὸ καὶ
κατὰ σκελῶν ἐφόρει τὸ ἱμάτιον, ὡς Θεόπομπος ἐν
Παισί.

ΠΑΜΦΙΛΗ

41 Athenaeus 485b

σπόγγος, λεκάνη, πτερόν, λεπαστὴ πάνυ πυκνή,
ἣν ἐκπιοῦσ᾽ ἄκρατον Ἀγαθοῦ Δαίμονος
τέττιξ κελαδεῖ.

42 Athenaeus 485e

λεπαστὴ μάλα συχνή,
ἣν ἐκπιοῦσ᾽ ἄκρατον Ἀγαθοῦ Δαίμονος
περίστατον βοῶσα τὴν κώμην ποιεῖ.

43 Photius ε 1756

αὐτὴ δ᾽ ἐκείνη πρότερον ἐξηπίστατο
παρὰ τῆς ἐπιτηθῆς.

39 In fact all good things have come to men from associating with me.

40 He [Laispodias] had some problems with his legs . . . which is why he wore a cloak down to his ankles, as Theopompus says in *Boys*.

PAMPHILE

Athenaeus (591d) records that Pamphile (love-all) was the name of a hetaera who supported the actor Satyrus. As Satyrus belongs to the middle of the fourth century, she is unlikely to have been the subject of this comedy, but there could easily have been more than one Pamphile in the fourth century. As F 41 and 42 sound very much alike, it has been suggested that the comedy was presented in a revised version or that Athenaeus (or his sources) has turned one citation into two.

41 A sponge, a basin, a feather, a very sturdy limpet cup, from which she drinks unmixed wine in honour of the God of Good Luck and chirps like a cicada.

42 A very sturdy limpet cup, from which she drinks unmixed wine in honour of the God of Good Luck, and with her bawling gathers the village round her.

43 She herself learned well in the past from her great-grandmother.

44 Photius p. 484.4

τούτων ἁπάντων ὁ ῥαχιστὴς Δημοφῶν

ΠΑΝΤΑΛΕΩΝ

46 Pollux 10.41

ὠνητιῶν τὸ δέρμα τοῦ θηρός

ῥάψας ὅλον
σάξαι κνεφάλλων

44 Demophon, the boaster about all these things.[1]

[1] Prominent Demophons of the early 4th c. include a general in 379/8 (*PAA* 321635), the guardian of the young Demosthenes (321715), and a poet (dramatic?) mentioned at Ephippus F 16 (321650).

Brief fragment: (F 45) "sandals."

PANTALEON

Athenaeus (20b) mentions planoi (wandering entertainers), including a Pantaleon (PAA 764430), and elsewhere (616a) cites the comic poet Theognetos (F 2) for Pantaleon's peculiar verbal delivery and the philosopher Chrysippus for a Pantaleon who on his deathbed deceived his sons about the location of his buried treasure. This may, of course, have nothing to do with the subject of this comedy, but a distinctive popular entertainer would have made an excellent target. The name is not rare in the fourth century, perhaps a dozen examples, the best known of which is a man accused by the speaker of Lysias 10.5 of defrauding his brother (PAA 764425).

46 Wanting to buy the skin of the beast

To stitch and stuff all of the pillow.

Brief fragment: (F 47) "little cave."

ΠΗΝΕΛΟΠΗ

48 Photius (b, z) α 163

καί σε τῇ νουμηνίᾳ
ἀγαλματίοις ἀγαλοῦμεν ἀεὶ καὶ δάφνῃ.

49 Athenaeus 657a

καὶ τὴν ἱερὰν σφάττουσιν ἡμῶν δέλφακα.

ΣΕΙΡΗΝΕΣ

51 Photius ε 1797

αὐλεῖ γὰρ σαπρὰ
αὕτη γε κρούμαθ᾽ οἷα τἀπὶ Χαριξένης.

THEOPOMPUS

PENELOPE

*Penelope was the subject of tragedies of that name by Aes-
chylus and Philocles. Of the latter only the title is known,
of the former one fragment (F 187) survives, in which a
character claims that he is "of an ancient race, a Cretan"—
compare* Odyssey *19.165ff. where the disguised Odysseus
tells Penelope a story in which he claims to be a Cretan. It is
possible that Theopompus'* Odysseus *and* Penelope *could
be the same play. If there are two different comedies, it is
possible that F 34 belongs to* Penelope.

48 On the day of the new moon we shall always honour
you [sing.] with images and laurel branches.

49 They are slaughtering our sacred piglet.

Brief fragment: (F 50) "spindle harp."

SIRENS

Nicophon wrote a Sirens *at roughly the same time as
Theopompus. Three fragments of that comedy survive, all
having to do with food and none apart possibly from F 21
having any real connection with the story of Odysseus and
the Sirens. This is yet another comic drama to exploit
the adventures of Odysseus from Homer. Traditionally the
Sirens are two or three in number. Could comedy have
expanded that number to create a chorus?*

51 She is playing some stale melodies like those from the
time of Charixena.

THE POETS OF OLD COMEDY

52 Athenaeus 399d

θύννων τε λευκὰ Σικελικῶν ὑπήτρια

53 Σ Aristophanes *Lysistrata* 45

ὑποδοῦ λαβὼν <   > τὰς περιβαρίδας.

54 Pollux 7.181

φρυγεύς, θυεία, λήκυθος

ΣΤΡΑΤΙΩΤΙΔΕΣ

55 Athenaeus 483e

ἐγὼ γὰρ ⟨ἂν⟩ κώθωνος ἐκ στρεψαύχενος
πίοιμι τὸν τράχηλον ἀνακεκλασμένη;

56 Pollux 9.64

καίτοι τίς οὐκ ἂν οἶκος εὖ πράττοι τετρωβολίζων,
εἰ νῦν γε διώβολον φέρων ἀνὴρ τρέφει γυναῖκα;

52 White under-slices of tunny fish from Sicily.

53 Take and put on these shoes [women's] of yours.

54 Roasting pan, mortar, oil flask.

SHE-SOLDIERS

The title, as well as the woman in command at F 57, suggests strongly a comedy of the sort as Lysistrata *and* Assembly-Women. *F 55 is spoken by a woman faced with drinking from a military canteen (kōthōn), a nice mixture of the bibulous nature of women and the hardships of the military life (cf. Eupolis'* Officers). *F 56 does sound rather close to the spirit of* Assembly-Women, *where the implications of the new order are worked out for the household. In F 57 "Thrasymachus" is probably not the sophist familiar from* Republic 1, *but a made-up name ("bold fighter") in the same way that the women's names at* Thesmophoriazusae *802–10 are chosen for their etymology. The iambic tetrameters of F 56–57 indicate a formal contest (agon), where one speaker is arguing in favour of having women join the army.*

Recent bibliography: A.K. Gravilov, MH 53 (1996) 100–105.

55 I [fem.] would twist my neck off by drinking from a twisted-throated canteen?

56 And furthermore what household would not fare well on four obols a day, if a man now keeps a wife while making two obols?

57 Priscian *Institutes of Grammar* 18.213

ἡ Θρασυμάχου ‹δ'› ὑμῶν γυνὴ καλῶς ἐπιστατήσει.

58 Σ (Arethas) Plato *Apology* 18b

Θεόπομπος δὲ Στρ‹ατι›ώτισιν ἐμβαδᾶν αὐτὸν εἶπεν παρὰ τὰς ἐμβάδας, ἐπεὶ καὶ Ἄρχιππος Ἰχθύσιν εἰς σκυτέα αὐτὸν σκώπτει.

ΤΕΙΣΑΜΕΝΟΣ

60 Harpocration p. 171.6

ἀλλ' ἡ μὲν Εἰλείθυια συγγνώμην ἔχει
ὑπὸ τῶν γυναικῶν οὖσα καταπλὴξ τὴν τέχνην.

61 Σ Aristophanes *Wasps* 1221

τὸν δὲ Μύσιον
Ἀκέστορ' ἀναπέπεικεν ἀκολουθεῖν ἅμα.

---

[1] Acestor (nicknamed Sacas—*PAA* 116685) was a tragic poet (*TrGF* I 25), whom the comic poets made fun of for allegedly not being a proper Athenian citizen (*Wasps* 1221, *Birds* 31; Cratinus F 92; Eupolis F 172.14–16; Metagenes F 14).

57 The wife of Thrasymachus will command you well.

58 Theopompus in *She-Soldiers* calls him [Anytus] "slipper" on account of his slippers, since Archippus in *Fishes* [F 31] makes fun of him as a shoemaker.

Brief fragment: (F 59) "slender."

TEISAMENUS

Does Teisamenus refer to an actual Athenian, in which case the comedy would have a strong topical and political theme (cf. the demagogue comedies of Platon), or is he a figure from myth (e.g., the son of Orestes), or is there some other significance? The matter is further complicated by Aelian's (T 2) report that Teisamenus was the name of Theopompus' father. The name is not rare at Athens, the best-known contemporary being PAA 877610, the son of Mechanion, who proposed a decree after the fall of the Thirty to reestablish the laws of Solon (Andocides 1.83, Lysias 30.28). Lysias' dismissal of Teisamenus and his fellow "undersecretaries" as men vastly inferior to their predecessors implies a notoriety that a comic poet could exploit. Others of the time include PAA 877720 (a tamias of Athena in 414/3), a man made fun of at Acharnians 603 (PAA 877645), and the father of the tragic poet Agathon (PAA 877635).

60 But Eileithuia will be forgiven by the women for being reticent about her craft.

61 He has persuaded Acestor the Mysian to go along as well.[1]

ΦΙΝΕΥΣ

63 Athenaeus 649b

παῦσαι κυβεύων, μειράκιον, καὶ τοῖς βλίτοις
διαχρῶ τὸ λοιπόν. κοιλίαν σκληρὰν ἔχεις,
τὰ πετραῖα τῶν ἰχθυδίων ἀπέσθιε.
ἡ τρὺξ ἄριστόν ἐστιν εἰς εὐβουλίαν.
5   ταῦτ᾽ ἢν ποῇς, ῥᾴων ἔσει τὴν οὐσίαν.

ΑΔΗΛΩΝ ΔΡΑΜΑΤΩΝ

64 *Etymologicum Genuinum* A

                    ὥς σοι δοκεῖν
εἶναι τὸ πρόθυρον τοῦτο βασανιστήριον,
τὴν δ᾽ οἰκίαν ζητρεῖον ἢ κακὸν μέγα.

65 Athenaeus 23e

ἐπίνομεν μετὰ ταῦτα <   >
κατακείμενοι μαλακώτατ᾽ ἐπὶ τρικλινίῳ
Τελαμῶνος οἰμώζοντες ἀλλήλοις μέλη.

66 Plutarch *Lysander* 13.7

                    τοὺς Ἕλληνας ἥδιστον ποτὸν
τῆς ἐλευθερίας γεύσαντες ὄξος ἐνέχεαν

Brief fragment: (F 62) "superstitious."

PHINEUS

Phineus is the blind prophet associated with the Harpies and the Argonauts and is the subject of a tragedy by Aeschylus and two by Sophocles.

63 Stop playing dice, kid, and in the future start eating blite. Your bowels are constipated. Stay away from rockfish. Wine-lees are best of all for clear thinking. If you do this, you will be healthier in your . . . wallet.

UNASSIGNED FRAGMENTS

64 With the result that this foreporch seems to you to be a torture chamber and the house itself a place of punishment or something really bad.

65 After that we started drinking, reclining very comfortably in a room with three couches, moaning the songs of Telamon to one another.

66 Having given the Greeks the sweetest taste of freedom they [the Spartans] served them up vinegar.

[*Barmaids?*]

67 Eustathius *On the Odyssey* p. 1604.4

ἄφωνος ἐγένετο,
ἔπειτα μέντοι πάλιν ἀνηνέχθη.

68 Athenaeus 50e

τρώγουσι μύρτα καὶ πέπονα μιμαίκυλα.

69 Athenaeus 62e

κἄπειτ᾽ ἰδὼν ἀσφάραγον ἐν θάμνῳ τινί

70 Clement of Alexandria *Miscellanies* 6.19.5

δὶς παῖδες οἱ γέροντες ὀρθῷ τῷ λόγῳ.

71 Σ Aristophanes *Wealth* 1138c

{Α.} εἴσω δραμὼν αἴτησον. {Β.} ἀλλ᾽ οὐκ ἐκφορά.

72 Pollux 2.234

ἄπνους, ἄνευρος, ἀσθενής, ἀνέντατος

73 Photius (b, z) α 632

ὃς αἱμασιολογεῖν ἄριστ᾽ ἠπίστατο.

74 Orus *On Orthography* fol. 281ʳ 3

ὁ δὲ ταῦρός ἐστιν ἀγόμενος πρὸς τῷ νεῷ.

67 He became silent, and then, however, came back to his senses.

68 They are munching myrtle and ripe arbutus berries.

69 And then seeing asparagus on a bush.

70 That saying is right: old men are children for the second time.

71 (A) Run inside and ask.   (B) But nothing's being given out.   [*Barmaids*?]

72 Without breath, without nerve, without strength, without exertion.

73 Who knew how to lay walls very well.

74 Here is the bull being led beside the temple.
[*Phineus*?]

75 Photius (S²) α 3097

αἰσχρῶς ἀτιμώσαντες ἐξελαύνετε

76 Athenaeus 68d

μαλθακωτέρα
πέπονος σικυοῦ μοι γέγονε.

77 Zonaras p. 920

ἀλλ' εἰ δοκεῖ, χρὴ ταῦτα δρᾶν· εὐοδεῖν πορεύομαι.

78 Athenaeus 264a

δεσπότου πενέστου ῥυσὰ βουλευτήρια

79 Zonaras p. 388

τοὺς βιβλιοπώλας † λεύσομαι.

80 Pollux 2.18

πρεσβῦτις, φίλοινος, μεθύση, οἰνομάχλη, κοχώνη.

75 You people are driving [him, them, her] out after shamefully dishonouring [him, etc.].

76 She [it] has come to me, softer than a ripe cucumber.

77 Well, if that's what you think, that's what must be done. Farewell, I am off.

78 The wrinkled councillors of a serf turned master.

79 I shall stone (?) the booksellers.

80 An elderly woman, fond of wine, drunk, full of wine lust, bottoms up.

Brief fragments: (F 81) "an aggressive person," (F 82) "navy women," (F 83) "a dish of little birds," (F 84) "prone to tears," (F 85) "hold up," (F 86) "will be purchased," (F 87) "bag," (F 88) "with one's own hand," (F 89) "ritual branches," (F 90) "Galena" [name of hetaera].

(F 91) "servile demeanour," (F 92) "centaur" [of the female genitalia], (F 93) "puppy dog," (F 94) "drunken woman," (F 95) "first-timer" [of a virgin being married], (F 96) "quivering necklaces,"(F 97) "take account of."

ΘΟΥΓΕΝΙΔΗΣ

Testimonium

i *IG* ii² 2325.55

.........]s¹ I

¹ Θουγενίδης or Μενεκράτης Körte; Ξενόφιλος Wilhem.

Fragments

ΔΙΚΑΣΤΑΙ

THUGENIDES

*As one might expect, the name of this shadowy comic poet
was confused in the tradition with Thucydides, but Pollux
(citing F 1, 3) and the Antiatticist (citing F 2) do know of a
poet called Thugenides, for whom one title (Jurors) was at-
tested. If his name is rightly restored on the victors' list for
the Dionysia (T 1)—although Xenophilus is a better candi-
date—then he won one victory around 440, probably with*
Jurors, *before vanishing from the scene.*

Testimonium

i [From the list of victors at the Dionysia, from the late
440s or 430s]

Thougenide]s 1

Fragments

JURORS

*Perhaps an inevitable title for an Old Comedy, especially
in view of the theme of jury service in* Wasps *and the con-
stant jokes in Aristophanes about the Athenians' fondness
for litigation. If* Jurors *is as early as the 430s, then it shows
that the dicastic stereotype in comedy predates Aristoph-
anes by at least ten years.*

355

1 Photius (b, S^z) α 2096

τί ὦγάθ᾽ ἀντιδικοῦμεν ἀλλήλοις ἔτι;

2 The Antiatticist p. 114.22

τριαχθῆναι

ΑΔΗΛΩΝ ΔΡΑΜΑΤΩΝ

3 Pollux 6.38

ᾔτησεν εἰς ὀψώνιον τριώβολον.

4 The Antiatticist p. 107.30

μὴ νόμισον

5 Zonaras p. 1294

Λειβηθρίων ἀνοητότεροι

THUGENIDES

1 Why do we go back and forth at law, my friend?

2 To be beaten three times.

UNASSIGNED FRAGMENTS

3 He [she] asked for three obols as a salary.

4 Don't think.

5 More foolish than the people of Leibethra,[1]

[1] A city in Macedon, at the foot of Mount Olympus.

ΞΕΝΟΦΙΛΟΣ

Testimonia

i *IG* ii² 2325.55

.........]ς Ι

Θουγενίδης or Μενεκράτης Körte; Ξενόφιλος Wilhem.

ii *IG* ii² 2325.118

[Ξ]ενόφιλος Ι

iii *IG Urb. Rom.* 215

Ξενόφιλος[- - - -
- - - - ἐπὶ τὰ τ]ρίτα καὶ ἐπὶ τὰ [τέταρτα - - - -

XENOPHILUS

*Given his first-place finish at the first Lenaea competition
(c. 440–T 2), Xenophilus is rather more likely than Thu-
genides or Menecrates to be the name ending in sigma on
the list of victors at the Dionysia (T 1). On the Lenaea list
his name comes right before that of Teleclides, on the Dio-
nysia list it would come right after. We have definite proof,
then, of a minor comic poet named Xenophilus active
around 440. His work was clearly an early casualty, as we
have no recorded titles or fragments extant.*

Testimonia

i [From the list of victors at the Dionysia, from the late
440s or 430s]

Xenophilu]s 1

ii [First name on the list of victors at the Lenaea, c. 440]

X]enophilus 1

iii [From a Roman inscription listing comic poets and
their plays, grouped in order of their placings]

Xenophilus . . . as regards third- and ⟨fourth-place⟩ re-
sults . . .

ΞΕΝΟΦΩΝ

Testimonia

i Diogenes Laertius 2.59

γεγόνασι δὲ Ξενοφῶντες ἑπτά· . . . ἕβδομος κωμῳδίας ἀρχαίας ποιητής.

ii *IG* ii² 2325.135

Ξενο[φ]ῶν Ι

XENOPHON

*Diogenes Laertius (T 1) records a poet of Old Comedy as
the seventh known Xenophon. His existence is confirmed
by the presence of that name on the list of victors at the
Lenaea (T 2). At this point the list is presenting winners at
that festival in the 390s. Xenophon was thus a very minor
poet of the last phase of Old Comedy, whose plays had
ceased to be remembered.*

Testimonia

i There have been seven men named Xenophon . . . the
seventh is a poet of Old Comedy.

ii [From the list of victors at the Lenaea, from the 390s]

Xeno[ph]on 1

COMIC ADESPOTA

The reader will find nearly a thousand "book" fragments in PCG VIII. Sometimes we are told quite firmly that a fragment is found "in Old Comedy" (F 242, 806), but in many instances the attribution to comedy is uncertain and the result of judgements made by the nineteenth-century editors of the comic fragments. Several fragments (e.g., F 154, 221, 461, 729) are attributed to "the comic poet," which often means Aristophanes or Menander, but on occasion can mean another comedian.

Personal humour provides an important criterion. While keeping in mind that personal jokes may certainly be found in Middle and even New Comedy, one may certainly claim for Old Comedy jokes at Alcibiades (F 123) or Cleon (F 461, 846) or Euripides (F 421, 860), and very probably the reference to the clean-shaven man on whom a horrible fate is invoked (F 154). Then there are fragments very much in the spirit of Old Comedy, with its fondness for

COMIC ADESPOTA

bold and inventive compound forms (as at F 176, 514), vulgar language and reference to bodily functions (F 173, 474), and plays on words (F 83). On some occasions an unusual metre will suggest possibly a parabatic context, as at F 209, 245–46, where a metatheatrical tone seems to be present. Parody of Euripides has been detected in a couple of places (F 421, 445), and while Middle and New Comedy certainly knew and cited their Euripides, I have chosen to include these here. Then there are places where a comic fragment recalls in word or spirit a passage that we know for certain belongs to Old Comedy, as F 100 immediately brings Eupolis F 316.1 to mind, and the description "oak Acharnae" (F 498) recalls Aristophanes' first extant comedy. I have included also those fragments for which scholars have reasonably suggested an attribution to a particular author or lost play from Old Comedy. Finally, many fragments are often lexical notes about an unusual form; I have generally included these as "brief fragments."

COMIC ADESPOTA

8 Photius δ 762

ἐκωμῳδοῦντο γὰρ οἱ Ἀχαρνεῖς ὡς ἄγριοι καὶ σκληροί,
Ποτάμιοι δὲ ὡς ῥᾳδίως δεχόμενοι τοὺς παρεγγράφους.
Θυμοιτάδαι καὶ Προσπάλτιοι ὡς δικαστικοί.

45 Origen *Against Celsus* 6.78–79

ἑξῆς δὲ τοιαῦτά τινα λέγει ὁ Κέλσος· "ἔτι μὴν εἴπερ
ἐβούλετο ὁ θεὸς ὥσπερ ὁ παρὰ τῷ κωμῳδῷ Ζεὺς ἐκ
τοῦ μακροῦ ὕπνου διϋπνίσας ῥύσασθαι τὸ τῶν ἀνθρώ-
πων γένος ἐκ κακῶν, τί δή ποτε εἰς μίαν γωνίαν
ἔπεμψε τοῦτο, ὅ φατε, πνεῦμα; δέον πολλὰ ὁμοίως
διαφυσῆσαι σώματα καὶ κατὰ πᾶσαν ἀποστεῖλαι τὴν
οἰκουμένην. ἀλλ' ὁ μὲν κωμῳδὸς ἐν τῷ θεάτρῳ γελω-
τοποιῶν συνέγραψεν ὅτι Ζεὺς ἐξυπνισθεὶς Ἀθηναίοις
καὶ Λακεδαιμονίοις τὸν Ἑρμῆν ἔπεμψε· σὺ δὲ οὐκ οἴει
καταγελαστότερον πεποιηκέναι Ἰουδαίοις πεμπόμε-
νον τοῦ θεοῦ τὸν υἱόν;" ὅρα δὴ καὶ ἐν τούτοις τὸ
ἄσεμνον τοῦ Κέλσου, ἀφιλοσόφως κωμῳδίας ποιητὴν
γελωτοποιὸν παραλαβόντος καὶ τῷ παρ' αὐτῷ διϋπνι-
σθέντι πέμποντι Ἑρμῆν παραβάλλοντος τὸν τοῦ παν-
τὸς δημιουργὸν θεὸν ἡμῶν. . . . ὁ μὲν οὖν κωμῳδὸς
γελωτοποιῶν τὸν Δία κοιμώμενον πεποίηκέ τε καὶ
διϋπνιζόμενον καὶ πέμποντα πρὸς τοὺς Ἕλληνας τὸν
Ἑρμῆν.

8 The Acharnians were made fun of in comedy as fierce and truculent, Potamians as easily admitting illegal aliens, and the Thymoetidae and Prospaltians as fond of litigation.[1]

[1] *Acharnians, Potamians,* and *Prospaltians* are all demes of Attica and the titles of comedies by Aristophanes, Strattis, and Eupolis. We do not know of any comedy called "Thymoetidae."

45 Celsus continues with something along these lines, "Furthermore if God, like Zeus in the comic poet, waking up from a deep sleep, wanted to protect the human race from evil, why did he send that spirit you speak of to just one corner of the world? He should have breathed it into many bodies in the same way and sent them out throughout the whole civilised world. The comic poet wanting to get a laugh in the theatre wrote that Zeus woke up and sent Hermes to the Athenians and the Spartans. But do you not find it more ridiculous to have the son of God sent to the Jews?" Notice here in particular the lack of respect from Celsus, enlisting in a very unphilosophical manner a laughter-loving comic poet and comparing our God, the creator of all, with a Zeus who wakes up and sends Hermes . . . The comic poet, keen on laughter, has created a sleeping Zeus waking up and sending Hermes to the Greeks.[1]

[1] Clearly the summary of the "great idea" of a comic play, it could belong to a mythological burlesque of the 4th c., but the mention of "Athenians and Spartans" suggests the latter half of the 5th c.

47 Choricius *Orations* 2.63

τοιγαροῦν εἰ κωμῳδίαν ἐπηγγελλόμην, εἰσῆγον ἂν ἐν
εἴδει γυναικὸς ἑκατέραν, ὥσπερ τὴν Νύκτα τῶν κωμι-
κῶν τις, καὶ βασκαίνουσαν τῇ Νυκτὶ τὴν Ἡμέραν
ἐποίουν

72 Aelian *Historical Miscellany* 13.15

φασὶ παχύτατον γενέσθαι τὴν διάνοιαν οἱ τῆς κωμῳ-
δίας ποιηταὶ τὸ δέρμα ἔχοντα ἀδιακόντιστον Πολύ-
δωρόν τινα, καὶ ἄλλον Κοικυλίωνα ὄνομα, ὅσπερ τὰ
κύματα ἠρίθμει ὑπὸ τῆς ἄγαν μανίας. λόγος δέ τις καὶ
Σαννυρίωνα τοιοῦτον γενέσθαι, ὃς ἐν τῇ ληκύθῳ τὴν
κλίμακα ἐζήτει. καὶ Κόροιβον δὲ καὶ Μελιτίδην καὶ
ἐκείνους ἀνοήτους φασίν.[1]

> [1] Πολύδωρόν MS, Πολύωρόν Leutsch; μανίας MS, ἀνοίας
> Jacobs.

80 Ammonius *On the Difference between Synonyms* 267

ἀλλὰ θύε τοῦ κέδρου

83 Anonymous *On Comedy* (Koster VI.8)

ἕκτον κατὰ ἐξαλλαγήν, ὡς τὸ "ὦ Βδεῦ δέσποτα" ἀντὶ
τοῦ "ὦ Ζεῦ."

47 If I were producing a comedy, I would bring on each of them [Night and Day] in the form of a woman, just like one of the comic poets ⟨did with⟩ Night, and I'd make Day having words with Night.[1]

[1] Platon's *Long Night* has been suggested as the play in question.

72 The comic poets say that there was a certain Polydorus, who had an impenetrable skin, very dense in intellect, and so also another man named Coecylion, who was so crazy that he kept trying to count the waves. There is also a story that Sannyrion was like this too, "who kept looking for the tempest in the teapot." They say that Coroebus and Melitides were stupid as well.[1]

[1] In the Greek the phrase "tempest in a teapot" is actually "ladder in a *lēcythus*," both words being terms of rhetoric flourish—see Calder, *Philologus* 117 (1973) 141f. Sannyrion could be the comic poet, and the reference to something in a comedy by him, or it may be a *nom parlant* from *sannas* (crazy—see Cratinus F 489).

80 But add some juniper berries to the sacrificial flame.

83 The sixth ⟨source of verbal humour⟩ lies in wordplay, such as "O Lord Juice" for "O Lord Zeus."[1]

[1] In Greek the wordplay is on "Zeus" and "Bdeus" (farter).

COMIC ADESPOTA

100 Athenaeus 20b

τὴν λαμπροτάτην πόλεων πασῶν ὁπόσας ὁ Ζεὺς
ἀναφαίνει.

102 Athenaeus 39d

οὔτ' ἂν σκώμματα
γένοιτ' ⟨ἂν⟩ οὔτ' αὐτοσχέδια ποιήματα

112 Athenaeus 307f

μὴ καὶ ἡμεῖς ἄγομεν Θεσμοφορίων τὴν μέσην, ὅτι
δίκην κεστρέων νηστεύομεν

116 Athenaeus 401b

φροντιστὰ καὶ λογιστά

119 Athenaeus 415d

Ἀρχίλοχος δ' ἐν Τετραμέτροις Χαρίλαν εἰς τὰ ὅμοια
διαβέβληκεν, ὡς οἱ κωμῳδιοποιοὶ Κλεώνυμον καὶ Πεί-
σανδρον.

123 Athenaeus 574d

Ἀλκιβιάδην τὸν ἁβρόν, ὦ γῆ καί θεοί,
ὃν ἡ Λακεδαίμων μοιχὸν ἐπιθυμεῖ λαβεῖν.

100 . . . the most glorious city of all those that Zeus illumines.[1]

[1] Compare "O fairest city of all that Cleon oversees" (Eupolis F 316.1).

102 [Athenaeus' speakers are describing the benefits of wine]

‹From dry sustinence› no jokes would come nor improvised poems.[1]

[1] From Cratinus' *Wine-Flask?*

112 We are celebrating the middle day of the Thesmophoria, because we are fasting like mullets.[1]

[1] Another instance of comedy's use of *nēstis* (hungry) to describe grey mullets (*kestreis*). The fish was caught with no food in its stomach, hence "hungry."

116 Thinker and reckoner.

119 Archilochus in his tetrameters [F 167 West] has attacked Charilas in the same way [for gluttony], just as the comic poets do to Cleonymus and Peisander.[1]

[1] Cleonymus is made fun of for his appetite at *Knights* 956–58, 1290–99, and *Birds* 289; Peisander at Eupolis F 99.1–4.

123 Earth and gods, pretty boy Alcibiades whom Sparta lusts to have as her lover.

COMIC ADESPOTA

145 Demetrius *On Style* 142–43

{A.} δέσποτα Πλούτων μελανοπτερύγων,
{B.} τουτὶ δεινόν. π<υρ>ροπτερύγων
αὐτὸ ποίησον

154 Dion of Prusa 33.63

εἶτα ἐξύρων μέχρι τῶν παρειῶν· οὐδὲ τοῦτό πω δεινόν·
ἀλλ' ὅμως ὁ κωμικὸς καὶ τοῦτον ἐκέλευσε κατακαίειν

ἐπὶ φαλήτων συκίνων ἑκκαίδεκα.

173 *Etymologicum Genuinum* λ 34

λαπιδόρχας· ὁ μεγάλους ὄρχεις ἔχων. Ἀριστοκράτης
δὲ οὕτω διεβάλλετο.

196 Eustathius *On the Iliad* p. 971.39

ὀκνεῖς λαλεῖν; οὕτω σφοδρ' εἶ τηθαλλαδοῦς;

209 Eustathius *On the Odyssey* p. 1522.66

ὦ μόνοι ὦτοι τῶν Ἑλλήνων

221 Eustathius *On the Odyssey* p. 1910.10

πικρότερον δὲ τούτου εἰς σκῶμμα τὸ εἰρῆσθαι κένταυ-
ρον, ὃς κεντεῖ ὄρρον τὸν παρὰ τῷ κωμικῷ.

145 (A) "Pluto, black-winged Lord."
(B) That's awful. Make him "with wings of fiery red."

154 Then they started shaving right down to the cheeks. Now this wasn't so terrible, but still the comic poet ordered that even such a man be burned "on sixteen phalli made of fig wood."

[1] This reminds one of the jokes against such clean-shaven men (hence "women") as Agathon, Cleisthenes, and Epigonus. From Eupolis' *Demes* or Aristophanes' *Triphales?*

173 "Slack balls." Having large testicles. Aristocrates is attacked in this way.[1]

[1] More than a hundred holders of this name are known, the most prominent in comedy being the son of Scellias (*PAA* 171045), a right-wing politician of the 410s.

196 You are reluctant to speak? You are such a mama's boy.

209 [to the Athenians] You people, the only gulls in Greece.[1]

[1] In Greek the short-eared owl (*ōtos*) is used of people easily taken in, hence "gulls." The line can be scanned as anapaestic dimeter and has been assigned to the opening of a parabasis.

221 More galling than this is to be called "centaur" [*kentauros*] as a joke, who in comedy "pricks the butt" [*kentei* + *orros*].

233 Harpocration p. 22.16

ἄλλος δέ ἐστιν Ἀλκιβιάδης οὗ μνημονεύει Ἀντιφῶν ἐν τῇ πρὸς τὴν Δημοσθένους γραφὴν ἀπολογίᾳ· μνημονεύουσι δ' αὐτοῦ καὶ τῶν ἄλλων ῥητόρων τινὲς καὶ οἱ κωμικοί. ἔστι δὲ Φηγούσιος, Ἀλκιβιάδου ξένος.

ξένος codd., ἀνεψιός Sauppe.

237 Harpocration p. 86.2

Ἐρατοσθένης δὲ ἐν τοῖς περὶ τῆς ἀρχαίας κωμῳδίας πόθεν τὸ πρᾶγμα εἴρηται δηλοῖ οὕτω λέγων "Λύκος ἐστὶν ἥρως πρὸς τοῖς ἐν Ἀθήναις δικαστηρίοις, τοῦ θηρίου μορφὴν ἔχων, πρὸς ὃν οἱ δωροδοκοῦντες κατὰ ι′ γιγνόμενοι ἀνεστρέφοντο, ὅθεν εἴρηται Λύκου δεκάς."

238 Harpocration p. 135.9

ὅτι δὲ ἐκαλοῦντό τινες καὶ Ἱππάρχειοι Ἑρμαῖ ἀπὸ Ἱππάρχου τοῦ Πεισιστράτου εἴρηται ἔν τε τῇ ἀρχαίᾳ κωμῳδίᾳ καὶ παρὰ Πλάτωνι ἐν τῷ Ἱππάρχῳ.

244 Hephaestion *Handbook* 6.4

οὐδ' Ἀμειψίαν ὁρᾶτε πτωχὸν ὄντ' ἐφ' ἡμῖν.

ὑμῖν A, ἡμῖν DIH.

233 There is another Alcibiades, whom Antiphon mentions in his *Defence against the Law-suit of Demosthenes* [F 8 Blass]. Certain of the orators mention him, also the comic poets. He was Phegusius by deme, a cousin (?) of Alcibiades.[1]

1 This Alcibiades (*PAA* 121652) is known from Andocides 1.65–66 and Xenophon *Hellenica* 1.2.13, and the sale of his property is recorded on *IG* i³ 428.

237 "In tens": Eratosthenes in *On Old Comedy* [F 89] explains where the term comes from as follows: "Lycus is a hero, in the form of an animal, by the law courts in Athens, where those willing to be bribed would hang out in groups of ten, hence the phrase "Lycus' tens."[1]

1 Lycus (wolf) was an Athenian hero, likely identified with the son of Pandion. A statue of Lycus was located beside one of the Athenian law courts (*Wasps* 387, 819).

238 That certain ⟨Herms⟩ were called "Hipparchus' Herms" after the son of Pisistratus is stated in Old Comedy and in Plato's *Hipparchus* [228d–229a].

244 And you people don't even notice a beggar Ameipsias among us [you?].[1]

1 Meineke, followed by K.-A., read the name as "Amynias," the *pseudoploutos* at *Wasps* 1267–74, instead of Amepisias the comic poet.

COMIC ADESPOTA

245 Hephaestion *Handbook* 6.6

τῶν πολιτῶν ἄνδρας ὑμῖν δημιουργοὺς ἀποφανῶ.

246 Hephaestion *Handbook* 16.5

εὐφράνας ἡμᾶς ἀπέπεμπ' οἴκαδ' ἄλλον ἄλλοσε.

278 Hesychius α 5716

Ἀνδροκλέα τὸν ἀπ' αἰγείρων

283 Hesychius α 7248

Ἀριστόδημον οἱ κωμικοὶ τὸν πρωκτὸν καὶ Θεόδωρον καὶ Τιμησιάνακτα ἔλεγον, ἀπὸ τῶν ἡταιρηκότων. Φορμισίους δὲ τὰ γυναικεῖα αἰδοῖα καὶ Βασιλείδας, καὶ Λαχάρας

288 Hesychius α 7900

ἀστράψῃ διὰ πυκνός.

297 Hesychius β 1329

βυρσόκαππον· τὸν Κλέωνα

245 I shall demonstrate to you that . . . are the fashioners of citizens.[1]

1 It has been suggested that it is comic poets who are "fashioners of citizens." Compare *Acharnians* 641–42.

246 He would send us away happy, some this way, some that.[1]

1 This line is cited by Hephaestion as a eupolidean, strongly indicative of a parabasis. It sounds very like Aristophanes' description of the comedy of Crates at *Knights* 538. It is likely that "he" is another comic poet.

278 Androkles from the poplars.

283 The comic poets call the arsehole "Aristodemus" and "Theodorus" and "Timesianax," from homosexual perverts. They call the female genitalia "Phormisius" and "Basileides" and "Lachares."[1]

1 Aristodemus is so called at Cratinus F 151 and Aristophanes F 242 (*Banqueters*—427), and Phormisius at *Ecclesiazusae* 97. Theodorus is a very common name, while the other three are found at Athens only in later centuries.

288 ⟨Whenever⟩ it [he?] lightens through the Pnyx.[1]

1 The description of Pericles as Zeus casting lightning- and thunder-bolts at *Acharnians* 531 suggests that he might be the subject here.

297 Leather-cappus: Cleon.[1]

1 [*byrsoknapheus* (leather dresser) or *byrsokapēlos* (leather seller) have been suggested for the unknown form *byrsocappus.*]

310 Hesychius δ 859

Δημοκαλλίας· τοὺς περὶ τὰ δημόσια ἀναστρέφοντας

311 Hesychius δ 869

Δημοκλεῖδαι· οἱ ξένοι καὶ μοιχοί, ἀπὸ Δημοκλείδου τοιούτου ὄντος, καθάπερ καὶ τοὺς ἡταιρηκότας Τιμάρχους ἔλεγον, τοὺς δὲ πονηροὺς Εὐρυβάτους, Κιλλικῶνας δὲ τοὺς προδότας.

337 Hesychius ε 3839

Ἐξήκεστος· ἡταιρηκώς. ὅθεν καὶ τοὺς πρώκτους ὁμωνύμως Ἐξηκέστους ἔλεγον.

338 Hesychius ε 3840

Ἐξηκεστιδαλκίδαι· παρὰ τὸν Ἐξηκεστίδην καὶ Ἀλκίδην.

363 Hesychius κ 2266

κεραμικὴ μάστιξ· τὸν ὀστρακισμὸν λέγουσι· μάστιγα μὲν διὰ τὸ βασανίζειν τοὺς ὀστρακιζομένους καὶ κολάζειν, κεραμικὴν δὲ διὰ τὸ ἐκ κεράμου τὰ ὄστρακα εἶναι

310 Democallias: those who upset public affairs.[1]

1 Compare the similar form *dēmopithēcus* (People + monkey) at *Frogs* 1085, used of "big-talkers who deceive the people," and the notice in the *Suda* (κ 215) that a monkey could be called a "Callias," which suggest that Callias, the infamous son of Hipponicus, was likened to a monkey (an unpleasant comparison) in Athenian politics.

311 Democlidae: foreigners and adulterers, from a certain such Democlides, just as they would call homosexual perverts "Timarchuses" [cf. Aischines 1.157], wicked men "Eurybatuses" [Aristophanes F 242], and traitors "Cillicons" [*Peace* 363].

337 Execestus: homosexual pervert, for which reason they give the name "Execestus" to the arseholes.

338 Execestidalcidae: from the lyre players Execestides and Alcides.

363 "Lash of the pot": they mean ostracism, "lash" because they are "testing" and "punishing" those who are up for ostracism, and "of the pot" because the ostraca were potsherds.[1]

1 As the last ostracism was that of Hyperbolus in 416, it could be argued that this fragment predates that event. But a character in a later comedy could be recalling the defunct use of the "lash of the pot."

377

380 Hesychius λ 158

Λαισποδίας· ὄνομα κύριον. ἔνιοι δὲ τὸν Ἀλκμέωνα ᾠήθησαν λέγεσθαι. οἱ δὲ τὸν δρεπανώδεις πόδας ἔχοντα.

396 Hesychius o 454

Οἰωνίχου μουσεῖον

399 Hesychius o 920

ὀνοστύππαξ· διὰ μὲν τοῦ ὄνου τὸν μύλωνα ὀνειδίζων· διὰ δὲ τοῦ στύππακος, ὅτι στυππειοπώλης ἦν

421 Hesychius σ 844

σκάνδιξ· λάχανον ἄγριον, παρ᾽ ὃ καὶ σκανδικοπώλην τὸν Εὐριπίδην λέγουσιν, ἐπειδὴ λαχανοπωλητρίας υἱὸν αὐτὸν εἶναί φασιν.

461 Lucian *You Are a Prometheus in Words* 2

Κλέων Προμηθεύς ἐστι μετὰ τὰ πράγματα.

473 Origen *Against Celsus* 6.49

παίζοντες οἱ τῆς ἀρχαίας κωμῳδίας ποιηταὶ ἀνεγράψαντο· "Προῖτος ἔγημε Βελλεροφόντην, ὁ δὲ Πήγασος ἦν ἐξ Ἀρκαδίας."

380 Laespodias: proper name. Some thought that Alcmaeon was meant, others that he had crooked legs.[1]

1 Laespodias, a general and political figure in the 410s (*PAA* 600730), was made fun of for having deformed legs (*Birds* 1594, Eupolis F 107, Theopompus F 40).

396 Oeonichus' music house.[1]

1 For Oeonichus (*PAA* 741555) see *Knights* 1287.

399 "Hemp-donkey." Insulting the mill through the donkey, and through hemp, because he sold hemp.[1]

1 There are several jokes in Aristophanes (*Knights* 129, 253–54, F 149, F 716) aimed at a politician of the 420s named Eucrates (*PAA* 437755), who owned a mill and sold hemp and bran.

421 "Parsley": a wild herb, for which reason they call Euripides a parsley seller since they say he was the son of a woman who sold herbs.

461 Cleon is a Prometheus . . . after the fact.

473 The poets of Old Comedy wrote in fun, "Proteus married Bellerophon and Pegasus came from Arcadia."[1]

1 Compare Trimalchio's mangling of the Trojan story at *Satyricon* 59.

COMIC ADESPOTA

474 Manuel Philas 2.78

"χεζητιᾷ" γὰρ κατὰ τὴν κωμῳδίαν
"εἰς τοὺς βαθεῖς πώγωνας ὁ χρόνος βλέπων"

498 Photius δ 762

Δρυαχαρνεῦ· δρύϊνε Ἀχαρνεῦ, ἀναίσθητε· ἐκωμῳδοῦν-
το γὰρ οἱ Ἀχαρνεῖς ὡς ἄγριοι καὶ σκληροί.

511 Photius p. 192.12

Κυσολάκων· ὁ Κλεινίας ὁ τῷ κυσῷ λακωνίζων· τὸ δὲ
τοῖς παιδικοῖς χρῆσθαι λακωνίζειν λέγουσιν· Ἑλένη
γὰρ Θησεὺς οὕτως ἐχρήσατο, ὡς Ἀριστοτέλης.

Μελαίνη cod., Ἑλένη Ruhnk; Ἀριστοτέλης cod., Ἀρίσταρ-
χος Ruhnken, comparing Hesychius κ 4735.

514 Photius p. 204.14

λακκοσκαπέρδαν

536 Photius p. 500.2

σάραβον τὸ γυναικεῖον αἰδοῖον οἱ κωμικοὶ καλοῦσι·
καὶ σάκταν· καὶ σάβυτταν· καὶ σέλινον· καὶ ταῦρον
καὶ ἕτερα πολλά.

474 For according to comedy, Time looking at such long beards takes a shit.

498 "Oak-Acharnian": Acharnian, thick as oak, stupid, since the Acharnians were made fun of as hard and uncultivated people.

511 "Laconian arse-bandit": Clinias, who had anal sex like a Laconian. They call having sex with a boyfriend "love Laconian style." This is how Theseus did it with Helen, according to Aristarchus.

514 Cistern-arsed.

536 The comic poets call the female genitalia *sarabus* and "bag" and "shaving ground" and "garden" and "bull" and many other things.

572 Photius (b, z) a 372

ἀδολεσχεῖν· σημαίνει μὲν τὸ φιλοσοφεῖν περί τε
φύσεως καὶ ‹τοῦ› παντὸς διαλεσχαίνοντα. οἱ μέντοι
ἀρχαῖοι κωμικοὶ λεσχαίνειν ἔλεγον τὸ διαλέγεσθαι,
καὶ λέσχαι οἱ τόποι, εἰς οὓς συνιόντες λόγοις
διημέρευον.

692 Plato *Phaedrus* 236c

ἵνα μὴ τὸ τῶν κωμῳδῶν φορτικὸν πρᾶγμα ἀναγκα-
ζώμεθα ποιεῖν ἀνταποδιδόντες ἀλλήλοις.

695 Plutarch *Alcibiades* 10.4

καὶ ὅτι μὲν δυνατὸς ἦν εἰπεῖν, οἵ τε κωμικοὶ μαρτυ-
ροῦσι καὶ τῶν ῥητόρων ὁ δυνατώτατος.

696 Plutarch *Aristides* 5.7

Καλλίας ὁ δᾳδοῦχος· τούτῳ γάρ τις ὡς ἔοικε τῶν
βαρβάρων προσέπεσεν, οἰηθεὶς βασιλέα διὰ τὴν
κόμην καὶ τὸ στρόφιον εἶναι· προσκυνήσας δὲ καὶ
λαβόμενος τῆς δεξιᾶς, ἔδειξε πολὺ χρυσίον ἐν λάκκῳ
τινὶ κατορωρυγμένον· ὁ δὲ Καλλίας ὠμότατος ἀνθρώ-
πων καὶ παρανομώτατος γενόμενος, τὸν μὲν χρυσὸν
ἀνείλετο, τὸν δ᾽ ἄνθρωπον, ὡς μὴ κατείποι πρὸς ἑτέ-
ρους, ἀπέκτεινεν. ἐκ τούτου φασὶ καὶ λακκοπλούτους
ὑπὸ τῶν κωμικῶν τοὺς ἀπὸ τῆς οἰκίας λέγεσθαι.

572 *Adoleschein*: means to talk in a philosophic manner about nature and everything else. The poets of Old Comedy, however, would say *leschainein* for having a conversation. *Leschai* are places where people would get together and spend the day in gossip.

692 So that we are not forced to adopt that vulgar practice of the comic poets of replying "back at you."

695 That he [Alcibiades] was a powerful speaker is attested by the comic poets and the most accomplished of the orators [Demosthenes 21.145].

696 Callias the Torch-Bearer: [at the battle of Marathon] one of the Persians, as it happened, fell down before him, supposing him to be a king because of his long hair and his breast-band. Prostrating himself, he took Callias' right hand and showed him a great deal of gold that had been buried in a cistern. Callias, who was a very cruel and wicked man, took the gold and killed the man so that he would not tell anyone else. They say that's why people from that family are called "cistern-rich" by the comic poets.

697 Plutarch *Crassus* 36

κατὰ τὸν κωμικόν, "ἀνὴρ ἄριστος εἶναι τἆλλα πλὴν ἐν
ἀσπίδι."

700 Plutarch *Pericles* 7.8

ὑφ' ἧς ὥσπερ ἵππον ἐξυβρίσαντα τὸν δῆμον οἱ κωμῳ-
δοποιοὶ λέγουσι

  ἐξυβρίσας πειθαρχεῖν οὐκέτι τολμᾷ,
ἀλλ᾽ † δάκνει † τὴν Εὔβοιαν καὶ ταῖς νήσοις
ἐπιπηδᾷ.

701 Plutarch *Pericles* 8.4

δεινὸν δὲ κεραυνὸν ἐν γλώσσῃ φέρειν

702 Plutarch *Pericles* 13.14

δεξάμενοι δὲ τὸν λόγον οἱ κωμικοὶ πολλὴν ἀσέλγειαν
αὐτοῦ κατεσκέδασαν, εἴς τε τὴν Μενίππου γυναῖκα
διαβάλλοντες, ἀνδρὸς φίλου καὶ ὑποστρατηγοῦντος,
εἴς τε τὰς Πυριλάμπους ὀρνιθοτροφίας, ὃς ἑταῖρος ὢν
Περικλέους αἰτίαν εἶχε ταῶνας ὑφιέναι ταῖς γυναιξὶν
αἷς ὁ Περικλῆς ἐπλησίαζε.

697 According to the comic poet, "an excellent man in all respects, except in his shield."[1]

[1] Nicias and Cleonymus have been suggested as the person meant.

700 As a result of which [this freedom] the comic poets say that the people are like a violent horse:

in its violence it no longer dares to do what it's told, but snaps at Euboea and lunges at the islands.[1]

[1] Eupolis F 246 describes Chios as a "horse that never needs the whip." *Clouds* 211–13 records an expedition against Euboea, while Cleon's concern with the islands (i.e., with the *archē*) is noted at *Knights* 170, 1034. Also see Aristophanes' (or Archippus'?) *Islands* and Eupolis' *Cities*.

701 [of Pericles] Wielding a terrible thunderbolt on his tongue.[1]

[1] For the celebrated oratorical abilities of Pericles see *Acharnians* 531, Eupolis F 102, and perhaps *PCG* VIII F 288.

702 When the comic poets got hold of the story, they heaped all sorts of indecency on him, making charges about the wife of Menippus, his friend and subordinate commander, and about Pyrilampes and his pet birds. Pyrilampes was a friend of Pericles and was accused of using peacocks to entice the women whom Pericles was seducing.[1]

[1] Menippos (*PAA* 646185) may be the man called "swallow" at *Birds* 1293. Pyrilampes (*PAA* 795695) had been an ambassador to Persia, where he presumably acquired the peacocks. See Antiphon F 57 and *Acharnians* 62–63.

COMIC ADESPOTA

703 Plutarch *Pericles* 16.1

καίτοι τὴν δύναμιν αὐτοῦ σαφῶς μὲν ὁ Θουκυδίδης
διηγεῖται, κακοήθως δὲ παρεμφαίνουσιν οἱ κωμικοί,
Πεισιστρατίδας μὲν νέους τοὺς περὶ αὐτὸν ἑταίρους
καλοῦντες, αὐτὸν δ᾽ ἀπομόσαι μὴ τυραννήσειν κελεύ-
οντες, ὡς ἀσυμμέτρου πρὸς δημοκρατίαν καὶ βαρυ-
τέρας περὶ αὐτὸν οὔσης ὑπεροχῆς.

704 Plutarch *Pericles* 24.9

ἐν δὲ ταῖς κωμῳδίαις Ὀμφάλη τε νέα καὶ Δηάνειρα
καὶ πάλιν Ἥρα προσαγορεύεται.

729 Plutarch *On Exile* 602b

ὅπου φησὶν ὁ κωμικὸς τὰ σῦκα ταῖς σφενδόναις
τρυγᾶσθαι καὶ πάντ᾽ ἔχειν ὅσων δεῖ τὴν νῆσον.

741 Plutarch *Precepts of Statecraft* 811e

Μητίοχος μὲν < - > στρατηγεῖ, Μητίοχος δὲ τὰς
    ὁδούς,
Μητίοχος δ᾽ ἄρτους ἐποπτᾷ, Μητίοχος δὲ τἄλφιτα,
† Μητίοχος δὲ πάντα κεῖται,† Μητίοχος δ᾽
    οἰμώξεται.

747 [Plutarch] *On Music* 1142a

καὶ ἄλλοι δὲ κωμῳδοποιοὶ ἔδειξαν τὴν ἀτοπίαν τῶν
μετὰ ταῦτα τὴν μουσικὴν κατακεκερματικότων.

386

703 Thucydides describes Pericles' power clearly, while the comic poets make the point maliciously, calling those around him "the new Pisistratids" and telling him to take an oath "not to be a tyrant," since his preeminent position was rather harsh and inconsistent with democracy.

704 In comedy she [Aspasia] is called "a new Omphale" and "Deianeira" and also "Hera."

729 [Seriphus] where the comic poet says that figs are gathered in slings and the island has all it needs.

741 Metiochus is general, Metiochus ⟨minds⟩ the streets, Metiochus inspects the bread, Metiochus ⟨supervises⟩ the grain, Metiochus does everything (?), Metiochus will be sorry.[1]

[1] The name Metiochus is very rare at Athens, one instance being a son of Miltiades (*PAA* 650615), who was captured by the Persians, the other a friend of Pericles (*PAA* 650600), who is very likely the man meant here.

747 And the other comic poets shown the absurdity of those who have minced up music even more.

771 Pollux 3.56

κἂν δόξῃ πολίτης εἶναί τις οὐκ ὤν, παρέγγραπτος,
παρεγγεγραμμένος. τὸν δὲ τοιοῦτον καὶ ὑπόξυλον
ὠνόμαζον οἱ νέοι κωμικοί. καὶ ὑπόχυτον δ' οἱ παλαι-
ότεροι τὸν κακῶς γεγονότα, καὶ παρημπολημένον, ὡς
ἀποφύλιον τὸν φυλὴν μὴ ἔχοντα.

809 Pollux 8.133

θόρυβον πυκνίτην

827 *Bodleian Proverbs* 550

Κορυδέως εἰδεχθέστερος· ἐπὶ δυσμορφίᾳ ἐκωμῳδεῖτο
καὶ οὗτος καὶ οἱ παῖδες αὐτοῦ ὧν ἕνα τὸν Ἀρχέστρα-
τον φασιν.

831 Proverbs of the Codex Laurentianus 58.24

τί δ' ἀσπίδι ξύνθημα καὶ καρχησίῳ;

832 Macarius 4.36

ἡ γλῶττ' ἀνέγνωχ', ἡ δὲ φρὴν οὐ μανθάνει

771 And if someone seemed to be a citizen who wasn't ⟨he was termed⟩ "illegally enrolled" or "illegally registered." The poets of New Comedy would call such a man "counterfeit," while the older poets ⟨would call⟩ a false citizen "doctored" or "an intruder" or as "tribeless," for having no tribe.

809 A hubbub at the Pnyx.

827 "Uglier than Corydeus": this man was made fun of for his ill features, and his sons as well, one of whom they say was Archestratus.[1]

1 The name Corydeus is not known at Athens, although an Archestratus (*PAA* 211047) is made fun of at Eupolis F 298.4 for having a squint.

831 What is this compact between a shield and a drinking cup?[1]

1 This is based partly on a line supposedly describing Socrates' military service, "What is this compact between a shield and a staff?" (Athenaeus 215e) and the confrontation between Lycurgus and Dionysus in Aeschylus' *Edonians* [F 61], parodied at *Thesmophoriazusae* 136–45. As the drinking cup (*karchesios*) is associated with Dionysus at Cratinus F 40, I suspect that this comes from Eupolis' *Officers*, where Dionysus embarks on military training.

832 My tongue it was that read, my mind . . . doesn't understand.[1]

1 Euripides *Hippolytus* 612, "It was my tongue that swore, my mind remains unpledged," was parodied three times by Aristophanes (*Thesmophoriazusae* 275–76, *Frogs* 101–2, 1471).

COMIC ADESPOTA

842 Σ Aristophanes *Birds* 281

ἔστι δὲ ὁ Φιλοκλῆς τραγῳδίας ποιητής, καὶ Φιλοπεί-
θους υἱὸς ἐξ Αἰσχύλου ἀδελφῆς. ὅσοι δὲ Ἀλμίωνος
αὐτόν φασιν, ἐπιθετικῶς λέγουσι διὰ τὸ πικρὸν εἶναι.
ἅλμη γὰρ ἡ πικρία.

860 Σ Euripides *Orestes* 554

ἄνευ δὲ μητρός, ὦ κάθαρμ' Εὐριπίδης

940 Zenobius *Athoos* 2.48, Photius δ 389

κεῖται δ' ὁ τλήμων τὸ στόμα παρεστραμμένος,
ὃ τὸν διάμορφον Σωκράτην ἀπώλεσεν.

951 Zenobius *Common Proverbs* 3.177

ἐν δὲ διχοστασίῃσι καὶ Ἀνροκλέης πολεμαρχεῖ

ἐν γὰρ ἀμηχανίῃ καὶ Καρκίνος ἔμμορε τιμῆς

957 Orus F A 65

Φορμίων τρεῖς ⟨ἀργυροῦς⟩ στήσειν ἔφη
τρίποδας, ἔπειτ' ἔθηκεν ἕνα μολύβδινον

*Brief fragments: (F 176) "work the tongue" [sens.obsc.],
(F 184) "stingy," (F 213) "boastful tongue-charmer,"
(F 242) "complete feast," (F 270) "pound up in a pestle" [of
Cleon?], (F 505) "success," (F 551) "whoremonger,"*

842 Philocles is a tragic poet, the son of Philopeithes and of the sister of Aeschylus. Those who call him "son of Brine" are speaking metaphorically because he was bitter and brine is bitter.[1]

[1] Philokles was the nephew of Aeschylus and a tragic poet himself (*TrGF* 24). He was a frequent target in comedy: Cratinus F 323, Teleclides F 15, Aristophanes *Wasps* 460–61 (relevant to this fragment), *Birds* 279–83, 1245, *Thesmophoriazusae* 167.

860 And without your mother, Euripides, you filth.

940 There he lies the wretch with the twisted lips that destroyed the multiform Socrates.[1]

[1] Photius claims that this is a parody of Euripides' *Meleager* (F 531a). If Meletus the accuser of Socrates was also the tragic poet (*TrGF* 48), he would be a good candidate for the "he."

951 In times of dissension even Androcles can take command.

In a time of uncertainty even Carcinus has a share of honour.

957 Phormion said that he would set up three silver tripods, then put up one . . . of lead.

(F 560) *"get one's prick up,"* (F 638) *"donkey-paunch,"* (F 688) *"like Phrynondas,"* (F 758) *"female spectator,"* (F 766) *"erection,"* (F 803) *"porters,"* (F 806) *"stagehands,"* (F 847) *"city of Coesyra."*

COMIC PAPYRI

PCG VIII presents over 150 fragments on papyrus, which
in their view may reasonably be assigned to comedy. Many
are too fragmentary to yield any clues as to which period
they might belong, most of the rest seem characteristic of
the later Greek comedy of romance and errors. But some

1005 *Pap. Lit. Lond.* 86 = CGFP 226

αὗται λαλοῦσαι τον[
τρύχουσι πολλοῖς τ[
κακουμέναις γὰρ .[
ὑπὸ μητρυῶν τε κα[ὶ
5 οὐκ ἦλθ' ἀρήξων ἀλ[λ
νῦν οὖν ἄποινα τ[
κατὰ τὴν Μελανίπ[πην
ἀλλὰ ξεστῶν ετ[

COMIC PAPYRI

are very much in the spirit of Old Comedy, either because they contain personal jokes (not by itself an indication of Old Comedy) or obscene or colloquial language, or because they seem "political" in tone or subject. Some engage with tragedy (especially Euripides), something not ruled out for later comedy, but more common to Old Comedy.

1005 *In the original publication this was described as a "fragment of a tragic text with scholia," but was later regarded as comedy referring to tragedy. Aristophanes'* Gerytades *and second* Thesmophoriazusae *have been suggested, but Strattis should not be ruled out, and Eupolis does cite Euripides'* Melanippe the Wise *in* Demes *(F 99.78). The first seven lines are in iambics, the eighth is perhaps the beginning of a lyric response.*

(A) These chattering women . . . they wear ⟨us?⟩ out with all their advice (?) . . . for to women in distress . . . by both stepmothers and by . . . he did not come to bring support, but . . . now then in recompense . . . according to Melanippe . . .

(B) But of polished . . .

1024 P. Oxy. 1176 = *CGFP* 294b

{A.}   ο]ὐχὶ τ[ο]ῦτον τ[ὸν τ]ρόπον,
ἀλλ' ο[ὐδὲ τ]ῆι πονηρ[ίαι] π[ρ]οσχρώμεθα,
ὅτ]ε τωι μάλισ[θ' ὅσ'] ἂν λέγη[ι] πισ[τεύ]ομεν
λέγ[οντ]ες οὐ πονή[ρ‿‿]α‿λ‿[‿] δεχρω[
5   κἄπειτ[α τῆς] ἐκκλησία[ς κα]τηγορεῖ
ἕκασ[τος] ἡμῶν, ἧς ἕκασ[τος] αὐτὸς ἦν.
{ΔΙΟΔΩΡΟΣ.} πολλὰ καὶ παρὰ τῶν κωμικῶν, ὡς
ἔοικε, ἅμα αὐστηρῶς λέγεται καὶ πολιτικῶς.
{A.} πῶς γὰρ οὔ;

1033 P. Oxy. 1611 = *CGFP* 295

"]ον νῦν γ' ὁρᾶι[ς] ἡμᾶς δύ' ὄντας, τέτταρ[α]ς καὶ τοὺς
κριτάς," δηλῶν οὕτως τέτταρας ὄντας, Λύσιππ[ο]ς δ'
ἐν Βάκχαις ε΄, ὁμοίως δὲ καὶ Κρατῖνος ἐν Πλούτῳ
λέγει.

1062 *PSI* 1175 = *CGFP* 215

{ΡΕΑ.} "τί οὖν ἐμοὶ τῷν σ[ῶν μέ]λει;" φαίη τις ἂν

1024 *This comes from Satyrus' Life of Euripides (F 39 col. iv 1), constructed as a dialogue through which the information about and citations from Euripides (and from other authors) is provided.*

(A) " . . . not in this way, but do we not take advantage of someone else's wickedness, when we put our trust completely in the man who speaks, not saying wicked things ourselves, but certainly taking advantage? Then each one of us criticises the assembly of which each one of us was a part."

(DIODORUS) Many other things, it would seem, are spoken by the comic poets in this vigorous and political manner.

(A) Yes indeed.

1033 "And now you see us, two in number, and the judges four," thus making it clear that there were four, but Lysippus in *Bacchae* [F 7] says five, and Cratinus in *Wealth-Gods* [F 177] the same.

1062 *Some have assigned this to Middle Comedy, and if the "line from Sophocles" refers to* Oedipus at Colonus *892, it would date this comedy after 401. But it is very much in the Old Comic manner that Rhea can swear "by Zeus" (l. 12) and mention a prophecy by Apollo (ll. 9–13), when neither has yet been born. This will have come from the prologue, when Rhea informs the spectators of the play's subject (cf. "you" of the spectators at* Wasps *65;* Peace *20, 55). Phrynichus wrote a* Cronus *and Philiscus a* Birth of Zeus, *the latter of which Austin (CGFP 215) and others have suggested as the source of the fragment.*

(RHEA) "Why should I care about your problems?",

ὑμῶν. ἐγὼ δ᾽ ἐρῶ [τ]ὸ Σοφοκλέους ἔπος·
"πέπονθα δεινά." πάντα μοι γέρων Κρ[όνος
τὰ παιδί᾽ ἐκπίνει τε καὶ κατεσθίει,
5 ἐμοὶ δὲ τούτων προσδίδωσιν οὐδὲ ἕν,
ἀλλ᾽ αὐτὸς ἔρδει χειρὶ καὶ Μεγαράδ᾽ ἄγων
ὅ τι ἂν τέκω ᾽γὼ τοῦτο πωλῶν ἐσθίει.
δέδοικε γὰρ τὸν χρησμὸν ὥσπερ κυν[
ἔχρησε γὰρ Κρόνωι ποθ᾽ Ἀπόλλων δραχ[μήν,
10 κᾆτ᾽ οὐκ ἀπέλαβε. ταῦτα δὴ θυμὸν πνέ[ων
ἑτέραν ἔχρησε[ν οὐκέτι] δρα[χ]μῶ[ν ἀ]ξ[ίαν,
οὐ σκευάρια, μὰ τὸν Δί᾽, οὐδὲ χρήματα,
ἐκ τῆς βασιλείας δ᾽ ἐκπεσεῖν ὑπὸ π[αιδίου.
τοῦ]τ᾽ οὖν δεδοικὼς πάντα καταπί[νει τέκνα.

1088 *PSI* 1281 = *CGFP* 231

..........].ρ.[....]τ̣ο[.]τ̣ρ...[
. οὐ]κ ἀνακέκυ[φ]ε̣ τοῦ χρ[ό]νου τ[
πλὴ]ν πέρυσιν ᾔτησ᾽ ἀμίδα.[
εἰ ν]ῦν καθεύδων οὗτος, οἶμαι, τ[
5 ἄν]ω γεγένηται καὶ κάτω τὰ π[ράγματα.
ἀλλ᾽] αὐτὸν ἐγερῶ κεἴ με δεῖ πληγ[ὰς λαβεῖν,
ἵνα] μὴ γένηται πλεῖον ἔτι τω[
καὶ] μὴν ὑπορρέγκει καθεύδων[

one of you people might say. I will reply with that line
from Sophocles, "I have suffered terrible things." For old
Cronus has gulped down and eaten up all my kids, and
doesn't let me have even one of them. But he just waves
his hand at me, goes straight off to Megara, sells the child
that I have borne, and gobbles up the money. He's afraid,
you see, of the prophecy, as ⟨a hare fears⟩ a dog (?), for
Apollo once loaned Cronus a drachma and then didn't get
it back. So with anger seething in his heart Apollo ⟨would
no longer⟩ loan him anything valuable,[2] nor household
goods, no by Zeus, nor any property, but that he would be
deposed from his throne by a child of his. He's afraid of
this, and that's why he gulps down all ⟨his children⟩.

[1] This is the only use in extant Sophocles, but the phrase oc-
curs four times in Euripides and twice in Aristophanes. It could
easily have been used in an earlier play by Sophocles.   [2] There
is an untranslatable pun in the Greek on the verb χρᾶν, which can
mean "to lend" and "to give a prophecy,"

1088 *The similarity between "last year he asked for a jar"
and* Thesmophoriazusae *627–33 ("last year . . . Xenylla
asked for a basin, for there wasn't a jar") has led most
scholars to consider this as Old Comedy. Austin suggests
that the sleeping man might be Endymion (see Alcaeus'
comedy with that title), but the speaker sounds more like a
slave blessed with an irascible master.*

And he did not raise his head up during ⟨that⟩ time, ex-
cept last year he asked for a jar . . . this man now asleep, I
think, . . . matters are upset from top to bottom. But I will
go and wake him up, even if I get a beating for it, ⟨so that⟩
. . . any more happen . . . snores in his sleep.

1095 *PSI* 1388 = *CFGP* 232

```
  .]. γιγνώσκω[ν τ]ὴν ἐργασίαν[
  τί γὰρ ..... [τ]ῆς ὁμονοία[ς
  ἐθέλουσιν ν[.].νητη ...[
  καὶ τῶν αὐτῶν ἐπιθυ[μ]η[ς
5 ἐ]ν ταῖς ἀρχαῖς. :: τότε .[.]...[
  τοῦτο πονηρὸν τοίνυν[
  ἀ]λλὰ δίκαιον τοῦτο νο[μ]ι̣[ζ
  σ]κεύη δ' ἐθέλει γείτο[νο]ς̣ .[
  ..]ησαι ταχέω[ς] ὥσπερ ....[
10 ...].α τὴν γῆν γιγ[ν]ώσκουσ[ι]ν [τ]ὴν[
  ...]τοιμα.[..]ν τῶν ἀρχαί[ίω]ν.[
  .....] πενιχροὶ τῶν ἀνθ[ρώ]πων οὐκ[
  ...]ν σκευαρίων ἐπιθυμ.....[
  .....] ἁθρόοι συλλεχθέντες κ.[
  ἐς τὰς α]ὐλὰς ἐσπηδῶσιν μιλτωσάμ[ενοι τὰ
15 πρόσωπα
  κᾆτ' αἴρ]ουσιν κλίνας, δάπιδας, χ.[
  κοὐκ] ἀντιλέγει ταῦτ' αἰρομένων οὐ[δ
  οὐδ' οἶ]δε τί δρᾷ[ν] ταῦτα φ[ε]ρόντων .[
  ὁ δ' ἀνὴ]ρ σι[γ]ᾷ[ι] κοὐδὲν γρύζει κ[
20 νὴ τὴν] Δήμητρ', ἀγαθους.[
```

1095 *The metre is anapaestic tetrameter catalectic, a meter favoured by Old Comedy for the agon, parabasis proper, and elsewhere. As this is a dialogue (note the changes of speaker at ll. 4,5 8) and as there are hints of argument in 6–8, an agon seems perhaps the most likely. The business about property and poor men in ll. 9–12 might suggest something like the debate with Poverty in* Wealth, *but the passage goes on to describe the actions of a plural group (the "poor men" in 12?) who invade and plunder the home of a wealthy man who does nothing to protect his property. This does sound rather like what seems to have happened to Callias in Eupolis'* Spongers *(see F 161–62, 169). If this fragment does come from that play, then the oath "by Demeter" acquires an ironic tone in view of Callias' role as* dadouchos *of the Mysteries.*

(A) . . . he knowing the activity . . . for why . . . of unanimity . . . they want, yes by (?) . . . (B) And you desire the same . . . in positions of authority. (A) At that time . . . consider then this wicked act . . . but this just act. (B) A neighbour's goods tend to . . . quickly just as . . . they recognise the earth . . . of olden . . . poor men do not desire the goods . . . gathering together they burst into the courtyards, their faces painted red, and then they pick up couches, carpets . . . and he says not a word against them while they take this stuff and does not even know what to do as they carry it away, but the fellow keeps silent and utters not a peep, by Demeter . . . good men.

1104 P. Oxy. 2742 = *CFGP* 74 [the text below is that in
CFGP 74]

```
    - - - - - - -
         ].̣.̣[
       ]ειρης[
    τ[.̣].̣ραδοπαρ[      ἔ-
    λεγον δ᾽ οὕτω[
5   μακρὰν ἐξ ἧς[
    μένους ἀνω[      ]ελε-
    .̣.̣]ν προσδεσ̣.[.̣].̣ομενων
    Στρ]άττις Ἀταλ[άν]τωι "ἀπὸ τῆς
    κράδης, ἤδη γὰρ ἰσχὰς γίν[ομαι,
10  ὁ μηχανοποιός μ᾽ ὡς τάχιστα
    καθελέτω." <καὶ> ἐν Φοινίσσαις·
    "Διόνυσος ὃς θύρσοισιν αὐληταὶ
    † δει·λ † κω[...] ἐνέχομαι, δι᾽ ἑ-
    τέρων μοχθ[ηρ]ίαν ἥκω κρε-
15  μάμενος ὥσπερ ἰσχὰς ἐπὶ κρά-
    δης." Ἀριστοφάνης Γηρυτάδῃ·
    "περιάγειν ἐχρῆν τὸν μηχα-
    νοποιὸν ὡς τάχιστα τὴν κρά-
    δην." "οὕτω δὴ τὸν Πολυδέκ[την
20  βάλλεις τοῖς σκώμμασινειε.̣[
    Περσεὺς καὶ τοῦ ποδὸς ἕλκεις
```

---

[1] Or reading Περσεῦ with the original editors, "So then,
Perseus, with your jokes . . . ", thereby making Perseus a character
in the comedy.

1104 *This comes from a commentary to an Old Comedy,
the first part of which (1–19) is concerned with the appear-
ance of a character on the* mēchanē *calling attention to his
situation. The author cites Strattis'* Atalantus *(F 4),* Phoe-
nician Women *(F 46), and Aristophanes'* Gerytades *(F
160), where the* mēchanē *is called a "branch"* (kradē). *The
metre of the lemma at ll. 19–22 seems to be paroemiacs, for
which compare Crantinus F 151. The mention of both
Polydeuctes and Perseus and the implied presence of a
character on the* mēchanē *have led scholars to conclude
that the comedy in question was Cratinus'* Men of
Seriphus. *But Aristophanes in* Thesmophoriazusae *paro-
dies an aerial scene from Euripides'* Andromeda, *and we
know also of that early comedy by Phrynichus parodying
the story of Andromeda (and presumably Perseus). The
fragment is an odd mix of an address by a character on the*
mēchanē *and a metatheatrical allusion to a less than en-
thusiastic chorus member.*

that *kradō* from *kradē*. That's what ‹the comic poets›
used to call the large ‹*mēchanē*› from which above . . . peo-
ple fastened, of which Strattis in his *Atalantus* (F 4), "Let
the crane man get me down from the branch as quickly as
possible, for I am turning into a fig already," and also in his
Phoenician Women (F 46), "I am Dionysus, involved with
thyrsuses, *aulos* players and revelries (?); here I am,
trapped by the wickedness of others, hanging like a fig
upon a branch." Aristophanes in his *Gerytades* (F 160),
"The crane operator should have moved the branch about
as quickly as possible." "So then with your jokes you [sing.]
pelt Polydeuctes like Perseus[1] and you drag the sheet cor-

καὶ τῆς ὑπέρας, ἵν᾽ ἄκρ᾽ ἴῃς." "το[ῦ
ποδὸς ἕλκεις" οἷον εὐρύθμως
τιθεὶς τὸν πόδα, ὡσανεὶ "ἄντι-
25 κρυς" ἔφη· καὶ τοῦ ῥυθμοῦ ἕλκε[ις,
εἶθ᾽ ἑξῆς ἡ ὑπέρα ψυχρῶς πρὸς
τὸν πόδα. γνώσει μέντοι κα-
τὰ τῶν πτερνῶν. ἐναφίῃς
κατὰ τῶν σκελῶν μέχρι τῶν
30 π]τε[ρ]ρῶν. "ἀλλὰ χορευτὴς
φ]οιτᾶν ὕστατος αἰεὶ πλὴν
ἐπὶ δεῖ]πνον" ἐπειδὴ εἰς
τὰς μελ]έτας μόλις ἐφοίτων
καὶ πο]νηρῶς οθε.[   ].[
35   ]ωνη[
– – – – – – –

1105 P. Oxy. 2743 = *CGFP* 220

(a) 1–18

            ]φανῆναι[
      ]   [
      ]νεακαλ[
      ]ης κόρης[
5   ].ραγονικ[
      ].οσοστισε [
Χῖος π]αραστὰς Κῷον [οὐκ ἐᾷ λέγειν
      ]ν τοιοῖσδε συν.[
      ].ικες ὄντες ω.[

ner and the brace to release the ends." "You drag the
sheet" like putting the foot[2] in a rhythmical fashion, as if he
said "straightforwardly." You drag the rhythm and then
"brace" ⟨goes⟩ coldly with "foot." "You [sing.] will realise,
however, down to the heels." You will let down over the
legs as far as the heels. "The chorus member always the last
to arrive, except for dinner," since they would arrive at re-
hearsals with difficulty and badly . . .

[2] There is a pun here on *pous* as "foot" (both anatomically and
metrically) and as "lower rope of a sheet or sail."

1105 *Over 30 fragments combine to produce parts of
more than 250 lines of this comedy, but most in very poor
shape and yielding little sense or continuity. Line 7 cites a
proverb, which is found at Strattis F 24* (Lemnomeda), *but
proverbs can be found in more than one comedy. Luppe
suggested Eupolis'* Demes, *pointing out that a character is
called "just" at 129–30 and comparing the meagre remains
at 59–60 with F 99.32–33; certainly the political tone of
63ff. and 101–3 would not be out of place in that comedy.
Austin and Perusino argue for Cratinus'* Runaways *on the
basis of the joke at Lampon (cf. F 62), but Lampon is a fre-
quent target of the comic poets. Tammaro (MCr 10/12
[1975/77] 101–2) has proposed Cratinus'* Thracian
Women. *If the address to Wealth (l. 104) has any connec-
tion with the larger plotline, then we might consider
Aristophanes' first version of* Wealth *(408), Cratinus'*
Wealth-Gods, *or Archippus'* Wealth.

(a) A Chian stands by and shuts the Coan up. (7)

10   ]ν κῶμον οικ[
            ].μεν σαφῶσ[
            ]κωσπουδης.[
            ]ρασει καὶ γὰρ σα[
            ].ων ἐστι δο.[
15   ]τραχηλ[
            ]βλέψαι δυν[
            ]ρ ἴσας πληγ[
            ].ν ἄνδρα χ.[

(b) 63–78

                ]βριζων ε[
            ].αρ δίκην
65   ]ἔχων ἄρ᾽ ἦν φρόνησιν
        ]φαίν[.]ται πᾶσιν ἐναργῆ
        ]λοκα καὶ πολυμήχαν᾽ ἰδεῖν
        ]ομεν οὐδὲν ἔχοντα πέραι
        ]ν γὰρ ἁπλοῦν τι πέφυκε βροτοῖς
70   ]τελουμένοισιν ἔργοις
            ]ουμενον οὐκ ἴσασιν οὐδ᾽ ὁρῶσιν
            ]νδε πόλιν βλέπουσι
            ].ας ἔχειν ὅλον δὲ μηδὲν ὀρθῶς
            ]λίαν εἶναι νόμον τίθενται
75   ]..αμένοις· τοὺς πάντας † ἐξιοῦντες
            ν]είκη χολὴν μέλα[ιν]αν
            ]νηγιαν ἀνῆκεν
                ]ν λέγω τὸν [ἄν]δρα

(b) . . . Using violence . . . justice . . . he indeed had good sense . . . clear to all and intricate and well-planned to behold . . . having nothing extra . . . has been something simple for mortals . . . with their tasks completed . . . they do not know nor do they see . . . but look at the city . . . to have but nothing at all correctly . . . they pass a law that there be . . . for those having. And putting everyone on equal terms . . . black bile he has sent forth . . . I mean the man. (63–78)

COMIC PAPYRI

(c) 94–106

καὶ μὴν ἄρα φύλλον ἀπὸ ῥύπου πάδοσ . . [.]ν[
95   σὺ δ᾽ οὖν † διαχν † ἐπὶ ταῖς πτέ[ρ]ναισι π[ ] . [
σεμνὸν διακυσοσαλεύων τῆδ᾽· ἐμοὶ δαλ[
μακρὸς γὰρ ἄγαν περὶ πόρνης μῦθος ἠγο[ρεύθη·
Λάμπωνα δὲ τὸν κόρακος θεῶ π[. .] . . . . κ[
τίς οὐκ ἂν ὁρῶν παρατίλαιτ᾽ ἐν κακοῖσιν . [
100 παίδων τ᾽ ἔραται μετὰ τυμπάνων τεπα . [
πόλεις δὲ βαρὺ στενάχουσι χρήμαθ᾽ ἀ[
μισθοὺς ξυνελέξατο πολλῶν ῥήσεω[ν
ὥστ᾽ οἰκοδομεῖν πάρα καὶ παίδων . [
          πολυώνυμε Πλοῦτε καὶ σὺ δη[
105   ξενικὸς χορο[ς . . . . .] . . [ ]τυρω . [
          ὀλίγον . [ ] . . . [ ]επεισασ[

(d) 124–35

]γὰρ ἡμῶν τὴν προ . [
125] . ς εὐωχοῦ χάριν δ[
μ]έντἂν, ὡς ἐγῷμαι, τήμ[ερον
Δι]όνυσον τοῦ τράγου τουτ[
]ιους σκώληκες εἰ λυπου[
]θοινῶ σε γὰρ δίκαιον ὦ πρε[
130]υχαις καλει. :: πρεπονтασω[
] . ν κύκλωι φέρων ὁ τὴν . [
]σι χρὴ τάδε πάντα με . [
]εν καιρῶι
]οι πρῶσον εστεμ[
135]δευρι[

406

(c) And furthermore then a leaf from a filthy . . . but you
[sing.] walking on your heels (?) [waddling like a goose?]
swing your butt arrogantly for her. Enough for me. For too
much talk has been uttered about a whore. Look at Lam-
pon, the son of a crow . . . who would not tear their hair out
on seeing . . . in troubles? He lusts after boys with tambou-
rines.[1] Cities deeply resent the money which . . . has col-
lected as payment for his many utterances, and so he can
construct also . . . of boys . . .

Wealth, god of many names and you . . . foreign chorus
. . . a little bit . . . (94–106)

[1] Possibly "he loves to . . . boys with tambourines."

(d) (A) . . . For our . . . feast sumptuously for the sake of . . .
however, in my opinion, today Dionysus of the goat . . .
worms if grieved . . . I entertain, since ‹I think› you just,
old man (?) . . . calls.[1]

(B) In a fit manner . . . carrying in a circle . . . it is neces-
sary for me ‹to do› this . . . at the proper time . . . push for-
ward . . . this way.

[1] If the fragment does come from *Demes,* then the "old man"
could be Aristides (one of the Four) or, perhaps more likely,
Pyronides, being hailed as "just" by the archetype of Justice him-
self.

1109 P. Oxy. 2806.1–11 = *CFGP* 76

```
         ]..[ ]...[
        ]ωνετ.[     ]
        ]ενησετ[     ]μετεκ-
  βάλωσι τοῦ νυνὶ τρόπου.
```
5 ἀλλὰ τῶν λοιπῶν ἄκουσον, ἄξιον γ[άρ] ἐστί σοι.
  πᾶσι γὰρ τέξουσιν ὑμῖν αἱ γυναῖκες πα[ι]δία
  πεντέμηνα κα[ὶ] τρίμηνα καὶ τριακο[ν]θήμερα,
  [ὁ]πόσ᾽ ἂν ἐπιθυμῶσι πλῆθος, ἄρ[ρ]ενά τε καὶ
     θήλεα.
9 ταῦτα δ᾽ ἡβήσει πρὶν εἶναι πεντεκαίδεχ᾽ ἡμερῶν
11 καὶ γενειάσουσιν ἑτέρων πεντεκαίδεχ᾽ ἡμερῶν
10 κᾆτα βινήσουσιν ἄλλων πεντεκαίδεχ᾽ ἡμερῶν

1110 P. Oxy. 2807.1–20 = *CFGP* 75

1109 *Line 4 is an iambic dimeter, followed by seven tro-
chaic tetrameters catalectic, the metre often found in the
epirrhematic sections of an Aristophanic parabasis. We get
the same combination in Eupolis F 99.1–34, a choral song
followed by an epirrhema. As the first section describes
an accelerated process of the production of children, the
speaker should be a divine being or hero. Handley argued
that this is part of a parabasis from Cratinus'* Dionys-
alexander, *which had a chorus of satyrs, and where on one
reading of the hypothesis the chorus "talked to the specta-
tors on the creation of children."*

E. W. Handley, BICS 29 (1982) 109–17; W. Luppe, ZPE
72 (1988) 37–38.

(A) . . . that they may divert you from your present ways.

(B) But listen [sing.] to what else is in store—it's worth
it for you. Your wives will bear children for all of you, five-
month ones and three-month ones and ones of just thirty
days, in number as many as they may desire, both boys and
girls. They will come to maturity within fifteen days, grow
their beards within the next fifteen days, and they'll be
screwing before another fifteen days have passed.[1]

---

[1] A note in the margin attests that in some ancient texts l. 11
preceded l. 10. Line 10 could be the interjection of a *bōmolochos.*

1110 *Line 17 contains the word* ὡραιζομενο[*(being in
one's prime), which is found in comedy at Eupolis F 393, of
a woman playing coy, and at Cratinus F 298, from his* Sea-
sons *(Horai). As it is followed here three times by the word
"seasons"* (ὡρέων/ὧρας), *it has been argued that this frag-
ment comes from that comedy by Cratinus. The inserted*

```
   ]μιν. {Β.} ἦλθέ τις διφ.[
   ].’ ἄνθρωπος ἦλ[θ
   ]τερον οἴχετα[ι
   ]σθαι καὶ γα..ον.[
 5 ]ν ἔφασκε ταυτα[
   ].ν[..]λωσινα..[
   ]ο.[.]στω παντ[
   ]μέ[γ]α σεμνὴ .ο.[
   πό]τνα δὲ κἀνδρῶν θηλυ[
10 πό]τνι’ αιδοι..δι[.]εκο.[
   καὶ] μὴν ἀτεχνῶς γ’ ἐστ[
   ]ντας δεπεμο.και.[
   ]κλασθῆναι κἀπι[
   ]κνισθῆναι
15 ].ληην γ’ εὔχει κατα.[
   ].[ ]φιλαι πολλας.[
   ]ελθεῖν ὡραϊζομενο[
   ]ων ὡρέων ἑτέρας ὥρας
   ].ν ὡρέων
20 ]ου θαρρῶν
```

1146 *Pap. Duk.* F 1984. 7 = "Comoedia Dukiana"

colon in the first line indicates a change of speaker. The metre seems to be iambic in lines 1–8, but anapaestic thereafter. In lines 8–10 someone addresses the goddess Shame, offering a prayer of some kind. The genitives ὡρέων in lines 18–19 for some reason are Ionic.

(A) . . . (B) Someone came . . . a person came . . . goes away . . . and kept saying these things . . . great awesome lady . . . queen of men and women, lady Shame . . . is completely . . . to be broken and pounded . . . you pray for many . . . to come in his [its?] prime for seasons to come upon seasons . . . upon seasons . . . taking courage [masc.].

1146 *This piece in trochaic tetrameters catalectic is a hymn of praise (1–19) to the* silouros *(sheatfish), a very large catfish, found in the Black Sea and in the Nile, followed by a treatise (20–50) on how to cook and eat this delicacy. The latter is couched in the language of a religious initiation. It was suggested by Willis, the initial editor, and strongly argued by Csapo, that this is a scene from Archippus' Fishes and that speaker A, the expert, was in fact Melanthius, the gourmand handed over to the fishes in the course of the comedy. This would date the comedy to the 390s, too early in the eyes of some for the reference to Isocrates' Praise of Helen (18–19), but must every work by Isocrates be dated after he founded his school in 392? Austin found the Egyptian references troubling (Nile fishes in l. 1, a nonclassical form in l. 15, the technical term "treasury official" in l. 38, the mention of Isis in 39, and the comparison to the Horus child in 44) and postulated an Alexandrian poet writing in the manner of earlier comedy.*

411

COMIC PAPYRI

{B.} τί σὺ λέγεις; γλαυκοῦ σίλουρον κρείττον' εἶναι
νενόμικας;
{A.} τῶν μὲν οὖν ὅλως ἀπάντων ἰχθύων σοφώτατον
φημὶ τὸν σίλουρον εἶναι κοίρανον τῶν ἰχθύων,
ἡγεμόνα, μόναρχον, ἀρχόν· τοὺς δὲ λοιπούς,
ἐπιβάτας
5 ὥστε μὴ ἀξίως ἐνεγκεῖν τῷ σιλούρῳ τὰ δόρατα.
{B.} καὶ τετόλμηκας σιλούρῳ συγγράφειν ἐγκώμιον;
{A.} ἢ σίλουρος ὄνομ' ἔχων Ἄδωνίς ἐστιν ποτάμιος.
εἰ γὰρ ἤθελεν σίλουρος μὴ κυβεύειν μηδ' ἐρᾶν,
οὐκ ἂν ἤδη δέκα ταλάντων περιέκειτ' ἀρτύματα
10 οὐκ ἂν ἤδη πέτασον εἶχε κἂν ἐφήβοις ἤψετο.
κᾆτα δή τις ἐστὶν ἰχθῦς ὅστις αὖ πρὸς ταῖς θύραις
ταῖς σιλούρου δόγμ' ἔχων ἔστηκεν ὄρθρου καὶ λέγει
"εἰ νένιπτ' ἤδη σίλουρος ......ις εἰσπορεύεται·
γέγονε ἆρα τοῖς μαιώταις πάντα περὶ ὧν ἠξίουν;
15 ἐντετεύχασ' οἱ λάβρακες ἀπὸ τοῦ πετρηρικοῦ
καί τὸ τῶν χοίρων μάτευμα τἀπὸ τοῦ σαγηνικοῦ."
⟨B.⟩ Ἰσοκράτης ἐγκώμιον τοιοῦτον οὐδεπώποτε
καθ' Ἑλένης εἴρηκεν ὡς σὺ περὶ σιλούρου. πρὸς
θεῶν
ἡ δὲ διατριβὴ τίς ἐστιν; θαυμάσαι γὰρ ἄξιον.
20 ⟨A.⟩ ὦ πόνηρ', οὐ παντὸς ἀνδρὸς ἐς σίλουρον ἐσθ'
ὁ πλοῦς.
ἀλλὰ καὶ προεγγραφῆναι καὶ μυηθῆναί σε δεῖ

1 γλαυκος σιλουρου Pap., γλαῦκον σιλούρου Willis and
others, γλαύκου σιλοῦρον K.-A.

412

W. A. Willis, GRBS 32 *(1993) 331–53; W. Luppe*, ZPE 98 *(1993) 39–41; E. Csapo*, ZPE 100 *(1994) 39–44; Rothwell 128–30, 194–97.*

(B) What are you saying? Have you concluded that the sheatfish is superior to the dogfish?

(A) I say that the sheatfish is the cleverest of all the fishes, the king of the fishes, their leader, their monarch, their ruler. All the rest, just foot soldiers, not worthy to carry a spear before the sheatfish.

(B) Have you undertaken to compose a hymn of praise to the sheatfish?

(A) Indeed, the sheatfish does have quite the reputation, a veritable Adonis of the rivers. For if the sheatfish were not willing to gamble and make love, ten talents' worth of seasonings wouldn't be surrounding him now, and he wouldn't be now wearing a wide-brimmed lid and be broiling among the cadets. And what's more, there is a fish that stands before the sheatfish's door, bright and early, decree in hand, and says, "Now that the sheatfish has finished his bath, ... going in. Did the maeots get all they were asking for? The sea bass from the Rocky Quarter have had their audience, so too the catch of pigfish from the Nets."

(B) Isocrates has never composed such a hymn of praise about Helen as you have over the sheatfish. But what's this discourse? It is certainly worth wondering about.

(A) You poor fellow, a voyage to the sheatfish is not for everybody. You must first be enrolled and initiated into the

τοῖς Σιλουρόθραιξι παισὶ καὶ μαθεῖν ὡς ἕψεται.
καταλαβεῖν σε τὴν πλύσιν δεῖ, δεῖ δὲ μὴ 'κτὸς
    μουσικοῦ
καὶ πλυνεῖς, ὡς ἡ γραφή, λεπτοῖς ἁλῶν ἀθύρμασι,
25 λεπτὰ σωλῆνος πτερίζων αἵματος μελαγχίμου
πέντε κρήνης πεντενίκου πεντεπακτωτοῖς ῥοαῖς.
ὡς δ' ἂν ἐκτρίβων ποιήσῃς οἱονεὶ κύκνου πτερὸν
. . . . η στίλβοντα λαμπρὰ φαλακρὸν ὡς ἀνθήλιον,
γίνεθ' ἡ πρόσοψις οὕτως ὡραία τῶν βραγχίων
30 ὥστε λευκομηρίδος δόκει θεωρεῖν ἰσχίον
παρθένου . . . . . ρως. ⟨Β.⟩ τοιαύτης ἄρα τὰ λοιπά,
    πρὸς θεῶν,
λευκότητος . . . ἄνυσον. σὸν γὰρ νικητήριον.
⟨Α.⟩ ἡ λοπὰς νῦν εἰσφερέσθω πέντ' ἐφήβων
    ὠλέναις.

γῦρον αὐλήτου ποίησον καὶ κολυμβητοῦ βυθόν,
35 ἐνθέσει θρῖόν τε νεαροῦ ποικ[ί]λων ⟨θ'⟩ ἡδυσμάτων,
πολυλεπίστων κρομμύων σκόρδων ὀριγάνου κλάδων,
Νηρέως τε χύμα πηγὸν κἀπὸ κρήνης μέλαν ὕδωρ.
καὶ λάβ' ὄξος δριμὺ λεπτὸν ὡς διοικητοῦ νόον.
ἐκ δὲ ληκύθου βαθείας παρθένου ταυρώπιδος
40 νᾶμα δαψιλὲς πρόχευσον μὴ κακιζούσῃ χερί,
ἀλλ' ὅλην μετάρσιον ἄρας τῶν σκελῶν κατάστεφε.
ὡς δ' ἂν ἐφθῇ σοι γένηται καὶ τὸ πῶμα κουφίσῃς,
σεῖε, πρὸς μυκτῆρας ἕλκων πενταδράχμους ἡδονάς,

ranks of the children of Silouro-thrace, and learn how it shall be boiled. You must undertake the washing, and you must do it with musical accompaniment, and you will do the washing, according to the recipe, with light sprinklings of salt, fledging lightly with the dark blood of a razor clam in five five-dammed streams from a five-times victorious fountain. Just as when by polishing you make . . . like the wing of a swan or a gleaming bald head reflecting the sun, so then the aspect of the gills becomes so lovely that it seems to be more appealing than . . . of a maiden with white thighs.

(B) By the gods, get on with the rest about the whiteness. The prize is yours.

(A) Let the cooking dish now be brought in the arms of five cadets. Make it as round as a house steward's girth and as deep as a diver can dive, with the addition of a fresh fig leaf and all sorts of seasonings, many-layered onions, garlic, and branches of marjoram, the salty stream of Nereus, and dark water from a spring. Take vinegar, sharp and subtle, like the mind of a treasury official. From a deep jar with the image of the bull-faced maiden pour out a generous stream with a steady hand; lift the jar right out of its legs and turn it upside down. When you think it is cooked and you remove the lid, stir it and draw to your nostrils the ex-

---

23 καταλαβεῖν σε δεῖ δὲ τὴν πλύσιν δειεκτος μουσικοῦ Pap. I have printed the conjecture of Austin and Handley.
26 πεντενίκου πεντεκρήνης Pap., πεντενίκοις πεντεκρήνοις Austin, πέντε κρήνης πεντενίκου Luppe.   34 αὐλητοῦ Pap., αὐλήτου Luppe.

καὶ ποίησον Ἀρποχράτου θηλάσας τὸν δακτυλον.
<Β.> Ζεῦ πάτερ, πέφρικ' ἀκούων καὶ δέδοικα μήποτε
τὴν κατάζηλον Βοιωτὸν ἡ λοπὰς παρεκβάλῃ.
<Α.> πρὶν δὲ γεύσαθαι τεράμνων κλεῖε λαίνων
    μοχλοὺς
καὶ κέλευε τοὺς μὲν ἔσθειν, τοὺς δ' ἐν ὅπλοις
    περιπατεῖν
μὴ 'πανάστασις γένηται τῶν ἀχάλκων γειόνων,
50 μὴ κύκνος γενόμενος ὁ Ζεῦς ἐπὶ κρυφαῖον κωμασῃ

1148 *Pap. Colon.* 342 = *Kölner Pap.* VIII (1995) nr. 330,
       31–33.

            ]βασι[λ]ευ[
        ἦ]μιν Ἀρχίας κρατεῖ
            ]ελεῖται κατακρισιν
            ]τε καὶ σοφῶς τά τε
5   ]σα....ἄλλον παρακαλει
     ]πων τρὶς θεαῖς σώσουσί σε
         ]τα παραζῶν θεῶν
     ] πιστόν, ἀσφαλῆ
     ].ς μ' ἑτέροις κρίσιν
         ]....[.]λιον καὶ ποικίλον
10].τοι μηδὲ λοιμὸν προσλάβῃς
     ].......για.α... εἰσὶν βίου

pensive savour, and do so while sucking your finger like Harpochrates.[1]

(B) Father Zeus, as I listen I shiver and I fear that my cooking dish will hereafter reject the envious eel of Boeotia.

(A) Before you have a taste, close the bars on your marbled doors, and bid the people inside to eat, and those under arms to patrol outside so that our penniless neighbours will not invade or that Zeus turn himself into a swan and secretly crash our party.

1 The child of Isis and Osiris frequently depicted in Egyptian art, especially in the Hellenistic and Roman periods. His characteristic pose was with a finger to his lips.

1148 *The link with Old Comedy depends on reading the unusual form ἥμιν in line 2, found at Phrynichus F 38, and on seeing "Archias rules among us" as an allusion to the archon of that name in 419/18. We seem to have the ends of lines in iambic trimter. Is the combination of "judgement" (3, 9), "thrice," and "goddesses" (6), and "multicoloured" (10) enough to suggest an allusion to the Judgement of Paris?*

. . . king . . . Archias rules among us . . . he takes care in accordance with judgement . . . encourages another . . . three times for goddesses they will save you [sing.] . . . merely existing . . . of the gods [goddesses?] . . . trusty, secure . . . me judgement for others . . . and multicoloured . . . and that you might not catch the plague . . . they are of life.

1151 P. Oxy. 4301

```
___.[.].ω[
___β[ο]υλησετ[
   ἦ μὴν σὺ θ[
___ἑταῖρον ητη.[
   Κλεώνυμος δ[
___γραφαῖσιν οδε.η[
   ἀλλ' οὐχὶ Δημαρατ'[
___οὐκ ἂν προδω.[
   ὦ μῶρε, καὶ τα[
   ως χαυν[
   ε..[
```

P. Oxy. 2738 = CGFP 237

```
   αι[..]........
πυρριχίζων, ἐν δὲ Αἰξὶν Εὐ-
πόλ[ιδος] τὸ μαλακὴν κε-
λ]εύ[ειν] τὴν Ἀθηνᾶν ποεῖν. σκλη-
ρ]ῶς ποιοῦντο[ς] τοῦ ἀγροί-
```

1151 *The mention of the familiar comic target Cleony-mus in line 5, together with "indictments" in the next, the fact that one speaker calls another "you idiot" in line 9, and the possibility that we read "wide-arsed" in line 10 suggest we have Old Comedy here. The* paragraphoi *in the margin make it clear that this is dialogue, the metre probably iambic trimeter. The hand of the copyist is very much like that of* PSI 1213 (= Eupolis F 260 *[Prospaltians]), and we should consider Eupolis as the first candidate for the source of this battered fragment.*

W. Luppe and I. C. Storey in Rivals *163–71.*

. . . (A) he (she) will want . . . (B) But for a fact you [sing.] . . . requested a companion . . . (A) But Cleonymus . . . with indictments, and he might get . . . (B) but Demaratus would not . . . to betray . . . (A) You idiot . . . for whom wide-arsed . . .

P. Oxy. 2738 = CGFP 237. This comes from a commentary on Old Comedy, which seems to be concerned with the epithets and associations of Athena. The author cites Eupolis F 18 (Nanny-Goats) *for an Athena dance, Aristophanes* Clouds *989 for the epithet "Triton-born," and Cratinus F 433 for a marvellous coinage "awaiting the Gorgon dragon." Borthwick* (Hermes 98 *[1970] 318–31) wonders if the epithets refer to poses or stances within the Athena dance, which may have reenacted her slaying of the Gorgon (cf. Euripides* Ion *1478).*

. . . doing the Pyrrhic dance, and in *Nanny-Goats* by Eupolis there is the instruction to perform the Athena dance in a fluid manner. When the farmer performs the

κου τὸ σχῆμα τῆς Ἀθηνᾶς
ὁ διδ[ά]σκαλος ἐκέλευσεν μα-
λακῶς αὐτὸ ποιεῖν. ὡς οὖν
ὁ Ἀρ[ισ]τ[ο]φ[ά]νη[ς] τῷ Τριτογέ-
νεια μόνῳ ἐπιθέτωι ἠρκέ-
σθη καὶ ὁ Κρατ[ῖ]νος τῷ Γοργο-
.ρακον.οδοκα.[ ] ἠρκέσθη
τ[ὸ] αὐτὸ δηλοῦντι πρᾶγμα
ὅτι ἀποκλινω[..]ηι κεφαλῆ[ι
τὸ τ[ῆς] θε[ο]ῦ σχῆμα πο.[ ]..
λεφι[ ].[ ].ται· .μοι[
μυνον[
].εν[
].[

TrGF II 646a = P. Fackelmann 5 + P. Köln 242 = *TrGF* V,
pp. 1135–37

Athena dance very awkwardly, the teacher ordered him to do it in a fluid manner. So then Aristophanes was content with the epithet "Triton-born" on its own and so too Cratinus with his "awaiting the Gorgon dragon," which shows the same thing that the form of the dance . . . nodding with the head.

TrGF II 646a = P. Fackelmann 5 + P. Köln 242 = *TrGF* V, pp. 1135–37. *The publication of the second fragment showed that the speaker was Silenus, the tutor and companion of Dionysus, who in lines 1–18 recounts his service to and for his god, in a manner rather like the opening of* Cyclops. *But in the last nine lines the dramatic illusion is broken by a mention of "the great bard of Salamis," an address to "goddesses," who must be the Muses, the phrase "the present labour of tragic songs," and what appears to be a request to avoid a third-place finish "in the contest" (agon—v. 27). The possibilities are: (1) to regard the source as a satyr drama and accept the rupture of the dramatic illusion, (2) to regard the play as an Old Comedy with a Dionysian theme, in which case the breaking of the illusion presents no problem, and (3) to consider the piece as a Hellenistic pastiche. We have the last two-thirds of twenty-seven anapaestic tetrameters catalectic, a metre found in the agon and parabasis of Old Comedy, and at Eupolis F 205 in an address to the spectators "at the beginning of the play." Unless the play had a chorus of satyrs (for which see Cratinus'* Dionysalexander, *and* Satyrs *by Ecphantides, Callias, Cratinus, and Phrynichus) of which Silenus could act as chorus leader, it is unlikely that this comes from a parabasis.*

ε]ὶς οἶδμ᾽ ἀπολίσθο[ι
]τορ....ις
]νασε....ιαις
]Σεμέλης [τέ]κ[ος] ὕμνον
5   ].βλα [.].[..] θεὸς Ἀρκάς
]σκεπτομεν[....]
].υλε....δησ.........ει παρέδωκεν
] πεφευγὼς ἤθυρον ἐγὼ νέος ἄντροις
]ουργος ἁπλοῦς, πάσης κακίας ἀμίαντος
10   ] .οσισου καρπὸν μὲν ἑλὼν τὸν ὄρειον
]αι τὸ πάλαι θηρῶν ἐφόδοις ἀκόμιστον
] παιδεύσας ὥριον ἥβην ἐφύλαξα
καρπὸ]ν ὀπώρας ἦρα βαθείας ἐπὶ ληνούς
]ν εἰς θνητοὺς ἀνέφηνα ποτὸν Διονύσου
15   ]σος ὁ μύστης οὔποτε λήγων ἐπὶ Βάκχῳ
]δε θεοῦ πρώτη πλοκάμοις ἀνέδησεν
]ων λήθη χάρισιν κείναις ἀνέλαμψεν
]αι θίασος· τοιάδε κομπεῖν ἐδιδάχθην.
].μέγας φησὶν ἀοιδὸς Σαλαμῖνος
20   ]ης ταμίας, νῦν δ᾽ εἰς ἀπάτας κεκύλισμαι
]ας παῦρος ὑπουργῶν ταῖς ψευδομένα[ις
]αραπέμψει τὸν ἀπ᾽ ὀθνείας ἐπεγείρων
]γνωτε, θεαί· τραγικῶν ὁ παρὼν πόνος
ὕμνων
].ος ὁρίζει· μὴ τὰ δικαίως καλὰ μόχθῳ
25   ]φθέντα μόλις θῆτε παρέργου τρίτα φόρτου
]αδεν ὀρθῇ Διόνυσος
β]ραβεύσας γ᾽ ἐν ἀγῶνι

A. Bierl, *GRBS* 31 (1990) 353–91; M. di Marco, in M. Martina (ed.), *Scritti di filologia classica e storia antica* (Trieste 2004) 41–74; L. Battezzato, in ΚΩΜΩΙΔΟΤΡΑ-ΓΩΙΔΙΑ 19–68.

. . . he slipped off into the surge . . . a hymn to (?) the son of Semele . . . the Arcadian god[1] . . . observing . . . handed over . . . after getting away I played as a youth in caves . . . a simple . . . -worker untouched by any vice . . . picking the harvest on the mountain-side . . . so long untouched by the attacks of wild beasts . . . I educated and watched over the youthful prime ‹of Dionysus›[2] . . . I lifted the fruit of harvest time into the deep vats . . . I displayed to mortals the drink of Dionysus . . . the initiate never ceasing on my Bacchic . . . and the first maenad of the god bound up ‹her locks› with bands of wool . . . forgetfulness gleamed forth in those delights . . . thiasos. I was taught to boast of such things.[3] . . . says the great bard of Salamis[4] . . . the steward, and now I am rolled into deceits . . . an insignificant person serving those women who lie . . . will wake and escort this one from a foreign land . . . show mercy [you know?], goddesses. This present labour of tragic songs . . . puts a limit on . . . do not . . . what is rightly attractive with toil . . . with difficulty winning the third prize of such trash . . . Dionysus with just (decision?) . . . having served as the judge in the contest.

[1] Hermes or Pan. [2] Bierl takes this as referring to the young vine. [3] The verb "I was taught" is *didaskein,* used of a poet putting on a play. There could well be a metatheatrical play here, "This is the speech written for me by the poet." [4] Euripides or Homer, "bard" (*aoidos*) is more easily used of the latter, unless the actual dramatic poet himself is meant (cf. Aristophanes and Aegina at *Acharnians* 652–54).

OLD COMEDY ON VASES

Athenian red-figure vases often show scenes based on tragedy, although what we see is not a representation of an actual tragic performance. While the story line may depend on a tragic original, the characters are not shown in dramatic dress, but in the heroic mode, males naked or nearly so, and often with various scenes from a play depicted together. They resemble more the collage advertising a modern film than an accurate reproduction of a dramatic moment. But only a few Athenian vases appear to show scenes from Attic Comedy. V 2 (c. 420) shows two men watching a dancer. Some have supposed this to be a performance of a contemporary comedy, but other explanations are possible. V 1 may show Phrynichus the comic poet with four singers and an *aulos* player (indicating that the scene is a musical performance, and not a comedy). If V 3 does show a comic actor, it would be the earliest such representation that we possess. V 26 presents two very atypical Athenian vases, which may depict aggressive birds from a comic play.

There is, however, a wealth of fourth-century vases from South Italy that show grotesquely costumed actors (wearing a wrinkled body suit, distorted mask, padded paunches and buttocks, and dangling phalli) in all sorts of bizarre scenes. These were usually assumed to be depictions of a crude Italian farce known as *phlyakes* and attributed to Rhinthon of Tarentum (late 4th/early 3rd c.). But since the late 1980s it has become apparent that some, if not most, of these vases represent scenes from Athenian Old and early Middle Comedy and that, contrary to what we had been taught, Old Comedy did travel from Athens to the West and was re-performed there. Often the artist has drawn a stage with steps leading up (V 10), a marker that this is a dramatic production, while some vases have a pair of inward-opening doors that represent the dramatic central doors of the *skēnē* building. In other cases a comic mask hangs about the scene.

Trendall (*PhV*²) includes more than two hundred such vases in his collection, and it is tempting to look at one of these and imagine how it might fit a known scene from Aristophanes or another poet of Old Comedy. For instance, Bieber *Theater* fig. 514 shows an old man before a teacher and a female scribe—perhaps the old farmer in Eupolis' *Goats*? Or fig. 517, where an old man leads a drunken younger man—the father and the wayward son in Aristophanes' *Banqueters*? The problem is complicated because for the ancients there was no break between what we call "Old" and "Middle Comedy." Green speaks well of a continuum here. This is especially problematic when dealing with the burlesques of myth that come into their own during the last phase of Old Comedy and last well into the Middle Comedy. A vase from 375–350 showing a burlesque of myth or of tragedy might be inspired by an Old Comedy, or equally well by one from the Middle period.

I have included below about thirty vases, choosing those that with reasonable justification may (or have been) seen as depicting scenes from Old Comedy. In some cases a particular comedy has been suggested.

The principal studies are M. Bieber, *The History of the Greek and Roman Theater*, 2nd ed. (Princeton 1961) 129–46; A. D. Trendall and T. B. L. Webster, *Illustrations of Greek Drama* (London 1971); and O. Taplin, *Comic Angels* (Oxford 1993), to which should be added D. Walsh, *Distorted Ideals in Greek Vase-Painting: The World of the Mythological Burlesque* (Cambridge 2009) and J. R. Green, "Greek Theatre Production: 1996–2006," *Lustrum* 50 (2008) 185–218; "The Material Evidence," in *Companion* 71–102.

*ARV*² = J. D. Beazley, *Attic Red-Figure Vase-Painters*, 2nd ed. (Oxford 1963)
*PhV*² = A. D. Trendall, *Phlyax Vases*, 2nd ed. (London 1967) [*BICS* Supp. 19]
RVAp = A. D. Trendall and A. Cambitoglou, *The Red-Figured Vases of Apulia* (Oxford 1978, 1982)
RVP = A. D. Trendall, *The Red-Figured Vases of Paestum* (British School at Rome 1987)

Kassel and Austin (*PCG* VIII 56–68) list only the vases with written text, usually the names of the characters (but see V 5).

V 1   Attic red-figure bell *krater* by the Cleophon painter, c. 425. *ARV*² 1145 no. 35.

Harvey, in *Rivals* 91–134, with full bibliography at 116 n. 1; Green "Production" 196.

The vase shows two singers (labelled "]peinikos" and "Pleistias") + "Phrynichus" (wreathed with ivy and wearing

427

a headband) + "Amphilochus" the *aulos* player + two sing-
ers ("Theomedes" and "Chremes"). This in all likelihood
shows the victorious poet at a dithyrambic contest, with
aulos player and four of the singers. Harvey argues that
this is Phrynichus the comic poet, who (it would appear)
also wrote dithyrambs.

V 2   Attic red-figure *chous,* c. 420. *ARV*² 1215. ("Perseus
Dance Vase" or the "Anavyssos Perseus").

Illustrations IV.1; Bieber *Theater* nr. 202; Hughes, *Oxford
Journal of Archaeology* 25 (2006) 413–33; Green "Produc-
tion" 200; Csapo, *Actors and Icons of the Ancient Theater*
(Oxford 2010) 25–27.

This vase shows two spectators seated on elegant chairs, an
older man with a beard, the other younger and beardless—
the gender is not certain. Before them on a platform with a
ladder cavorts a naked man, his right arm raised, a robe
over his left shoulder, and in his left hand a bag and what
looks like a sickle. Since on early vases Perseus is shown
wielding the sickle with which he slew the Gorgon, the
scene here has often been identified as a comic burlesque
of the story of Perseus. Beside him is a mysterious curved
object with lines suggesting panels or sections, variously
identified as a curtain, the side of a ship, or a stage build-
ing. If this is a comic performance, then this performer
lacks the usual body suit, padded costume, mask, and ex-
aggerated phallus, characteristic of the comic performer.
Csapo wonders if the two seated figures represent judges,
or the *chorēgus* and poet, or Dionysus and Ariadne as the
ideal spectators (as on the Pronomus Vase).

V 3   Attic red-figure cup, 450–430.

Webster, in *Hesperia* 29 (1960) 261 (B 1, pl. 67B); Moore, *The Athenian Agora. Volume XXX, Attic Red-figured and White-ground Pottery* (Princeton 1997) 326 (nr. 1449, pl. 136); Green "Production" 199–200.

Only pieces of this cup survive, showing what seems to be a *kōmos* of young revellers and the right arm and torso of a male figure wearing a bodysuit, a long-sleeved garment, and padding. Green 212–13 dates the cup closer to 430 than to 450.

V 4   Apulian bell *krater*, c. 370s. ("Würzburg Telephus"). *RVAp* 65, 4/4a.

Taplin *Comic Angels* 11.4 (pp. 36–41, 112); *PCPhS* 33 (1987) 92–104; Csapo, *Phoenix* 40 (1986) 379–92; Kossatz-Deismann, in Cahn and Simon (eds.), *Tainia: Festschrift für R. Hampe* (Mainz 1980) 281–90; Walsh *Distorted Ideals* 74–79, 102–3; Green in *Companion* 77–78.

The vase shows on the right a figure dressed as a woman, with one knee on an altar and holding a short sword in the right hand and a wineskin with baby boots in the other. Careful examination of the face shows the remnant of stubble. On the left a woman moves forward holding a large bowl. Higher up between the figures is a mirror. Csapo and Taplin argued independently that this was not just a comic parody of Telephus taking refuge at an altar and threatening the baby Orestes, but a snapshot of a scene from Aristophanes' *Thesmophoriazusae* (687–764), where Euripides' kinsman seizes a baby and discovers it to be a wineskin, complete with Persian booties (734). This was the vase that "broke the logjam" in the reassessment of the so-called *phlyax* vases and led to the conclusion that these vases in fact represented scenes from Athenian comedy.

V 5   Apulian *kalyx krater,* c. 400. ("New York Goose Play"). *RVAp* 46 3/7, *PhV²* nr. 84, *PCG* VIII.57.

Taplin *Comic Angels* 10.2 (pp. 29–30, 62, 111); *Illustrations* IV.13; Beazley, *AJA* 56 (1952) 193–95; Gigante, *Rintone e il teatro in Magna Grecia* (Naples 1971) 71–74; Marshall, *Theatre Journal* 53 (2001) 53–71; Green in *Companion* 76–77.

The early date of this vase and the Attic dialect of the quotations ensure that the original was a scene from Old Comedy. In the centre an old man, with all the accoutrements of the comic character, stands on tiptoe with his hands clasped above his head. He is glancing apprehensively at the figure on the left, younger and dark-haired, and holding a long rod. At the right on a platform before a structure of some sort sits an old woman beside a basket containing two kids and a dead goose. A comic mask hangs in the upper centre-left. Words like the balloon-speech in a modern comic book are provided for each character: the old man, "He (she?) has tied my hands above me," or possibly "she has bewitched my hands up"; the old woman, "I will provide ‹the evidence›"; and the man on the left the apparently meaningless "noraretteblo." This last figure is usually considered to be a barbarian policeman like the one in *Thesmophoriazusae,* whose Attic Greek is less than adequate. The old man appears to have gotten himself into trouble, perhaps involving the goose and the kids, and the authorities have been summoned.

Complicating the matter is the final figure on the upper left, clearly not meant to be on the same level as the comic participants. He is youthful, a boy even, naked with a robe over his shoulder, without a mask, and is labelled *tragōidos,* which should mean "tragic actor" or "tragic singer." Why a boy? Why is he naked? In what way is he a spectator—see note at V 9? Is he an indicator of para-tragedy? Some engagement between the dramatic genres is clearly going on, but his role in the scene remains a mystery.

V 6   Apulian bell *krater,* c. 370. ("Boston Goose Play"). *RVAp* 100, 4/251.

Taplin *Comic Angels* 11.3 (p. 32).

On a raised platform are two comic figures, a white-haired old man pouring liquid from an aryballus into his hand, and a dark-haired younger male in a threatening pose, his left arm outstretched and resting on a long rod. On the far left is a Herm with a cloak placed on top, and on the right are two baskets, each containing a kid, and between them a live goose. The two figures correspond well with the male figures in V 5, while the basket, kids, and goose make it certain that this vase is representing a scene from the same play as on that vase. That the goose is alive and well shows that this comes from an earlier point in that play. It is instructive that two different vase painters, thirty years apart, chose to represent scenes from this comedy with such similar iconography.

V 7   Paestan bell *krater* by Assteas, mid-4th c. *RVP* 65 2/
19, *PhV*² nr. 58, *PCG* VIII.64.

Taplin *Comic Angels* 16.16 (p. 42). *Illustrations* IV.31;
Sestieri, *ArchClass* 12 (1960) 156–59; Gigante *Rintone e il
teatro* 74–76; Goulaki Voutari, *Apollo* 15 (1999) 13–15;
Storey, *Eupolis. Poet of Old Comedy* (Oxford 2003) 117,
169–70; Telò, *Philologus* 147 (2003) 13–25; Piqueux,
Apollo 22 (2006) 3–10; Green "Production" 212–13.

On the left a wreathed lyre player, labelled "Phrynis" and
leaning backward, is being dragged in an aggressive fash-
ion by an old man, holding a walking stick. He is labelled
"Pyronides." Phrynis should be the well-known dithyram-
bic poet, made fun of at *Clouds* 969–72 for his musical in-
novations and at Pherecrates F 155 as the third of those
to assault Music. He may also be speaker A at Eupolis F
326. Since Pyronides is the name of the main character in
Eupolis *Demes,* I have suggested that we have here an in-
truder scene from that play (compare Cinesias at *Birds*
1372–1409), where the unwelcome poet is removed force-
fully by Pyronides. Telò suggests rather a scene in the
Underworld, where Pyronides encounters the ghost of
Phrynis, equally unwelcome. Both Goulaki Voutari and
Piqueux reject any link with Eupolis' play and see Phrynis
as a reluctant young pupil dragged unwillingly to school by
an older authority figure. But since "Phrynis" is holding a
kithara, the formal instrument of a professional musician
and not the *chelys* lyre that a schoolboy would hold, this
figure should be the poet, familiar from comedy.

V 8   Apulian bell *krater,* 375–350. ("Berlin Heracles").
*PhV*² nr. 22.

Bieber *Theater* 133 (fig. 487); Taplin *Comic Angels* 13.7 (pp. 45–47); Walsh *Distorted Images* 234–6; Panofka, *Archäologische Zeitung* 7 (1849) 17–20; Bieber, *Die Denkmäler zum Theaterwesen im Altertum* (Berlin/Leipzig 1920) pl. 80; Gigante *Rintone e il teatro* 37. Earlier bibliography at *PhV²* nr. 22.

As this vase was lost during World War II, we are dependent on earlier photographs and on a drawing made by Panofka. On the left a Heracles figure, stage naked, stands at a door, holding a raised club in his right hand and trailing a robe from his left. He does wear the padding, bodysuit, and grotesque mask of comic actors, although the phallus is rather smaller than usual. Behind him on the right a figure with baggage on his back rides a donkey. Is this the opening scene of *Frogs*? Although we do not immediately see Dionysus disguised as Heracles (no *krokōtos* or soft boots), the parallels do outweigh the difficulties. How many ancient comedies would have a scene with a "Heracles" beating at a door and a donkey in the background carrying both a slave and baggage?

V 9   Apulian bell *krater,* c. 380. ("Chiron Vase"). *RVAp* 100 4/52, *PhV²* nr. 37. *PCG* VIII.60.

Bieber *Theater* 135 (fig. 491); Taplin *Comic Angels* 12.6 (pp. 61–62); Walsh *Distorted Images* 216–17. *Illustrations* IV.35.

An old man ("Chiron") with a walking stick is being pushed up a short set of stairs to a platform by an unnamed slave while another ("Xanthias") pulls from above. The combination of the old man with the lower slave does with imagination make the figure resemble a centaur to some degree. In a separate panel above and to the right are two female figures in comic masks labelled "Nymphs." It is generally thought that the play turned on a visit by Chiron to a place of healing presided over by the Nymphs, who may have formed the chorus. But Marshall (see V 5) points out that *nymphai* could also mean "brides." Aristophanes wrote a *Plays or Centaur,* Nicochares a *Centaur,* and Apollophanes a *Centaurs,* while Cratinus' *Chirons* and Pherecrates' *Chiron* were well-known comedies.

On the lower right stands a perplexing figure, a youth dressed modestly in a cloak, but without a mask. Is he a character in the play, perhaps the young Achilles, Chiron's best-known pupil? Did youths and children in comedy, then, not wear the comic costume? Is he a spectator, like (perhaps) the *tragōidos* on the New York Goose Play? Or perhaps a representative of tragedy, like Aegisthus on the *Chorēgoi* vase (V 10)? Or an indication that the scene is a parody of a tragic original?

V 10   Apulian bell *krater,* 400–380. ("*Chorēgoi* vase"). *RVAp* supp. ii, 7–8, 1/124; *PCG* VIII 59.

Taplin *Comic Angels* 9.1 (pp. 55–66); Gilula, *ZPE* 109 (1995) 5–10; Robertson, in M. Joyal (ed.), In Altum: *Seventy-Five Years of Classical Studies in Newfoundland* (St. John's NL 2001) 273–87; Green "Production" 208–9.

This splendid vase shows a group of figures on a platform with steps in the centre leading down. On a raised "soapbox" stands a figure ("Pyrrhias") with right arm raised, clearly in full oratorical flood. On either side are two figures, each with a crooked stick and each labelled *"Chorēgos,"* an older man with white hair on the left and a younger one with dark hair and beard on the right. The older *chorēgos* has his right arm raised, either to greet or dismiss a fourth figure, who has just entered through the open double doors on the extreme left. But this figure is wearing tragic dress, a splendid long robe, and holds two javelins. He is labelled "Aegisthus" and is clearly meant to be part of the ensemble. He is not watching like the boy on the Chiron Vase or the *tragōidos* on the New York Goose Play.

Taplin argued that *chorēgos* (note the Attic spelling on an Italian vase) had its Athenian meaning, the officially appointed sponsor of a play, and supposed that the two *chorēgoi* were members or leaders of two opposing sub-choruses, with one leaning toward tragedy (for him Aegisthus is symbolic of tragedy) and the other toward Pyrrhias, who symbolises comedy. Gilula is less certain that these are chorus members and identifies the figures with the *choragoi* known from Plautus *Trinummus* 858 and *Persa* 160), "equipment managers." In her view the vase shows preparations for a performance, and she wonders if the Aegisthus actor has dressed for a tragic role by mistake.

I agree that we have a scene from a comic drama about drama itself. Aristophanes wrote two comedies called *Plays* (with the secondary titles of *Centaur* and *Niobus*), but neither seems relevant to Aegisthus. Other possibilities are Platon's *Costumes,* Phrynichus' *Muses* or *Tragic Actors,* Alcaeus' *Tragicomedy,* Cratinus' *Dramatic Rehearsals,* and Aristophanes' *Proagōn.* Taplin entertains, but ultimately rejects this last possibility, but with Robertson I would give it more serious consideration. But the poet, who (along with Aristophanes) displays the greatest engagement between tragedy and comedy is Strattis, and I might suggest his *Orestes the Mortal,* where F 1 describes the selection of Hegelochus as the lead actor for *Orestes.* Compare Aristotle's complaint at *Poetics* 1453a26 about comedies in which Aegisthus and Orestes leave the stage together as friends.

V 11 Five unglazed Attic *oinochoai,* late 5th c.

Crosby, *Hesperia* 24 (1955) 76–84.; Webster, *Hesperia* 29 (1960) 261–63 (B 2–5, pl. 65); Bieber *Theater* nrr. 209–10 (pp. 49–50); Green and Handley, *Images of the Greek Theatre* (London 1995) 50–51; Storey, *Eupolis* 248, 260; Csapo *Actors and Icons* 28–29.

Four of these pots were found in an ancient well in the Agora in 1954, a fifth very similar pot was already known in the British Museum. The pictures are crudely painted onto the unglazed surface and in Crosby's judgement "almost certainly come from the same workshop." The scenes all seem to have to do with public performances at a festival of Dionysus, and Crosby wonders if they were meant to be sold at one of these festivals. Webster argues for a single winning comedy behind all five vases, but it would be difficult to imagine a play that combined Dionysus, a man rowing a fish, a solo dancer, two *obeliaphoroi,* and a parody of the myth of Tyro and her sons. We know that the *chorēgoi* would dispense food and drink before (and during?) the performance. Were these inexpensive vases part of that largesse, a souvenir decorated with a scene from the play? Green and Handley suggest "a set of wine-jugs made for a party to celebrate a particular production."

(a) Only the top part of this vases survives, showing the head of a male figure and the names, Pelia]s, Tyro, and Neleus. Sophocles wrote two versions of a tragedy about Tyro and her sons. Aristophanes alludes to the myth at *Lysistrata* 139 and parodies F 654 at *Birds* 275. We do not have enough of the scene to know whether we have a tragic scene or (more probably) a comic parody. There is no obvious candidate among the extant titles of Old Comedy.

(b) A crudely rendered single performer fills the scene on this vase, which shows a male dancer, either executing a *schēma* or resting on one knee. There are hints of padding and the exaggerated features of a comic mask. A scarf is draped over his right arm, his left holds a small wine jar, and he wears a white band around his head and elaborate boots with wide cuffs and turned-up points. He could be just a reveller with no dramatic context, but the comic features of his costume would suggest a memorable performance in a comedy (cf. the dancers at the end of *Wasps*).

(c) The scene on this vase remarkably resembles that on V 12. Two male figures are running while carrying a white object on a spit. There are hints of padding, certainly there are grotesque masks, and a long phallus seems to be visible for the figure on the left. This man wears a white cap and boots like those of the preceding vase. Both figures seem to be wearing short white chitons. The object they carry has been seen as a roast on a spit, but it is more likely an *obelias* loaf (see Athenaeus 111b, Pollux 6.75). These were carried in processions at festivals at Dionysus, but the fact that two vases with comic performers seem to show the same scene suggests that the original was a memorable scene in comedy. Both Aristophanes' *Farmers* (F 105) and

437

Pherecrates' *Forgetful Man* (F 61) mention the *obelias* loaf, but this is not sufficient evidence that either was the play in question.

(d) Two well-padded figures face each other on this vase. The one on the left (" . . .]onysus") is reaching out to the figure on the right, who seems to be retreating somewhat. He is labelled "Phor[. . . " It is very likely that these are the two principal characters from Eupolis' *Officers,* Dionysus and Phormion, although Webster does not comment on the possibility, and Crosby remains hesitant. Csapo is quite confident that this vase depicts two characters from *Officers.*

(e) This vase, in the British Museum, shows a well-padded figure, with hints of the grotesque mask, but with no visible phallus, seated backward on a large fish and rowing with two very long oars. His head is turned round so that he may see where he is going. I suggest that this represents another scene from Eupolis' *Officers,* where Dionysus returns in triumph at the end of the comedy. It might have been related in a brilliant messenger speech, but if Aristophanes can mount Trygaeus in *Peace* on a giant dung beetle or have Dionysus row a boat across the orchestra in *Frogs,* which scene seems to have its original in *Officers* (F 268 51–52, 54–55), could Eupolis not have actually staged this scene as represented here?

V 12 Apulian bell *krater,* 375–350. ("St. Petersburg *Obeliaphoroi*"). *RVAp* 148, 6/97, *PhV*[2] 34.

Taplin *Comic Angels* 14.12 (pp. 73, 76); Crosby, *Hesperia* 24 (1955) 80–81.

As the scene on this vase is so close to that on the *oinochoē* V 11 (c), we may legitimately consider whether the two vases, perhaps forty years apart, represent a scene from the same Old Comedy. On a platform are two male comic figures (with bodysuit, grotesque mask, padding, and phallus) carrying on a spit either a large roast of meat or an *obelias* loaf. They are led by a female *aulos* player. Taplin considers that they might be two members of the chorus, but the difference in masks suggests that they are actors, slaves or domestic servants.

V 13   Apulian bell *krater*, 400–380. ("Milan Cake-eaters"). *RVAp* supp. ii 7, 1/123, *PhV*² 45; *PCG* VIII 58.

Taplin *Comic Angels* 12.5 (pp. 42, 55); *Illustrations* IV.18.

The early date of the vase suggests that the original of this scene belonged to the last period of Old Comedy. While the names Xanthias and Charis belong to the everyday world of later comedy, Philotimides (note the Attic spelling) is a rare name at Athens, only one instance documented (*PAA* 950285, c. 380), and could qualify as a *nom parlant* of the sort common to Old Comedy ("Son of Ambition"). Three characters stand on a platform, with a pair of in-swinging double doors partly open on the left. In the middle stands a woman ("Charis") taking a bun or a cake from a tray held by the white-haired old man ("Philotimides") to the left. He himself is examining what appears to be a sausage or salami, while on the right the third figure ("Xanthias") is slipping a flat-cake into his clothing. Both Xanthias and Philotimides wear the familiar outfit of the comic performer, while Charis wears an unflattering mask.

Between Charis and Philotimides a low table rests on the platform and above hangs a wine jug.

V 14   Lucanian *kalyx krater,* late 5th c. by the Amykos Painter. *PhV*[2] nr. 75.

Illustrations IV.15.

On the left a figure crouches down, awaiting a beating from the standing figure on the right. Both are bearded with dark hair and both wear the usual outfit of the comic performer. The man on the right raises a crooked staff in his right hand, while his left hand holds a rope tied to the neck of the offender. At the top is the head of another male, apparently thumbing his nose at the scene below. Aristophanes complains at *Peace* 743–77 about the tired comic business of slaves being beaten but in *Frogs* does give us a scene (616ff.) where Dionysus and Xanthias are beaten by Aeacus. In view of the early date, if this scene does reflect Athenian comedy and not a local Italian farce, then its source will have been an Old Comedy.

V 15   Apulian bell *krater,* 400–375. *PhV*[2] nr. 24.

Illustrations IV.16. Bromberg, *HSCPh* 64 (1959) 237–45; Hoffmann, *Grabritual und Gesellschaft* (Rahden 2002) 170–77; Green "Production" 209.

A floor can be seen, but without supports or stairs, a column on the left and the double door, opening inwards on the right. From the left approaches a white-haired old man carrying a crooked staff and wearing the familiar comic costume (mask, phallus, padding, body suit) with a short cloak on top and a decorated headband. He is being greeted by an old woman with arms stretched out toward him. Above in the middle hangs a male comic mask, fitted with a white headband. Bromberg, Hoffmann, and Green favour a domestic scene, and the man's backward posture and her aggressive advance might suggest that she is in control of the situation. But a scene from myth is not out of the question: Odysseus and Penelope, or (better) Odysseus encountering Circe. Theopompus did write an *Odysseus,* while from Middle Comedy we know of a *Circe* by Ephippus and Anaxilas.

V 16   Apulian bell *krater,* c. 380.

Green, in Csapo and Miller (eds.), *Poetry, Theory, Praxis. The Social Life of Myth, Word and Image in Ancient Greece* (Oxford 2003) 179–85.

The figures on the vase possess the normal costume of comedy, and they perform on a platform supported by three posts. The figure on the left is that of an old man, stage naked, dancing and holding a rope stretched out in both hands. In the middle stands a slave figure, his arms held out straight to the person on the right. With his right hand he is tipping over a small vessel, while his left holds a sprig with three branches. The figure on the right is also a slave, seated on what looks like clothing or bedding, with his hands on his knees. On his forehead are tattooed the letters Σ Θ E (S TH E).

Green argues that these letters form the stigma of a wayward slave and that they stand for the name Sthenelus, a tragic poet of the late fifth century (*TrGF* 1 32), who is made fun of in comedy by Aristophanes (*Wasps* 1313 and F 158 [*Gerytades*]) and by Platon (F 136 [*Costumes*]). The reference in *Wasps* is to "Sthenelus shorn of his gear"; in Green's opinion he is the stage-naked figure on the left, and the scene depicts a wayward slave who has stolen from his master (Sthenelus), while Sthenelus dances for joy at the situation. As *Gerytades* had to do with a journey to the Underworld, it might be a less likely candidate, but *Costumes* remains a contender.

V 17   Paestan bell *krater,* by Assteas, 350–340. *PhV*[2] nr. 65.

Illustrations IV.19; Gigante *Rintone e il teatro* 86.

On the left a white-haired old man, wearing a small crown, carries a ladder up to a window, through which the head and upper body of a woman may be seen. That his head pokes through the rungs of the ladder implies that he is not an expert at this sort of thing. On the right stands Hermes, recognisable by his caduceus (left hand) along with a traveller's hat and cloak. In his right hand he holds out a very small lamp. The classic tale of seduction involving Zeus, Hermes, and a woman is of course that of Zeus and Alcmena, of which Heracles will be the result. Although this vase belongs later in the fourth century, Assteas did paint a scene from Eupolis' *Demes* some sixty years after its Athenian performance (V 7), and although the heyday of mythological burlesque lies in Middle Comedy, Platon's *Long Night* and Archippus' *Amphitryon* do belong to Old Comedy.

V 18   Apulian *kalyx krater* by the Varrese Painter, c. 350. *PhV*² nr. 81; *PCG* VIII 67.

Illustrations IV.21; Gigante *Rintone e il teatro* 95.

On a stage resting on posts and with a substantial set of steps sits a female figure ("Hera") on a throne, a long sceptre in her right hand. On either side two male figures, identified as "Daedalus" and "Enyalius" are engaged in armed combat, the stances showing that the former is prevailing. Each is armed with a shield and spear, Enyalius wearing a splendidly plumed helmet, reminding one of Lamachus in *Acharnians,* and Daedalus a cap resembling a wicker basket. "Enyalius" is another epithet for War ("Ares") and "Daedalus" ("skilled" of craftsmen) is used of Hephaestus at Euripides *Heracles* 471 and Pindar *Nemean* 4.59. The familiar comic costume is especially clear for the figure of Daedalus.

The myth is that represented on the François Vase and other sixth-century vases and recounted by Alcaeus (F 349) and Pindar (F 283), and more fully at Pausanias 1.20.3, Hyginus 166 and [Libanius] *Narrations* 6, how Hephaestus trapped his mother Hera in a chair from which she could not extricate herself, how Ares attempted without success to compel Hephaestus to release their mother (the scene represented here), and how finally Dionysus accomplished the freeing of Hera and the return of Hephaestus. Epicharmus dramatised the story in his *Revellers or Hephaestus,* and Aristophanes and Platon each wrote a *Daedalus* (so too Eubulus for Middle Comedy), but Aristophanes' comedy does seem to have more to do

443

with Zeus enlisting the services of the legendary crafts-
man, Daedalus.

V 19   Apulian bell *krater,* 375–350. ("Birth of Helen").
PhV² nr. 18.

Taplin *Comic Angels* 19.20 (pp. 82–83); *Illustrations* IV.26;
Bieber *Theater* 135 (nr. 492).

A platform on supporting posts and the open double door
on the left show that a dramatic scene is being repre-
sented. On the far left a woman (Leda?) is shown in the
doorway peering out. She is watching a white-haired old
man, in the standard comic costume, with a double axe
raised high above his head. Beneath him in the centre a fe-
male figure (Helen) is emerging from an egg, which has
already been cracked open. She raises her arm to ward
off another swing of the axe. On the right a younger male
figure (dark hair and beard), also in the comic costume,
stands with his right hand raised, presumably in astonish-
ment or possibly to halt a second stroke. A window fills the
space above the egg. The scene is thus outdoors.

   The identity of the female figures is straightforward:
Leda and Helen, but the male figures present more of a
problem. The figure wielding the axe might be Hephaes-
tus, who engineers the birth of Athena, but can the figure
on the right, who resembles the traditional comic slave
on vases, then be Tyndareus? Or is the axe-wielder more
likely to be Tyndareus? In that case the figure on the right
is a domestic servant, and why is he in the scene? We know
that Leda was a character in Cratinus' *Nemesis* and that the
egg was visible in that comedy.

444

V 20   Apulian bell *krater*, 375–350. *PhV*[2] 17.

Illustrations IV.27; Taplin *Comic Angels* 93–94; Walsh *Distorted Images* 140–42.

Apart from the comic costumes the only indication of a dramatic setting is a simple stage raised on three posts. On the left is an older man with a stick; in the centre and dominating the scene is a woman with right hand raised and a fillet in her left. On the right is a younger male with bulging eyes, holding a wreath in his right hand and a thyrsus in his left. Some conclude that the woman is waving farewell to the male on the left and thus this vase shows a scene associated with Cratinus' *Dionysalexander*, the departure of Helen with Paris-Dionysus, Menelaus then being the figure of the left. But no such scene is implied by the hypothesis to that comedy, and we would have to conclude that either the author of the hypothesis omitted this scene from his summary (unlikely since it would involve a double shift of location: Ida to Sparta and back to Ida), or that the vase painter portrayed a scene that was not in the play, or (most likely) that the scene has no connection with Cratinus' play or even with the story of Helen. While the body language of the scene could suggest that the female figure is being led away by the man on the right, it could also be the case that she is introducing a suppliant or a visitor (Dionysus on one of his comic adventures?) to the authority figure on the left.

V 21   Apulian bell *krater*, 380–370. *PhV*[2] 61.

Taplin *Comic Angels* 18.19 (pp. 82, 115); *Illustrations* IV.29; Gigante *Rintone e il teatro* 126ff.

Only the costumes of the two figures imply that this scene comes from a comic drama—there is no stage, double door, or comic mask. On the left an old man with a Phrygian cap is sitting on an altar and raising his left hand in what seems to be a gesture of protection from a younger male on the right, drawn sword in hand. The old man seems to be in the middle of a serious speech—the raised hand may then be a rhetorical flourish. To the extreme left stands a laurel tree. The most natural conclusion is that this is Priam under threat from Neoptolemus during the fall of Troy, but while the early date of the vase might suggest an Old Comedy as its inspiration, none of the titles that we possess suggests a comedy set during the fall of Troy. Strattis' *Myrmidons, Troilus,* and *Philoctetes* are parodies of tragedies with a Trojan setting.

V 22 Apulian bell *krater* by the Raimone Painter, 380–370. ("Santa Agata Antigone"). *PhV*² 59.

Panofka, *Annales de l'Institut archéologique* 19 (1847) 216–21; Taplin *Comic Angels* 21.22 (pp. 83–88, 115); *Illustrations* IV.33; Bieber *Theater* 134 (nr. 490); Walsh *Distorted Images* 221–22.

Only the costumes indicate a comic drama as the source of this scene, and while the masks, bodysuits, and phalli are suitably comic (that of the figure in the middle can be seen through the see-through gown that he is wearing), the padding is minimal. Dominating the scene is the old man in the centre, wearing a long *peplos,* holding a female mask in his right hand and clasping a hydria in his left close to his body. On the right holding a pair of spears and firmly leading the old man is a younger male dressed in an animal skin and wearing a cap. They are moving in the direction of a third figure on the left, who holds a staff or sceptre and wears a Phrygian cap. He wears a mask that resembles that of the old man in the centre.

Panofka was the first to suggest that this was a parody of the scene in *Antigone* where the guard brings the apprehended Antigone before Creon. The hydria would contain either the ashes of Polynices or something for the funeral, and the female mask would imply that an old man has usurped the role of Antigone in the same way that Euripides' in-law has disguised himself as a woman, and later in the play parodied both Helen and Andromeda. Taplin argues (implausibly to my mind) that this is an inversion of the myth, that Creon is sending out an old man to do the job of Antigone. He calls attention also to Eupolis' *Prospaltians*, where F 260 paraphrases *Antigone* 712–17, but Eupolis does not seem to have indulged in paratragedy to the extent that Strattis and Aristophanes do. I prefer the sceptical attitude of Walsh and Marshall (*G&R* [1999] 201 n. 49) that this has nothing to do with Antigone.

V 23   Apulian bell *krater*, 375–350. *PhV*² 31.

Illustrations IV.22; Bieber *Theater* 132 (nr. 482); Walsh *Distorted Images* 89–90, 255.

The floor at the bottom of the scene may represent a stage floor, but it could just be the floor of the temple of Zeus. On the left seated on a throne is a bearded small (almost dwarfish) figure, whose feet cannot reach the floor beneath the throne, brandishing a thunderbolt in one hand and

447

holding an eagle sceptre in the other—it is a very small eagle. In the centre is a stage-naked figure in full comic regalia (especially the padding), with a lion's-head cap and wolfing down a dainty from a shallow bowl. On the right, with his back turned to the action, is an old man, with a generously endowed phallus and a cloak over his shoulders, pouring a libation to a pillar altar.

The scene seems to show Heracles in the presence of his father, Zeus, eating the sacrificial offerings, while a tiny and impotent Zeus looks on in rage. This could come from one of the numerous comedies which featured Heracles, of which Pherecrates' *Heracles the Mortal* or *False Heracles* might be candidates, but I would suggest Platon's *Zeus Badly Treated*.

V 24   Apulian *oenochoe*, 375–350. *PhV*[2] 122.

Illustrations IV.23; Hoffmann *Grabritual und Gesellschaft* 170–77; Green "Production" 209; Walsh *Distorted Images* 224–25.

This vase depicts three characters dressed in the conventional comic costume. In the centre stands a well-padded figure wearing a lion skin with a club and a bow at his feet. This must be Heracles. In his hands he holds a love-wheel (*iynx*). On the right an older male with a walking stick points to the ground with some concern, while on the left in some agitation stands a crowned figure on crutches, while Heracles' club rests on his foot. The other two figures are sometimes identified as Iolaus (right) and Eurystheus (left), but see the comments of Hoffmann and Green. Whoever these other character are, the sense is

that Heracles is abandoning his labours for the pursuit of love. A lame Eurystheus (or whoever) might indicate a comic parody of a tragedy by Euripides, who was (in)famous for his dramatic portrayal of beggars and cripples. This could be a scene from any comedy (the beginning perhaps) involving Heracles' amorous adventures, but I might suggest *The Marriage of Heracles* by Archippus or *Heracles Gets Married* by Nicochares, or *Wool-Carders or Cercopes* by Platon, which seems to have dramatised Heracles' service to Omphale.

V 25 Apulian bell *krater,* c. 370, by the Lecce Painter.

Trendall, in Cambitoglou and Robinson, *Classical Art in the Nicholson Museum, Sydney* (Mainz am Rhein 1995) 125–31; Green et al., *Ancient Voices Modern Echoes. Theatre in the Greek World* (Sydney 2003) 49–50; Storey, in Phillips and Pritchard (eds.), *Sport and Festival in the Ancient Greek World* (Swansea 2003) 281–92; Walsh *Distorted Images* 230; Green "Production" 198.

The costuming of the two figures suggests a scene from comedy. On the left a stage-naked figure, wearing a white wreath, is running away with a flat-cake in each hand, while looking over his shoulder at his pursuer. This other figure advances aggressively, holding a raised club in his right hand, his left arm draped with an animal skin (fawn?, certainly not that of a lion). Storey identified the scene as an example of the sort of comedy rejected by Aristophanes at *Wasps* 60 ("Heracles tricked out of his dinner") and suggested that one such play might be Leucon's *Envoys* (L-422). Trendall, Green, and Walsh call attention to the

mask, which is that of a slave and not that of Heracles, and to the fawn skin in place of the lion skin, and suggest that this is a "pretend" Heracles (Pherecrates' *False Heracles?*) and the scene a parody of the familiar motif of Heracles robbed by thieves, whom he then pursues.

V 26

(a) Attic red-figure *kalyx krater,* 425–400. ("Getty Birds").

Taplin *Comic Angels* 24.28 (pp. 101–4); Green, *J. P. Getty Museum. Greek Vases* 2 (1985) 95–118; Taplin, *PCPhS* 33 (1987) 92–104; Csapo *Phoenix* 47 (1993), 1–28, 115–24; *Actors and Icons* 9–12; Rothwell 54.

An unusual and perplexing vase, "with poor quality glaze . . . [and] distinctly crude technique" (Taplin *Comic Angels* 101). An *aulos* player in a richly patterned robe stands in the centre between two figures costumed as birds. They wear bird masks with crests and impressive beaks and wattles, leotards with dot-filled circles, wings and shoes with spurs at their ankles. Each wears a pair of shorts, like the furry shorts worn by satyrs, to which are attached tail feathers and an erect phallus. Each figure has its arms raised as if making a point or threatening the opponent.

Five interpretations have been proposed: (1) that these are two members of the chorus of *Birds* (Green, who points out that the closest parallel in Attic vases are earlier vases with an *aulos* player accompanying dancers), (2) that these are the two *logoi* of *Clouds,* who according to Σ *Clouds* 889c were brought on stage as fighting birds, perhaps in the lost original of 423 (Taplin 1987), (3) that as the

shorts with phallus and tail attached are reminiscent of the costume in satyr drama, the vase depicts a chorus of satyrs as fighting-cocks, (4) that the vase depicts members of a comic chorus, from a play that we cannot identify (Csapo), and (5) that it is not even a dramatic performance at all (Taplin *Comic Angels,* Rothwell). The third is ruled out since there is no evidence for anything other than satyrs in a satyr play, and Csapo's preferred date for the vase (c. 425) eliminates *Birds* and perhaps also first *Clouds.* I would find (2) or less likely (4) as the most reasonable explanation.

(b) Athenian r/f *pelikē,* c. 425

Gaunt, in *Companion* xi; Csapo *Actors and Icons* 9–12.

By the same painter as 26a, this vase, now at Emory University, was not known until 2008. On one side there is a bearded *aulos* player, wearing a long formal chiton and a fillet on his head, and on the other a single dancing figure, very similar to the two "Getty birds," even to the details of the mask, spurs, and patterned shorts. This does show that the "Getty Birds" was not a one-off effort and that it does represent some sort of public performance at Athens. Csapo dates both vases around 425.

INDEXES

Fragments are cited by poet + number or play title. *CA* = Comic Adespota (cited by number), *CP* = Comic Papyri (cited by entry), *V* = Vases (cited by entry).

KŌMŌIDOUMENOI

The entries under a given name may not all refer to the same person.

KŌMŌIDOUMENOI

Demus: Eupolis 227
Diagoras: Hermippus 43
Dieitrephes: Cratinus 251;
 Platon 30
Diocles: Eupolis 192.170–71
Dioclides: Phrynichus 61
Diognetus: Eupolis 99
Dionysius: Callias 3; Polyzelus
 12
Diopeithes: Ameipsias 10;
 Phrynichus 9; Teleclides 7
Dracon: Cratinus 300
Dracontides: Platon 148

Ecphantides: Cratinus 361, 462,
 502
Elpinice: Eupolis 221
Epicrates: Platon 127, 130;
 Strattis 10
Euathlus: Cratinus 82; Platon
 109
Euclides: Archippus 27
Eudamus: Ameipsias 26;
 Eupolis 96
Eudemus: Cratinus 302
Euripides: CA 421, 860;
 Cratinus 342; Platon 29, 142;
 Strattis 1; Teleclides 41–42;
 Theopompus 35
Eurybatus: CA 311
Euryphron: Platon 200
Execestides: CA 338;
 Phrynichus 21
Execestus: CA 337; Eupolis
 259

Glaucetes: Platon 114
Glaucon: Platon 65
Gnesippus: Chionides 4;

Cratinus 17, 104, 276;
 Eupolis 148; Teleclides 36
Gorgias: Alcaeus 11

Hagnon: Cratinus 171
Hegelochus: Platon 235;
 Sannyrion 8; Strattis 1, 63
Hermaeus: Archippus 23
Hierocles: Eupolis 231
Hieroclides: Hermippus 39 (?);
 Phrynichus 18 (?)
Hipparchus: CA 238
Hippoclides: Hermippus 16
Hippocrates' sons: Eupolis
 112
Hippon: Cratinus 167
Hipponicus: Cratinus 492;
 Eupolis 20, 156
Hyperbolus: Cratinus 209, 283;
 Eupolis *Maricas,* 193–94,
 203, 207–9, 252; Hermippus
 Bread-Wives; Leucon 1;
 Platon *Hyperbolus,* 182–83,
 185, 203

Ion of Chios: Teleclides 18
Isaeus: Theopompus 19
Ischomachus: Cratinus 365
Isocrates: CP 1146; Strattis 3

Lachares: CA 283
Laespodias: CA 380; Eupolis
 107; Philyllius 8; Phrynichus
 17; Strattis 19; Theopompus
 40
Lagisce: Strattis 3
Lais: Cephisodorus *Rival of
 Lais;* Strattis 27
Lampon: Callias 20; CP 1105;

455

GEOGRAPHICAL NAMES

459

MYTHOLOGICAL NAMES AND SUBJECTS